Conflict, Culture and Communication

Conflict, Culture and Communication provides a coherent, research-informed overview of conflict and intercultural communication. Aimed at encouraging and enabling conflict prevention, this book contributes to a better understanding of the factors that create, foster and exacerbate conflict in intercultural interaction and discusses how conflict can be handled, managed and resolved once it has manifested. Furthermore, this book:

- Critically assesses the repercussions of prevalent conflict management approaches, providing insights into best practices and sustainable conflict resolution outcomes.
- Combines insights from multiple disciplines and cultures, including Asia, Europe, Oceania, and North and South America, in order to arrive at a holistic and balanced understanding of the complexities inherent in negotiating conflict across cultural contexts.
- Avoids cultural stereotyping by discussing both between-culture variation and within-culture variation.

Conflict, Culture and Communication is essential reading for students and researchers of applied linguistics, communication studies and international business, as well as anyone interested in learning more about this growing area.

Stefanie Stadler is an Assistant Professor at the Division of Linguistics and Multilingual Studies at Nanyang Technological University in Singapore.

Conflict, Culture and Communication

Stefanie Stadler

Routledge
Taylor & Francis Group

LONDON AND NEW YORK

First published 2020
by Routledge
2 Park Square, Milton Park, Abingdon, Oxon OX14 4RN

and by Routledge
52 Vanderbilt Avenue, New York, NY 10017

Routledge is an imprint of the Taylor & Francis Group, an informa business

© 2020 Stefanie Stadler

British Library Cataloguing-in-Publication Data
A catalogue record for this book is available from the British Library

Library of Congress Cataloging-in-Publication Data
Names: Stadler, Stefanie, author.
Title: Conflict, culture and communication / Stefanie Stadler.
Description: Milton Park, Abingdon, Oxon ; New York, NY : Routledge, 2020. | Includes bibliographical references and index.
Identifiers: LCCN 2019014787| ISBN 9781138328167 (hardback) | ISBN 9781138328174 (pbk.) | ISBN 9780429448850 (ebook)
Subjects: LCSH: Conflict management. | Intercultural communication. | Interpersonal conflict
Classification: LCC HM1126 .S72 2020 | DDC 303.48/2–dc23
LC record available at https://lccn.loc.gov/2019014787

ISBN: 978-1-138-32816-7 (hbk)
ISBN: 978-1-138-32817-4 (pbk)
ISBN: 978-0-429-44885-0 (ebk)

Typeset in Bembo
by Taylor & Francis Books

Contents

Introduction

With increased globalization grows a need for increased intercultural understanding. Multi-ethnic and multicultural workplaces have become a norm,
migration has reached an all-time high, and intercultural relationships and
international business endeavours are on the rise. The mono-cultural dynamics
that were once prevalent have become a thing of the past. Instead, inter-
culturality and plurilingualism have become the norm – if not in real life, then
at least via access to virtual realities. A mono-cultural, homogeneous existence
has become highly improbable, if not altogether impossible. However, an
increase in intercultural outlook does not in and of itself guarantee positive,
beneficial and constructive outcomes. Since the complexities of interactions
across cultures hinder understanding, the realities of intercultural interaction
invariably lead to lower levels of predictability and a lowered capacity for
interpreting others' behaviours in line with their respective intentions. This, in
turn, makes intercultural interactions more prone to conflict.

Conflict constitutes a natural by-product of communication. As conflict
typically arises from a misalignment in opinions and/or goals, it emerges on a
regular basis in any type of interpersonal communication. It should therefore be
considered a normal interactional process, even in *intra*cultural communication.
However, what causes problems in *intra*cultural communication typically causes
more – and more severe – issues in intercultural communication. This is of
course not to say that intercultural communication invariably leads to conflict.
Many intercultural exchanges are unproblematic. However, culture-based attitudes, norms and practices exist largely outside our conscious awareness, while
nevertheless influencing our behaviours to a greater extent than we can possibly
know. The lack of conscious knowledge of our own cultural scripts and those
of others not only implies that conflict is more likely to occur, but also that it is
harder to resolve.

Much has been said about the positive versus negative nature of conflict,
about organizational approaches to conflict management in business settings,
about spousal and family conflict, about the link between personality factors
and conflict, and about historical and political conflict. These approaches typically contain either a macro cultural perspective that lacks interpersonal

interactional considerations, or situate conflict on a micro level that lacks a wider cultural perspective. What causes and contributes to conflict across cultures in interpersonal communication therefore remains poorly understood.

This book sets out to systematically assess the intersection between culture, communication, and conflict, in order to underscore the complexities involved in conflict situations across cultures. The aim of this book is twofold. On the one hand, it hopes to contribute to a better understanding of the factors and dynamics that create, foster and exacerbate conflict in intercultural interaction. On the other hand, it discusses how conflict can be handled, managed and resolved once it has manifested. The first part of this book takes a look at how various contextual factors, demographic constituents, attitudes and mindsets impact on the interactants' stance towards disagreement, dissent, and ultimately conflict. First and foremost, it addresses whether cultures are inclined to engage in conflict or not, and how this is expressed in their communication patterns and behaviours. A multitude of factors are explored that can either create or proliferate conflict. Many of these may seem innocuous at first, but can exert powerful reactions upon closer examination. The reason they do is because they are often linked, in subversive ways, to wider, underlying cultural value systems. Essentially, this part of the book is dedicated to gaining a deeper understanding of the cultural and relational dynamics of interpersonal communication, and is aimed ultimately at how conflict can be prevented. Since conflict cannot always be avoided, the latter part of the book explores culturally preferred conflict negotiation approaches, and assesses best practices for synergistic solutions to effective conflict resolution. By drawing on examples from a myriad of cultures from across the globe, this book wishes to present a balanced view that takes into account cultural diversity on a broad scale.

While it is next to impossible to avoid cultural stereotyping altogether — owing largely to the fact that this is how culture has been discussed in much of the literature — this book does not wish to proliferate cultural stereotypes, but rather attempts to present a holistic image that combines wider cultural orientations with individualized predispositions to conflict. Although this book addresses cultural preferences, it emphasizes that culturally influenced behaviours exist on a continuum, and that individuals within a culture typically draw on a spectrum of acceptable practices, but may also chose to deliberately ignore them. The stance to culture which this book takes is that outliers do exist, but that, overall, people tend to choose to act along a range of culturally acceptable behaviours that lie within the boundaries of a culture's expectations of appropriateness.

Cultural comparisons in the literature often situate behaviours and attitudes along an East–West divide, or dogmatic dichotomies, such as the individualism–collectivism dimension. Representing these insights invariably necessitates reflecting these dichotomous stances to culture to some extent. However, this book sets out to question the validity of such rigid categories, and hopes to be able to present a picture of cultures, and the individuals within them, as dynamic, fluid, and forever changing entities, that combine traditions, norms, practices and expectations with adaptation, accommodation, and idiosyncratic choices.

Rather than representing conflict from a single perspective, this book hopes to portray conflict in a way that unifies the insights gathered over the decades across academic disciplines. This multidisciplinary approach combines ideas and corroborates findings from numerous fields in order to best represent conflict from multiple angles. While the predominant focus lies on communication disciplines, their insights are supplemented by research findings from fields as diverse as anthropology, psychology, sociology, business, management, marketing, healthcare, peace studies and law.

Ultimately, this book hopes to contribute to a better, more profound, holistic understanding of the dynamics involved in conflict, conflict management and conflict resolution in interpersonal communication. By better grasping the underlying factors that influence our attitudes and behaviours, this book can hopefully aid in preventing conflict from arising, and offer insights into effective ways in which to approach the resolution of conflict.

Chapter 1

Communication across cultural contexts

Communication is central to successful intercultural encounters and work of any kind, be it for travelling, interpersonal interactions or international business. Unfortunately, speaking the other party's language is not sufficient to guarantee successful interactions, and many of the discrepancies in communication are due to pragmatic differences and cultural preferences for particular ways of communicating, with language functioning merely as a tool (Stadler, 2011). As interactional partners rarely completely align in their views and goals, managing intercultural interactions and transactions is particularly prone to conversational conflict. The particularly high propensity for conflict in intercultural communication is documented in studies such as Spencer-Oatey and Xing (2008), which investigated business deals that went awry on the grounds of culture-based conflicts. The tendency for intercultural contact to lead to more, and more complex, conflict situations is also documented by Elmer (1993) and von Glinow et al. (2004). Conflict is not conducive to successful interactions and it need not come in the shape of a complete breakdown to adversely affect communication and relationships. Previous research demonstrated clearly that different cultures have starkly different orientations to disagreement and approaches to managing conversational conflict situations (Stadler, 2013a). Hence, it is imperative to gain a better understanding of culture-based attitudes towards conflict, as well as the cultural variables that underlie them, in order to arrive at smoother relations and more successful interactions and transactions across cultures.

1.1 Demographics, context and conflict

When we communicate, we invariably assess who we talk to. The interactional strategies we choose may be selected subconsciously, but just because this occurs predominantly outside our immediate awareness does not mean it is not subject to a complex decision-making process. Stadler (2007) outlines the elaborate processes utterance-production and utterance-interpretation undergo, both on a conscious and on an unconscious level. Banks (1998, p. 5) points out that we are all members of cultural communities where the interpretation of our life experiences 'is mediated by the interaction of a complex set of status variables, such as gender, social class, age, political affiliation, religion, and region'. Consequently, in interaction with other people there are a wide array of variables to consider, the most salient of which include age, status, power and gender.

1.1.1 Age

Although the precise way in which age affects communication is very much culture-dependent, in no culture do we address all individuals in the exactly the same manner. Confucian-influenced cultures with long-standing traditions of filial piety show a great deal of respect for age and seniority (Cho & Yoon, 2001; Lee, 2012; Sung, 2003). Chinese culture, for example, as Merriam et al. (2010) report, places greater value on age and on being male. This does not necessarily only refer to older generations, but can involve very complex structures where minimal age differences matter greatly. One thing that typically strikes visitors to Korea as rather odd is people's tendency to immediately inquire about a person's age. This is oftentimes perceived as somewhat intrusive. However, in Korean in culture, it is necessary to establish age differences precisely, as specific speaking and behavioural practices have to be observed when addressing an older person, whereby even a single year age gap carries implications of seniority and warrants deferential treatment. Consequently, establishing a conversational partner's precise age is a must. Reverence and respect for elders is a long-held social tradition and consequently, elders and seniority have vested rights in Korean culture (Cho & Mor Barak, 2008). A transgression of said rights can have serious repercussions, even in the social domain. I have witnessed several incidents among friends which make the potential for offence, that even minimal age gaps carry, very clear.

Case study: Age gap

A group of friends of 14 people (12 of them Korean) went on a trip to Busan. Due to the relatively large group size, we had to take multiple taxis. After one dinner, four of us went back to the apartment we all stayed in, while the rest went out for drinks, which they had forgotten to tell us about. Despite the fact that we tried to contact them, we could not reach them. Although none of the four of us were upset about this, when the rest of the group arrived back at the apartment a huge heated discussion broke out involving many accusations. After this had been going on for quite some time, one of the 'forgotten' four, a Korean male, made a remark along the lines of 'it's enough now' to a slightly older female. This was deemed so inappropriate that the female addressee was so livid with rage that she stormed out of the apartment and several group members had to run after her to console her, calm her down and convince her to come back. The following day, during a dinner, one male participant made a joke that another, also slightly older, female considered inappropriate, with the same resultant effect. She went out of the restaurant, only to be followed by several group members consoling her and persuading her to return, while the others scolded the offending male for his inconsiderate behaviour.

As these incidents demonstrate, even rather innocuous utterances across fairly small age gaps can incur serious consequences when norm-expectations are violated. The importance of age in such cultures should be viewed more in terms of what Merriam et al. (2010) refer to as 'positionality', i.e. how one stands relative to another person in terms of status. Park and Kim (2005) speak of an age-graded seniority system in Korean culture.

Although it has to be made clear at this point that foreigners are not subjected to the same expectations and scrutiny as locals, it is important to understand the dynamics at play in other cultures. While there may be some kind of 'foreigner allowance', providing a little bit of leeway for the non-initiated, there is a point beyond which transgressions are no longer forgiven. The repercussions for relationships can be disastrous, particularly in cultures that are bound by reciprocity and loyalty. While specific dynamics do not apply to foreigners to the same degree, a violation of reciprocity expectations affects foreigners every bit as much once they are included in the Korean in-group system.

While not all cultures are equally age-conscious, a sensitivity to age as a powerful determinant for communicative behaviour is advisable in nearly every context.

1.1.2 Status and power

LaFrance and Mayo (1978) consider status differences as one of the central factors in intercultural miscommunication. The notions of status and power are so prominent in our communicative strategies that very elaborate systems of deference marking have come into existence for the purpose of either exerting power or deferring to it. This is somewhat easier to negotiate in the English language, since it lacks an elaborate pronoun system. Therefore, power and solidarity of the speaker-hearer relationship cannot be analysed by the pronoun choice (Takenoya, 1999). Many Western cultures, however, have a T/V distinction, as Brown and Gilman (1960) defined the formal and informal second person personal pronoun address forms. Even to insiders, correctly identifying the most appropriate address form is not always straightforward, as it is subject to a complex interplay between either emphasizing closeness or status, and can therefore cause affront if misjudged. Pronouns can be found in most languages, but are 'perhaps the most diversified and complex in societies characterized by pronounced forms of hierarchical social organization and status' (Heine &

Song, 2011, p. 588). Pronoun choices, therefore, affect hierarchically structured societies more than egalitarian systems.

On the far end of the scale lies the extraordinarily complex Japanese honorifics system, which modulates power differentials and marks distinctions of rank or horizontal distance (Pizziconi, 2011). In Japan, power and/or distance 'are assigned markedly high values' (Fukada & Asato, 2004, p. 1997) and its society is characterized by extreme sensitivity to rank order (Nishiyama, 2000) and strict guidelines according to status and roles (Leung et al., 2002). According to Mitarai (1988, pp. 2–3), the 'concept of status pervades the lives of Japanese ... because no Japanese regards himself as the exact equal of any other person'. From a linguistic point of view then, 'the Japanese language does not allow any Japanese to so consider as there are only word forms that refer to superiors and inferiors. It is for this reason that a Japanese person almost always relates another person's status to his own by his choice of words. That is, a person of equal status is looked upon as a superior, and the speaker humbles himself' (Barna, 1973 cited in Mitarai, 1988, p. 3). The use of honorifics has been described as socio-pragmatically obligatory (Ide, 1989). Though this latter part has been contested, there is no doubt that status and power exert an extremely high influence on language choices in Japanese society.

The Japanese honorific system is so complex in structure and nature that even addressing someone with a personal pronoun becomes a dangerous minefield. A complex interplay between status, distance, age and gender render the decision-making process so treacherous and the consequences so serious, that Japanese people often avoid the use of personal pronouns altogether (Hinds, 1975). Suzuki (1978, p. 92) observed that 'there is a definite tendency to avoid their use as often as possible and to carry on a conversation using some other words to designate speaker and addressee'. In my observations, Japanese people do not necessarily even try to replace pronouns verbally. Rather, they show a preference for either replacing personal pronouns with a gesture, i.e. by politely pointing to the addressee (if present, predominantly to replace the personal pronoun 'you') or leaving the implication up to contextual inference. Japanese people largely avoid direct communication, not only in terms of pronoun use, and have thusly become extremely apt at guessing their interlocutor's intentions. Because of the homogeneity of Japanese society, Japanese 'are able to guess at each other's feelings from facial expressions, movements of the eyes and the slightest gestures, and their conjectures are not mistaken' (Eto, 1977, p. 75). This interactional style makes the burden on the addressee somewhat heavier, but avoids potential pitfalls.

The reason for the complexity of the Japanese system is that pronouns carry various semantic properties that are 'absent in the English parallels' (Hinds, 1975, p. 132). Each pronoun carries strong correlations to status and social distance. Barke and Uehara (2005) list *anata, anta, kimi, omae, kisama* and *temee* in rank order from most polite to least polite second person singular personal pronoun form. Each of these pronouns carries with it meaningful connotations.

Kimi, for example, carries connotations of informality and lower status; however, it also carries strong connotations of relative closeness and proximity (Mitarai & Moriyoshi, 2015; Takenoya, 1999). By using this pronoun one risks offending someone by not attributing a high status to them, because it can be perceived as speaking down to someone (Mogi, 2002). By avoiding it, one risks distancing the other and downplaying one's bond. According to Mogi, if a husband were to address his wife with *anata* (the more formal and more polite form) instead of *kimi*, it would sound ironic. Hence, both the use of a personal pronoun or the lack of use of a specific pronoun can be offensive.

Even addressing someone with *anata*, the most polite form, can be impolite, as it is still directly addressing a person. Tanaka (1999) cites a case of a foreign employee who was fired after referring to her boss with the pronoun *anata*. Kabaya et al. (1998) and Kurosawa (1972) outline that Japanese second person pronouns are not deferential; thus, even though *anata* is categorized as a polite word, it is not in and of itself functioning as an honorific. Mogi (2002) explains that someone might feel slighted through being addressed as *anata*, especially when a woman uses it, because then it often sounds informal and indicates social closeness (as apparently 'being female might be one part of closeness in the relationship' and invariably introduces an element of social proximity, according to Takenoya, 1999, p. 131). With this in mind, it is easy to see why Japanese people would rather avoid the use of personal pronouns altogether.

The Japanese system is only one such example, however. Heine and Song (2011) also list Thai, Burmese, Khmer, Vietnamese and Korean as languages with complex systems of personal pronouns based on distinctions of honorification. The Balinese language system even comprises of several entirely different registers that relate to various forms of hierarchical, status and caste considerations, with the highest register being reserved for priests and ritual language use (Fox, 2005). Fox (2005, p. 101) speaks of Javanese (a language system closely related to Balinese, and supposedly one that exerted influence on the Balinese system) 'as consisting of a layered number of speech levels reflecting distinct social gradations. These levels may vary from two to ten, depending on the analyst.' Though the same un-clarities exist regarding the Balinese system, a Balinese informant mentioned learning of four distinct registers: Basa Kepara (lowest), Alus Sor (strangers), Alus Mider and Alus Singghih (addressing priests/highest register), while Arka (2005) and Artawa (2011) speak of two or three registers. Due to the strictly hierarchical stratification, Arka (2005) claims that one cannot speak Balinese without knowing the relative social status of interlocutors. What makes it yet more complex to use is that how speech-level agreement works is inconsistent (Arka, 2005). Apparently, the notions of social stratification attached to the different registers in Balinese contribute to females avoiding Balinese language. Instead they rely mostly on Bahasa Indonesia (also because females report that Indonesian appears more sophisticated), while males use the lowest register of Balinese for solidarity purposes among males (which the females seem to avoid, as it sounds 'too crude' to them), but code-switch to Bahasa Indonesia when addressing females (Oktarini, 2018).

The complexity of these language systems leaves no doubt as to the salience status and power distinctions carry. The importance of giving due consideration to interactional partners from such backgrounds should therefore not be underestimated. While cultural variation may exist regarding the importance of hierarchical distinctions, a disregard for status and power is never well-received.

1.1.3 Gender

In these times of feminist movements towards gender equality it might be somewhat surprising that gender still forms an important category in inter-cultural communication, but with many cultures still holding on to a very tra-ditional role-based gender model, it does constitute a valid entity for consideration.

Some cultures have very strong linguistic dichotomies for what male and female speech should sound like and for what the acceptable parameters are. A characteristic feature is often that female language should be more polite. And while, for example, some Asian languages often have a greater gender gap, plenty of studies reveal that even in modern, Western workplaces, one can find what is commonly referred to as the double bind. More outspoken females are rebuked for coming across as overly aggressive and unfeminine, while females who speak more in line with gendered expectations are rebuked for not being sufficiently assertive and coming across as ineffective and weak (Lakoff, 2004; Jamieson, 1995; Oakley, 2000). These perceptions, though dated, still linger. Consequently, children are raised with the view of conforming to expectations of gender-appropriate, normative behaviour.

Norm-conform expectations are highly prominent in cultures where gender inequality is institutionalized. Cultures influenced by Confucian ideals still have very traditional expectations on gender-appropriate behaviours. According to Cho and Mor Barak (2008, p. 105), in the Korean cultural context 'gender is a particularly important diversity characteristic because of the pervasive dis-crimination against women'. In Japanese society, women are expected 'to avoid the deprecatory level of pronoun use and to display a polite demeanor' (Ide, 1997, pp. 73–74). Wasserman and Weseley (2009) point towards a link between grammatical gender in language and the relative social standing of men and women in society. Prewitt-Freilino, Caswell and Laakso (2012) clo-sely scrutinize this potential link between grammatical gender and perceptions of the gender of a person. They state that, given recent research that ties gender in language to gendered perceptions of the world

> one could infer that when language constantly calls attention to gender distinctions by discriminating between masculine and feminine nouns and pronouns – as is the case in gendered languages – that individuals may be

more apt to draw distinctions between men and women. If, in fact, language plays a role in how people organize their beliefs about gender, then it stands to reason that differences in the gendered language systems across different cultures could play a role in societal differences in beliefs, attitudes, and behavioural practices about the role and status of men and women. (p. 269)

Indeed, cultures that hold onto very traditional gender role models also seem to have very elaborate grammatical gender structures. Just like the aforementioned Japanese honorifics system applies to status and hierarchy, the same is true for gender. The second person singular pronoun *kimi* discussed earlier, for example, is chiefly used by men (Takenoya, 1999), in which case the pronoun carries connotations of social proximity. If a female speaker, on the other hand, were to use the address term *kimi*, she would sound like a male or come across as bossy (Mogi, 2002).

The use of the first person singular pronoun in Japanese also carries connotations of self-portrayal vis-à-vis one's interlocutors. The selection of a specific pronoun holds a vast amount of socio–pragmatic information. Ono and Thompson (2003) emphasize that self-reference is only a small part of the work that first person pronouns do. Though Martin (1988) lists *watakushi, watashi, atashi, atakushi, watai, wate, wai, atai, ate, watchi, ashi, asshi, washi, wasshi, boku, ore, ora, uchi, jibun, ono* and *onore* as first person pronouns, the most commonly used (first person singular) pronouns include *(w)atashi, boku* and *ore. (W)atashi* are feminine forms, *boku* is used by males only, while *ore* is used by males to emphasize masculinity. The connotations personal pronouns carry and the attached spectrum of appropriate usage was nicely outlined in the 2016 animated movie *Kimi no na wa* ('Your name').

Case study: Foregrounding masculinity

In the movie, a school girl finds herself waking up in the body of a male student in another city. As she has to try to blend in with the friends of the boy, whose body she inhabits, the following exchange takes place:

Girl: Etto...watashi...
  Well...I (feminine form)...
Boy 1: Watashi? (girl blushes and sweat pools on her forehead)
Girl: Watakushi?
  We?
Boy 1 & 2: mm? (sounding surprised, with a somewhat befuddled look on their face)
Girl: Boku?
  I? (plain male form)
Boy 1 & 2: hugh? (sounding utterly incredulous)
Girl: O::re? (Sounding probing and tentative)
Boy 1 & 2: Un (accompanied by nod)
   (Japanese vocalized form of agreement)

Girl: (continues narrative with an assertive) Ore tanoshikatta ye yo.
I had fun.

The boys' reactions to the girl's pronoun choices leave little doubt that her initial choices do not meet the societal gender expectations and conventions of the in-group. She realizes her mistake and tries to correct her initial choice, attempting to meet her interlocutors' expectations. Only when she finally switches to *ore* in a tentative and questioning voice do the friends signal approval and recognition.

This example, while not empirical, does highlight gendered expectations and conventions of language use, which leave but a narrow window of acceptance. While, traditionally, people follow these gendered patterns, apparently, this system is being challenged by younger generations.

The trend of younger women making use of non-stereotypical 'women's language' forms has been documented by Okamoto (1995), who states that women were found to use more neutral, less polite and mildly masculine forms of speech. Female junior high school students have also been observed using the plain male pronoun *boku* or even the other-deprecatory male pronoun *ore* (Miyazaki, 2004). Many girls also made up a new personal pronoun *uchi* for self-reference (which is normally used as a noun, meaning 'inside' or 'home') and according to Miyazaki (2004) is in use in the Tokyo area. It appears, from the students' comments that the use of *uchi* is preferred, as both *watashi* and *atashi* have stronger feminine connotations, which they seem to reject. This trend of younger women making use of non-stereotypical 'women's language' forms has also been documented by Okamoto (1995). Miyazaki (2004) posits that this non-traditional usage of personal pronouns is a daily challenge of positioning of femininity/masculinity, coolness, power, deference, solidarity, distance and intimacy. 'Girls and boys actively make sense of and negotiate these myriad, sometimes contested meanings within and outside their peer-groups' (p. 265). This study attests to both traditional expectations, as well as a movement to steer away from traditional conceptualizations of gendered language use. What this study also makes clear though is that gender, nevertheless, does exert a strong influence in language choices, even if it is in a deliberate effort to oppose the norms.

1.1.4 Language choice

While language choice does not constitute an addressee-specific variable in the way that age, status and gender do, an interlocutor's language background and cultural affiliation also exert a powerful influence on intercultural dynamics. Although this is rarely given sufficient thought, and possibly precisely for this very same reason, the choice of working language can cause a substantial amount of conflict.

With the pervasive spread of English, it is all too easy to assume that people will simply resort to English as a lingua franca. In fact, it can be considered a de facto assumption in intercultural work. Spencer-Oatey and Stadler (2009) caution though that the choice of working language requires careful consideration, because it is not merely a question of practicality. According to Janssens and Brett (1997), language is closely linked to power and a member's fluency will impact his/her capability to join and influence the internal team process. Language access and competence can therefore become a more determining factor than professional competence and skills.

> Choosing the working language can create winners and losers. Language is clearly associated with power, influence and emotional issues. Let us put it bluntly: the ability to master or not master English can create an unequal playing field. Sometimes language differences can be interpreted as personality problems and you can be treated as a deviant or simply ignored just because you do not seize all the linguistic subtleties (Berry, 1990). Beyond discouraging participation you tend to assimilate language fluency with scientific competencies. If you want to be the leader of the project, it is better if you have English as your mother tongue. Conversely, it is not always the scientific stars that represent a country or an institution but those who are relatively more apt in English.
>
> (Bournois & Chevalier, 1998, p. 207)

Everyone working in intercultural contexts would be well advised to reconsider this notion very carefully. HEFCE's eChina-UK project serves as a prime example for the damage that such an automatic assumption can cause to working relations. The Chinese project members were fairly upset about the fact that the topic of working language wasn't even broached and the British automatically assumed all interactions would be conducted in English. This left the Chinese side disadvantaged on various levels, including access to communication for some of the non-English speaking project members, the burden of having to translate all texts and documents from English to Chinese and back to English, and the cost associated with said translation services. The Chinese found this unacceptable and complained that it was the British people's turn to learn at least some basic Chinese, as they considered communication efforts to be a two-way street. For this very reason, taking language choice lightly can backfire considerably. The justified resentment of the Chinese was only resolved in Phase 2 of the Project, when the British participants started to enrol in language classes. Not that this had an immediate impact on communication (seeing as Chinese is not an easy language to acquire and the learning of any language requires a great deal of time investment and practice before it comes to fruition), but seeing the British put in time and effort on their side as well was very warmly received by the Chinese (Spencer-Oatey & Stadler, 2009).

The impact that a simple sign of willingness to engage with the other's language can have is demonstrated by the following example:

Case study: Host language use

A woman working as an auditor for a German pharmaceutical company, predominantly in South America, reported that due to the nature of her job (quality control), oftentimes she was received with a great deal of anxiety and wariness. Audits can be intimidating, because of the inherent risk for repercussions and reprimands. While she has no command of the Spanish language, she found that concluding her addressing speech with a simple *muchas gracias* ('many thanks') had a profound impact on peoples' attitudes towards her and their subsequent cooperativeness.

In the intercultural domain, an animosity towards cultural imperialism is tangible, and the use of English is seen as the embodiment of this resentment. While most people do not harbour negative feelings towards the use of English per se, the automatic assumption that this is the only language for consideration can ruffle feathers, as the eChina-UK project showed. In having said this, to some people, the very prospect of conversing with foreigners alone is anxiety-provoking even without the added language barriers. The use of foreign languages can cause issues in and of themselves, irrespective of power dynamics and concerns of imperialism. Even more modest considerations of language use should be taken into account in intercultural communication, as it is not only lingua franca choices alone that cause complications and friction.

Kowner (2002) reports of Japanese people that the mere thought of interacting in a foreign language (any foreign language) causes them anxiety. Speaking a foreign language is seen as a major barrier in their communication. In a country where perfectionism is institutionalized, it is perhaps unsurprising that the attitude prevails that one has to hone one's language skills to perfection before using them. Or as Kowner (2002, p. 341) puts it: 'the fear of failing in a mode of communication one believes one has to master but in reality does not'. To help understand how deeply engrained this thought pattern is in Japanese society, perhaps the following example helps to illustrate my point.

Case study: Ice cubes

A Japanese friend, who works as a bar keeper, told me that for the first three years of working in this profession, he did nothing but cut ice cubes by hand (a prevalent practice in Japanese bars). My friend spent three full years perfecting this skill before he was even allowed to mix a drink.

This kind of commitment to perfecting one's skill levels demonstrates very clearly the anxiety that speaking to foreigners induces, when the perception lingers that language skills are insufficient.

Japanese learners, however, are not the only ones affected. Studies have indicated that foreign language classes cause students considerably more anxiety than any other type of school classes (MacIntyre & Gardner, 1989). Cutrone (2009, p. 55) speaks of 'foreign language anxiety', even when no foreigner is present. According to Horwitz, Horwitz and Cope (1986), performance anxiety can be attributed to a mixture of communication apprehension, social evaluation and test anxiety that will affect most learners.

Seeing as language choice exerts a multitude of influences, a lot of empathy for the linguistic and cultural background of interactional partners is required. As I have outlined here, language is a very sensitive issue and is experienced as a (sometimes) insurmountable obstacle. Due to the high affective involvement of emotions, insecurities and anxieties, it is hardly surprising that the potential for offence and friction is also high. The impact of language and interlanguage communication should therefore not be taken lightly in intercultural encounters.

1.2 Implications for conversational conflict

Conflict can be triggered by virtually anything in intercultural settings. Ranging from inadequate hotel selection, mismanaged hosting practices, inappropriate seating arrangements (cf. Spencer-Oatey and Xing, 2008), to non-verbal expressions such as staring or pointing (cf. e.g. Stadler, 2007), transgressions regarding age, status, gender, language or simply a lack of verbal response. Wall and Callister (1995) provide an extensive list of conflict causes, including individual characteristics (personality, values, goals, commitment to position, stress, anger, desire for autonomy), interpersonal factors, such as perceptual interface (perception that other has high goals, other's intentions counter to party's, other's intentions counter to party's fairness norms, other's behaviour seen as harmful, distrust), communications (distortions and misunderstandings, hostility, dislikes, insults), behaviours (blocking party's goals, power struggles), structure (closeness, power imbalances, interdependence, status gaps, preferential treatment of one side), and previous interactions (past failures to reach agreement, history of conflict, locked-in conflict behaviours) (for a complete list refer to Wall and Callister 1995, p. 518).

What makes conflict arise is typically a mismatch between speaker intention and addressee interpretation. Interpretations are contingent on highly subjective perceptions and judgement processes. As the sections on age, status, power, gender and language choice have demonstrated, there are a myriad of factors that are subject to culturally influenced perceptions of appropriateness. These factors are graded according to importance in a culture, with as much variation as there are cultures in the world (and some more if we are to take individualized and subcultural preferences into account). Neustupný (2003) speaks of a deviation of expectations, and asserts that subjects apply expectations of their own interaction system to foreign systems. The resultant deviations triggered problems and negative evaluations. Kowner (2002) mentions the violation of expectation as causing alarm and distress. As such, it does not take more than a slight misalignment in perceptions to aggravate a situation.

An example for how easily conflict situations can be triggered by seemingly innocent behaviours can be seen in the following incident.

Case study: Conflict triggers

A passenger filmed an incident on the MRT (Singaporean public transport system) where an auntie (respectful address form towards older people in Singapore) and a girl (in her 20s) got into a very heated argument that involved a lot of shouting and swearing, which went viral (see wwwyoutube.com/watch?v=3cZ3WoQe3nl for the video link). While the incident started over the girl giving up the reserved seat for the auntie, the argument actually breaks out over the girl's staring. Even though she gave up the seat, reserved seats are either for the elderly (which the auntie is not), pregnant ladies (which the auntie is not), children (which the auntie is not), or injured people (which the auntie is not – not visibly anyways). The girl does not seem pleased about this, despite having given up her seat regardless – hence the staring. This makes the auntie very upset, who, as a consequence, tries to take a picture of the girl, in order to post it on a social media platform, with the intention to publicly shame the girl (a fairly common form of social justice in Singapore; Skoric et al., 2010). The following is a short excerpt of said altercation:

```
 I Aunty: I'm not happy when I ask for [the seat when standing ah]
 2 Girl:                              [Then you must take my pho]to for fuck
 3 Aunty: To- to let the public know what type of lady you are=
 4 Girl: =Then you don't take my photo, hello! (continuously keeps pointing
          finger at auntie)
 5     (10.0)
 6 Girl: Enough ah (pointing threateningly at the auntie and keeps finger pointed
          for several seconds)
 7     (4.0)
 8 Aunty: WHY YOU STARE AT ME! (snaps arm out)
 9 Girl: Why you take my photo?=
10 Aunty: =WHY YOU POINT AT ME!= (snaps arm out)
11 Girl: =Why you take my photo?=
12 Aunty: =WHY YOU [KEEP STARING AT ME!] (snaps arm out)
13 Girl:           [I'm telling you not ] to take photo you take photo for fuck
14 Aunty: For fuck you
15 Girl: Huh?
16 Aunty: You have nothing to [(unintelligible)]
17 Girl:                      [Give you seat al]ready you still said so much huh (.)
18 Auntie: Said so much
19 Girl: Huh! You making trouble or I making trouble?
```

While this scenario takes place between two Singaporeans, the auntie initially accuses the girl: 'most probably you are from China'. It is no secret that Singaporeans are not especially foreigner-friendly, what Gomes (2014, p. 23) describes as 'harbouring and expressing unbridled feelings of dislike, distaste and sheer loathing' towards 'foreign talent' migrants; exhibiting the most ire towards Mainland Chinese. However, the auntie's accusation highlights two immensely important, more widely applicable, points: when we encounter negative behaviours we dislike and do not want to be associated with, we are quick to attribute them to outsiders (Alarape, 2008). Secondly, with outsiders, there is a higher expectation of difficulties in communication (see e.g. Kowner, 2002).

This second issue has been hotly debated in the field of intercultural communication in recent years and increasingly, researchers have pushed for a dissociation of intercultural communication from miscommunication. This is a point that is as delicate as it is fascinating and deserves some closer exploration.

It is very true that intercultural communication does not always or necessarily involve miscommunication (see e.g. Sarangi, 1994), and I do not in any way wish to perpetuate the view that it does. If intercultural communication would directly equate to miscommunication, I assume no one would want to engage in it any more. Many encounters do go smoothly and many an encounter has forged friendships. However, just because not all intercultural communication is marred by miscommunication does not mean intercultural communication is not prone to it. The reason why I uphold the standpoint that intercultural communication holds a propensity for miscommunication is that the complexities involved in achieving effective and mutually satisfying interactional outcomes are simply much greater and more far-reaching. Because we cannot possibly be fully versed in all practices from all cultures of this diverse globe, it is much harder to interpret the behaviour of people from unfamiliar cultures than it is to interpret behaviours from our own culture, into which we have been socialized over many years since infancy. Due to the different parameters that are at work when people from different backgrounds interact, the likelihood for a lack of alignment increases (see Stadler, 2014). Warnecke, Masters and Kempter (1992) demonstrated that even slight cultural differences can elicit negative responses. Thorne (2003) speaks of clashes in expectations of behavioural rules and norms, which, he states, occur on a regular basis in an intercultural context. Francis (1991) also asserts that problems in intercultural communication can oftentimes be attributed either to variation in norms of behaviours acceptable to different cultures or a misinterpretation of such behaviours. According to Crawford, Candlin and Roger (2017, p. 65f.), miscommunication can result if interpretation is influenced by differing frames of reference which are culturally informed. Ulijn and St Amant (2000) compare differences in frames to optical illusions where the same picture can be interpreted in two ways, depending on how one looks at the picture. While neither perspective is wrong, different perspectives on the exact same item can and do, at times, lead to misalignment in communication. This applies to almost any context which involves diversity, be it cross-sector, inter-organizational or interdisciplinary (see e.g. Stadler & Choi, 2016), and intercultural communication is no exception.

Communication of any type involves a great deal of interpretation. As Heidegger (2001, p. 11) put it: 'What is spoken is never, and in no language, what is said.' What this means is that meaning intended or implied cannot be fully found in the utterances we speak. An addressee has to do substantial inferential work to arrive at the meaning behind the words that were spoken. In low-context cultures this is somewhat easier because communication is more direct and relies more on the speaker to communicate clearly, but even then a certain degree of interpretation is required. People always have to read between the lines. In other cultures, this can be taken to the extreme, where meaning is nearly always only implied and much, if not most, is left to the addressee to piece together. This can be difficult even for insiders.

Case study: Table settings

During a research exchange sojourn in Beijing, I was affiliated with a local Chinese university. During my two-month long research stay, my British boss came to Beijing for a week-long conference trip. While she visited the university where I worked, a lunch was held to welcome her. She had very close connections to the department through her former PhD student, who held a low-ranking position in the department. When the time came to go to the lunch, my boss wanted both me and her former student to join, though neither of us was sure if we were meant to attend. Although he was both a cultural insider and an insider to the departmental and institutional dynamics, he was unsure about the right course of action. We both ended up going, though we both felt nervous about it, but the number of table settings and chairs made it clear that one of the two of us was not meant to attend. Though they added an extra setting and chair, one person clearly committed a cultural transgression.

The fact that Japanese is largely a pro-drop language due to the potential face-threat involved in selecting the wrong form of address, and the fact that the Chinese local was not clear on who was meant to attend the lunch, show very clearly how difficult it is even for insiders to make the correct choices. And what causes problems to *intra*cultural communication, generally causes more severe problems to intercultural communication (Günthner & Luckmann, 2001). We simply lack the framework for interpretation that allows us to make inferences with the same degree of accuracy we could in our own cultures.

Even *intra*cultural communication is not error-free. In fact, perfect alignment in communication is an illusion. For some reason, we seem to hold the erroneous assumption that understanding is normal, and that, if it is not achieved, an interaction is in some way 'deficient'. The reality is that perfect under-standing is rarely, if ever, achieved. Misunderstandings are part and parcel of the linguaculture practice of conversation (House, 2007). Seeing as the interpreta-tion of a message is essentially constructed by the perceiver, message sent is almost never equal to message received (Johnston, 1985). There are simply too many thought processes involved that precede the speaker's utterance and too many interpretative processes involved post-utterance for complete alignment to constitute a realistic outcome. Limaye (2000) therefore asserts that, because human perception is selective, reality is only ever partially perceived. He refers to the diversity of perception as 'one of the most fundamental concepts in intercultural communication' (p. 27). Reception Theory, grounded in literary criticism, established that, while an author tries to communicate his intentions, the content of a written text may be perceived differently by the reader. The American writer and critic Edmund Wilson once said 'No two persons ever read the same book'. What he means by this is that while the text stands (unaltered), every person's subjective interpretation flavours the text in slightly (or even drastically) different ways. Though these statements may have been made relating to literary works, the same applies to the interactional realm. An utterance may stand, but its interpretation constitutes a subjective reading and evaluation. Cultural differences of course only exacerbate this effect.

The following example exemplifies how the same behaviour can be inter-preted very differently and how behaviours can be attributed to motivations (typically ill-will) that may not have been intended.

Case study: Overcharging

During a recent visit to Yogyakarta in Central Java, I observed the following incident as part of a small tour group. The tour involved visits to three temples, one of which was smaller, and not much visited. The group consisted of four Germans travelling together, a Polish couple and myself.

While the entrance price for Borobudur Temple and Prambanan Temple were strictly regulated, when our driver collected the entry fee from us at the beginning of the day, he also included the fee for Mendut Temple. He was a little unclear about the entrance fee and said that usually the fee is 25,000 Rupiah, but that they might charge us 35,000 Rupiah there on that specific day, because it was a public holiday. However, he said that if we paid the money to him he could get us admission for only 15,000 Rupiah. So we all gave him the 15,000 Rupiah. However, once we were at the temple, one of the German travellers in my group found out that the actual admission charge was only 3,500 Rupiah and that our driver had overcharged us. He got very upset over this incident and started a lengthy negotiation with the driver and insisted the driver pay us back 7,000 Rupiah (approximately 40 Euro cents).

I would argue that 40 cents is not a significant amount of money to anyone who has sufficient funds to afford a flight ticket from Germany to Indonesia and was hardly worth the time, effort and nerves it took to negotiate the reimbursement. I would argue, though, that there were different interpretative frames at work that caused this somewhat unnecessary argument.

From a German perspective, the driver was dishonest and deceitful. This goes against fundamental principles in German culture, which places a prime value on honesty (see e.g. Zeidenitz & Barkow, 2005; Stadler, 2007). All four of the German participants felt that the driver's behaviour was entirely inadequate and insisted on the rectification.

However, from an Indonesian perspective, tourists are wealthy and it is entirely appropriate for tourists to pay significantly higher prices than locals (van Son, 2014; Prasetya, 2017). This was very clear at Borobudur Temple and Prambanan Temple where they had separate entrances (and payment booths) for tourists and locals and blatantly obviously charged substantially different fees. However, the Germans paid the far higher fees of 524,000 Rupiah without complaint (showing clearly that money was not the issue so long as the overcharging was institutionalized). They only took offence and had issues with the implied misappropriation of funds where they perceived the overcharging as a malicious act of conscious deceit.

From the driver's perspective, however, I would not be at all surprised if he thought he was doing us a favour and treating us very kindly, because he did not charge us the customary 25,000 or the holiday-inflated 35,000, but only slightly more than the actual entrance fee. Seeing as customary overcharging for tourists is the standard, then overcharging only slightly can actually be viewed as a rather generous gesture. In fact, while we all paid for an eight-hour tour, the driver let us spend as much time as we desired at the temples and the tour took nearly twelve hours in the end, even though I am relatively certain he would receive the same fee irrespective of how long it took, extending considerable effort and kindness to us on his part.

While the overcharging is factual, the viewpoints of the Indonesian driver and the German tourists were very different. This incident shows how subjective interpretations of the same events can have a drastically different meaning to a person, depending on their interpretative frames.

1.3 Implications for effective communication

I have established earlier that it is both unreasonable and impractical to expect someone to fully understand every single culture one comes into contact with. It is simply not feasible, though some preparation and interest in another culture will certainly help. To understand Japanese reluctance to use a foreign language, for example, it helps to understand a little about the cultural history of isolation and homogeneity, as well as the resultant Japanese psyche that can still be found in many Japanese people. To understand Javanese attitudes towards tourist pricing, for example, it helps to understand the socio-economic situation of the country. To read some basic information about a culture, or to speak to cultural informants (if possible), can therefore be beneficial. After all, some understanding is better than no understanding. However, it also needs to be pointed out that half-hearted attempts at understanding a culture can also have the reverse effect, as it can lead to stereotyping. Stereotyping in and of itself is not problematic, but normal and necessary for uncertainty reduction purposes (Becker, 1962) and to lighten the cognitive load. Unfortunately, once stereotypes are formed, people are no longer very willing to update them, but simply look to confirm their stereotypes while discarding disconfirming information. As Barna (1994, p. 341) pointed out: 'stereotypes are sustained and fed by the tendency to perceive selectively only those pieces of new information that correspond to the image held'.

Another problem with this form of preparation is that people think they know about the culture, which increases their confidence level in their actions, but not their actual behaviours. In the realm of forensic linguistics this is known as 'investigator bias'. A study by Meissner and Kassin (2002), for example, showed that actual investigators did not outperform either students trained with police manuals by the researchers or by naïve (untrained) students; however, they were significantly more confident in their judgements. The same dynamics apply to unsubstantiated intercultural preparation.

The solution is not to rely on second-hand opinions (i.e. stereotypes) entirely, but on (a) a willingness to update pre-conceived notions about a culture based on first-hand experiences, and (b) a willingness to work on enhancing perceptiveness, awareness and attuning skills. These serve us far better in dealing with situations on an ad hoc basis and better enable us in effective communication. The importance of perceptiveness and attuning skills has been outlined in depth in Stadler (2013b) and Spencer-Oatey and Stadler (2009). The effectiveness of honing such skills lies in their adaptability to suit situation-based, circumstantial and context-befitting demands on behaviours. This stands in stark contrast to the rigid, unmodified, generic, presumed behaviours that inflexible stereotypes lead us to, not least because they stigmatize cultural norms into one-mould-fits-all behaviours. We seem to have a good understanding of individual variation in our own cultures, but somehow we cannot conceptualize individual variation to the same extent in other cultures, where we have a tendency to expect people to behave in a much more homogenized fashion than they do. For this reason, perceptiveness and attuning skills are all the more relevant, as they enable us to accommodate the individual we meet, rather than the cultural stereotype we expect to meet, thus allowing for individual variation as well as generalized cultural awareness. I would argue that we all prefer to be treated as individuals rather than as generic representatives of our cultures. Accommodating the people we encounter as individuals is therefore something I regard as chiefly important to effective intercultural communication.

1.4 Summary

In this chapter, I have outlined that even basic demographic and contextual factors may impact communication across cultures, or even incite conflict on their own accord, unbeknownst to us. Understanding that virtually any difference, however small, can contribute to conflict, forms a vital platform for exploring the dynamics of communication across cultural contexts. To ameliorate their impact, a willingness and ability to adapt and accommodate to social, situational and contextual circumstances constitute a basic pre-requisite for intercultural effectiveness.

References

Alarape, A.I. (2008). Xenophobia: Contemporary issues in psychology. *IFE Psychologia* 16(2), 72–84.

Arka, W. (2005). Speech levels, social predicates and pragmatic structure in Balinese: A lexical approach. *Pragmatics 15*(2/3), 169–203.

Artawa, K. (2011). 'Some topic' in Balinese. Lecture at ILCAA. (Available from: www.aa.tufs.ac.jp/documents/forums/forum_2011_03en.pdf).

Banks, J.A. (1998). The lives and values of researchers: Implications for educating citizens in a multicultural society. *Educational Researcher 27*(7), 4–17.

Barke, A. & Uehara, S. (2005). Japanese pronouns of address. In R.T. Lakoff & S. Ide (eds.), *Broadening the Horizon of Linguistic Politeness* (pp. 301–314). Amsterdam: John Benjamins.

Barna, L.R. (1973). *A Lecture Note on Intercultural Communication.* Portland, OR: Portland State University.

Barna, L.M. (1994). Stumbling blocks in inter cultural communication. In L. Samovar & R. Porter (eds.), *Intercultural Communication: A Reader* (pp. 337–346). Belmont, CA: Wadsworth.

Becker, E. (1962). *The Birth and Death of Meaning.* New York:Free Press.

Berry, J. (1990). *Emics and Etics: The Insider/Outsider Debate.* Newbury Park, CA: Sage.

Bournois, F. & Chevalier, F. (1998). Doing research with foreign colleagues: A project-life cycle approach. *Journal of Managerial Psychology 13*(3/4), 206–213.

Brown, R. & Gilman, A. (1960). The pronouns of power and solidarity. In P. Giglioli (ed.), *Language and Social Context.* Harmondsworth: Penguin.

Cho, S. & Mor Barak, M.E. (2008). Understanding of diversity and inclusion in a perceived homogeneous culture: A study of organizational commitment and job performance among Korean employees. *Administration in Social Work 32*(4), 100–126.

Cho, Y.H. & Yoon, J. (2001). The origin and function of dynamic collectivism: An analysis of Korean corporate culture. *Asia Pacific Business Review 7*(4), 70–88.

Crawford, T., Candlin, S. & Roger, P. (2017). New perspectives on understanding cultural diversity in nurse-patient communication. *Collegian* 24(1), 63–69.

Cutrone, P. (2009). Overcoming Japanese EFL learners' fear of speaking. *Language Studies Working Papers* 1, 55–63.

Elmer, D. (1993). *Cross-Cultural Conflict.* Downers Grove, IL: InterVarsityPress.

Eto, J. (1977). Japanese shyness with foreigners. In P. Norbury (ed.), *Introducing Japan* (pp. 74–77). New York: St. Martin Press.

Fox, J.J. (2005). Ritual languages, special registers and speech decorum in Austronesian languages. In A. Adelaar & N.P. Himmelmann (eds.), *The Austronesian Languages of Asia and Madagascar* (pp. 87–102). Abingdon: Routledge.

Francis, J.N.P. (1991). When in Rome? The effects of cultural adaptation on intercultural business negotiations. *Journal of International Business Studies* 22(3), 403–428.

Fukada, A. & Asato, N. (2004). Universal politeness theory: Application to the use of Japanese honorifics. *Journal of Pragmatics* 36(11), 1991–2002.

Gomes, C. (2014). Xenophobia online: Unmasking Singaporean attitudes towards 'foreign talent' migrants. *Asian Ethnicity* 15(1), 21–40.

Günthner, S. & Luckmann, T. (2001). Asymmetries of knowledge in intercultural communication: The relevance of cultural repertoires of communicative genres. In A. Di Luzio, S. Günthner & F. Orletti (eds.), *Culture in Communication: Analyses of Intercultural Situations* (pp. 55–85). Amsterdam: John Benjamins.

Heidegger, M. (2001). *Poetry, Language, Thought* (A. Hofstadter, Trans.). New York: Harper PerennialModern Thought. (Original work published 1971).

Heine, B. & Song, K.A. (2011). On the grammaticalization of personal pronouns. *Journal of Linguistics* 47(3), 587–630.

Hinds, J. (1975). Third person pronouns in Japanese. In F.C.C. Peng (ed.), *Language in Japanese Society: Current Issues in Sociolinguistics* (pp. 128–157). Tokyo: University of Tokyo Press.

Horwitz, E., Horwitz, M. & Cope, J. (1986). Foreign language classroom anxiety. *Modern LanguageJournal* 70(2), 125–132.

House, J. (2007). Talking at cross-purposes: Misunderstanding in intercultural communication. In M. Al-Haj & R. Mielke (eds.), *Cultural Diversity and the Empowerment of Minorities* (pp. 41–60). New York:Berghahn Books.

Ide, S. (1989). Formal forms and discernment: Two neglected aspects of universals of linguistic politeness. *Multilingua* 8(2/3), 223–248.

Ide, S. (1997). *Joseego no sekai* [The world of women's language]. Tokyo: Meiji Shoin.

Jamieson, K.H. (1995). *Beyond the Double Bind: Women and Leadership*. New York: Doubleday.

Janssens, M. & Brett, J.M. (1997). Meaningful participation in transnational teams. *European Journal of Work and Organizational Psychology* 6(2), 153–168.

Johnston, J.R. (1985). How personality attributes structure interpersonal relations. In J. Berger & M. Zelditch (eds.), *Status, Rewards, and Influence* (pp. 317–349). San Francisco, CA: Jossey-Bass.

Kabaya, H., Kawaguchi, Y. & Sakamoto, M. (1998). *Keigo-hyōgen* [Expressions of the honorific language]. Tokyo: Taishukan Shoten.

Kowner, R. (2002). Japanese communication in intercultural encounters: The barrier of status-related behavior. *International Journal of Intercultural Relations* 26(4), 339–361.

kurosawa, S. (1972). Japanese terms of address: Some usages of the first and second person pronouns. *Papers in Japanese Linguistics* 1(2), 228–238.

LaFrance, M. & Mayo, C. (1978). Cultural aspects of nonverbal communication. *International Journal ofIntercultural Relations* 2(1), 71–89.

Lakoff, R.T. (2004). *Language and Woman's Place* (M. Bucholtz, Ed.). Oxford: Oxford University Press.

Lee, C.Y. (2012). Korean culture and its influence on business practice in South Korea. *The Journal of International Management Studies* 7(2), 184–191.

Leung, K., Tremain Koch, P. & Lu, L. (2002). A dualistic model of harmony and its implications for conflict management. *Asia Pacific Journal of Management* 19(2/3), 201–220.
Limaye, M.R. (2000). Perception is the thing: Presenting variant worldviews in the
international business communication classroom. *Business Communication Quarterly* 63(3),
25–36.
MacIntyre, P. & Gardner, R. (1989). Anxiety and second language learning: Toward a
theoretical clarification. *Language Learning* 39(2), 251–275.
Martin, S.E. (1988). *A Reference Grammar of Japanese.* Rutland, VT: Charles E. Tuttle.
Meissner, C.A. & Kassin, S.M. (2002). 'He's guilty!': Investigator bias in judgments of
truth and deception. *Law and Human Behavior* 26(5), 469–480.
Merriam, S.B., Johnson-Bailey, J., Lee, M.H., Kee, Y., Ntseane, G. & Muhamad, M.
(2010). Power and positionality: Negotiating insider/outsider status within and across
cultures. *International Journal of Lifelong Education* 20(5), 405–416.
Mitarai, S. (1988). Language and culture relationships: Some aspects of Japanese society,
culture and interpersonal intercultural communication. *Culture and Language* 21(1), 1–10.
Mitarai, S. & Moriyoshi, N. (2015). Language and culture relationships: Japanese as a
second language. 比較文化論叢 32, 71–80.
Miyazaki, A. (2004). Japanese junior high school girls' and boys' first-person pronoun
use and their social world. In S. Okamoto & J.S. Shibamoto Smith (eds.), *Japanese
Language, Gender, and Ideology: Cultural Models and Real People* (pp. 256–274). Oxford:
Oxford University Press.
Mogi, N. (2002). Japanese ways of addressing people. *Investigationes Linguisticae* 8, 14–22.
Neustupný, J.V. (2003). Japanese students in Prague. Problems of communication and
interaction. *International Journal of the Sociology of Language* 162, 125–143.
Nishiyama, K. (2000). *Doing Business with Japan.* Honolulu, HI: University of Hawai'i
Press.
Oakley, J.G. (2000). Gender-based barriers to senior management positions: Under-
standing the scarcity of female CEOs. *Journal of Business Ethics* 27(4), 321–334.
Okamoto, S. (1995). 'Tasteless' Japanese: Less 'feminine' speech among young Japanese
women. In K. Hall & M. Bucholtz (eds.), *Gender Articulated: Language and the Socially
Constructed Self* (pp. 297–325). New York:Routledge.
Oktarini, K.R. (2018). Enriching and not simply competing: Balinese language in con-
versational interaction in Bali. In N. Sudipa, I.B.P. Yadnya, M. Budiarsa & N.D.
Putra (eds.), *Proceeding of International Conference on Local Languages 2018* (pp. 405–
414). Bali: Udayana University Press.
Ono, R. & Thompson, S.A. (2003). Japanese (w)atashi/ore/boku 'I': They're not just
pronouns. *Cognitive Linguistics* 14(4), 321–347.
Park, G.S. & Kim, E.A. (2005). Changes in attitude toward work and workers' identity
in Korea. *Korea Journal* 45(3), 36–57.
Pizziconi, B. (2011). Japanese honorifics: The cultural specificity of a universal
mechanism. In D.Z. Kádár & S. Mills (eds.), *Politeness in East Asia* (pp. 45–71).
Cambridge: Cambridge University Press.
Prasetya, J. (2017). Understanding 'Bule Prices' in Indonesia. *Indonesia Expat.* (Available
from: http://indonesiaexpat.biz/other/scams-in-the-city/understanding-bule-price
s-indonesia/).
Prewitt-Freilino, J.L., Caswell, T.A. & Laakso, E.K. (2012). The gendering of language:
A comparison of gender equality in countries with gendered, natural gender, and
genderless languages. *Sex Roles* 66(3–4), 268–281.

Sarangi, S. (1994). Intercultural or not? Beyond celebration of cultural differences in miscommunication analysis. *Pragmatics* 4(3), 409–427.

Skoric, M.M., Chua, J.P.E., Liew, M.A., Wong, K.H. & Yeo, P.J. (2010). Online shaming in the Asian context: Community empowerment or civic vigilantism? *Surveillance and Society* 8(2), 181–199.

Spencer-Oatey, H. & Stadler, S. (2009). The Global People competency framework: Competencies for effective intercultural interaction. *Warwick Occasional papers in Applied Linguistics #3.* (Available from: https://warwick.ac.uk/fac/cross_fac/globalp eople/resourcebank/gppublications/).

Spencer-Oatey, H. & Xing, J. (2008). Issues of face in a Chinese business visit to Britain. In H. Spencer-Oatey (ed.), *Culturally Speaking* (pp. 258–273). London: Continuum.

Stadler, S. (2007). *Multimodal (Im)politeness: The Verbal, Prosodic and Non-Verbal Realization of Disagreement in German and New Zealand English.* Hamburg: Verlag Dr. Kovač.

Stadler, S. (2011). Intercultural competence and its complementary role in language education. In C. Perez-Llantada & M. Watson (eds.), *Specialized Languages in the Global Village: A Multi-Perspective Approach* (pp. 259–284). Cambridge: Cambridge Scholar Press.

Stadler, S. (2013a). Cultural Differences in the Orientation to Disagreement and Conflict. *China Media Research*; Special Issue: Managing Language and Cultural Challenges in Cross-Border Deal-Making 9(4), 66–75.

Stadler, S. (2013b). Why intercultural interaction demands a dual role-relationship. *Language and Dialogue* 3(2), 167–185.

Stadler, S. (2014). Intercultural Perceptions – What do we really know about each other? In S. Poutiainen (ed.), *Theoretical Turbulence in Intercultural Communication Studies* (pp. 101–120). Cambridge: Cambridge Scholar Press.

Stadler, S. & Choi, S. (2016). Inter-cultural communication: Which culture? *British Journal of Interdisciplinary Studies* 2(4), 1–23.

Sung, S. (2003). Women reconciling paid and unpaid work in a Confucian welfare state: The case of South Korea. *Social Policy and Administration* 37(4), 342–360.

Suzuki, T. (1978). *Japanese and the Japanese: Words in Culture.* Tokyo: Kodansha.

Takenoya, M. (1999). Sociolinguistic study on terms of address: Effect of ascribed and acquired factors on speaker and addressee gender. *Journal of the Society of Humanities* 66, 117–136.

Tanaka, K. (1999). Keigo wa nihongo o sekai kara tozasu [The honorific language isolates the Japanese language from the world]. *Gengo* 28(11), 41–47.

Thorne, S.L. (2003). Artifacts and cultures-of-use in intercultural communication. *Language Learning and Technology* 7(2), 38–67.

Ulijn, J.M. & St. Amant, K. (2000). Mutual intercultural perception: How does it affect technical communication? *Technical Communication* 47(2), 220–237.

van Son, B. (2014). Should tourists pay more than locals at attractions? (Available from: wwwbrendansadventures.com/should-tourist-pay-more-than-locals-at-tourist-attra ctions/).

von Glinow, M., Shapiro, D.L, & Brett, J.M. (2004). Can we talk, and should we? Managing emotional conflict in multicultural teams. *Academic Management Review* 29(4), 578–592.

Wall, J.A. & Callister, R.R. (1995). Conflict and its management. *Journal of Management* 21(3), 515–558.

Warnecke, A.M., Masters, R.D. & Kempter, G. (1992). The roots of nationalism: Nonverbal behavior and xenophobia. *Ethology and Sociobiology* 13(4), 267–282.

Wasserman, B.D. & Weseley, A.J. (2009). ¿Qué? Quoi? Do languages with grammatical gender promote sexist attitudes? *Sex Roles 61*, 634–643.

Zeidenitz, S. & Barkow, B. (2005). *The Xenophobe's Guide to the Germans.* London: Oval Books.

Chapter 2

Conflict orientation

Conflict arising from communication is an entirely natural aspect of communication and not in any way restricted or tied to intercultural communication. However, how we deal with and respond to conflict – or indeed – if we engage in conflict at all, is very much a cultural construct.

I need to state very explicitly though that not all members of a culture behave in identical ways. I do not wish to purport that every single individual will pertain to the cultural trends I present here. Ultimately, we are individuals with our own characteristics and personalities, not cultural automata. 'All cultures (including subcultures) are characterized by internal variation' (Aguilar, 1981, p. 25). In addition, many individuals now travel, study or reside overseas for periods of time. And even those who do not, have the world at their doorstep via the internet. These external influences should not be overlooked and a Japanese national who lived in Austria and the UK for several years will probably have adopted some communication patterns characteristic of these regions. People do not necessarily even have to leave their home countries for such shifts to occur. Parker, Haytko and Hermans (2009, p. 134) explain that Chinese students of a US school's satellite campus demonstrated more Western thinking and values without ever even leaving China, describing them as 'not your typical Chinese'. As such, it is unreasonable to expect all members of a society to behave in exactly the same ways. We are not robots after all.

However, I do believe that cultures, as a collective of individuals, do show certain tendencies, trends and preferences that can be useful in understanding an individual's actions. Or as Matsumoto (1993, p. 121) put it (in response to criticism that cultural comparisons should not be made when based on the notion of countries): 'Differences, when found, are indeed reflective of something.' I believe (and argue here) that differences are reflective of cultural orientations. The reason I speak of cultural orientations rather than of cultural behaviours is that it allows the view that individuals within a culture act along a continuum of culturally appropriate behaviours, but that a general consensus of what is appropriate in a culture nevertheless exists. We all grow up being socialized into a particular society with its norms, regulations and expectations, and it is all but impossible not to be influenced by this to a certain extent. I once read that in Spain even the atheists are Catholic and this very much highlights the point that if you grow up in a society surrounded by its norms, they will rub off on you invariably. After all, 'culture is a key determinant in what it means to be a person' (Benet-Martínez & Oishi, 2008, p. 543). So while not all members of a culture follow the exact same behavioural patterns or subscribe to them with the same rigour and consistency, there are certain cultural trends and preferences. And even the outliers of a society are still more likely to follow these patterns to a certain degree, even if they do not subscribe to them fully. Hence, if I speak of a conflict-avoidant culture, this does not mean that all members of this culture always avoid conflict in all circumstances, but for the most part, members of this society prefer to avoid conflict in most situations and circumstances over raising or escalating conflict and are prone to employ interactional strategies that indicate a dispreference for conflict when they do engage in it. We owe our inclination to conform to cultural norms to human nature, which involves that we are liable to be influenced by other people's behaviours and judgements of us; essentially constituting an innate version of self-inflicted peer pressure.

In a study on tax repayments by Hallsworth et al. (2017), it became evident that 13% of the people who had failed to pay their taxes on time made payment within 3 days of receiving the SMS that 9 out of 10 people in their area made tax payments on time. This constitutes a substantial increase in payments when compared to a basic SMS reminder with no appeal for normative behaviour. In other words, most people do not want to deviate from the norm, but like to be seen as fitting in with the standard. Consequently, most people do follow normative behaviours, patterns, trends and expectations within the same culture, even when they do so to slightly different degrees, with slight variations and slight individualized preferences. While there are no cultural absolutes, there are visible cultural trends. It is these that I will discuss in this chapter.

2.1 Conflict: micro and macro level

Before I explore the notion of conflict orientations across cultures, it is necessary to establish what types of conflict there are and which aspects of conflict will form the central focus of this book. Conflict can arise on both a micro and macro level and these are often interconnected. Most macro conflicts also manifest on the micro level or even derive from individualized tensions, and most micro conflicts have the potential to escalate. All forms of conflict can have serious consequences, ranging from a loss of trust and damage of interpersonal relationships to international conflicts and wars.

Macro level conflicts tend to be mostly of a political nature and typically derive from a variety of socio-political issues, and from perceived or real injustices, involving elements of social exclusion, ethnic reconciliations, cultural claims to use rights and belonging, historical racial injustice, or generalized feelings of intercultural hatred, to name but a few. The nature of such concerns can be quite diverse, though many do carry cultural elements. Some such cultural and inter-ethnic disputes are, for example, over land use in Alaska and Finland regarding native rights and subsistence use of land and resources versus general public access and recreational use (Kluwe & Krumpe, 2003). The New Zealand foreshore and seabed controversy constituted a similar issue over Māori claims to customary ownership of land below the mean high-water mark, which led to what Gagné (2008) refers to as ethnicization of New Zealand politics and constituted a conflict between the minority population with both the majority population and the state. The North Dakota pipeline protest also constitutes an escalation between minority groups and the state over the threat to their culture, violation of sacred ground and historical injustices as well (Carasik, 2016; Burleson, 2017). Such inter-ethnic, cultural conflicts have the potential to escalate into wars, as was the case in former Yugoslavia, or countless times throughout history. However, macro level conflicts can also exist on smaller scales, such as debates over inclusion concerns of minority groups (not necessarily only of a cultural nature) that address general social injustices of exclusion of minorities and appeal for more fairness to governments and legislation (e.g. Mackett, Achuthan & Titheridge, 2007). Cuesta and Murshed (2008) emphasize that factors such as inequality, poverty, polarization, exclusion, ethnic tensions and natural resources all contribute to conflict. Addison and Murshed (2001) speak of a breach of what they refer to as 'social contract', i.e. a framework of widely agreed rules, both formal and informal. In Cuesta and Murshed's (2008) view, conflict arises as a result of non-cooperation.

Micro level conflicts, on the other hand, refer more to interpersonal and interactional conflicts between individuals, rather than to tensions with political and governmental institutions. What is interesting is that the linguistic and communication sector employs nearly identical terminology when discussing micro level conflicts. Fraser (1990) and Fraser and Nolen (1981) speak of a conversational contract, which they claim interactants abide by. Lakoff (1973) speaks of a social norm model, Grice (1975) talks about Cooperative Principles, and Yule (1996) of observing social rules. In other words, the dynamics that influence conflict on a macro level play out in very similar ways on a micro level. However, it is vital to point out that all macro conflicts always also include forms of micro level conflicts between individuals as well. Kluwe and Krumpe (2003) classify even cultural and political conflicts as both micro and macro, involving both tangible and intangible issues. This, they purport, includes interpersonal conflict and social value conflict between individuals, which constitutes a pertinent issue in intercultural interaction as well. As such, the value of studying interpersonal conflict on a micro level should not be underestimated, as it will invariably carry implications for macro level conflict situations, or as Martin and Nakayama (2011: 15) put it: 'It would be naïve to assume that simply understanding something about intercultural communication would end war, but these problems do underscore the need for individuals to learn more about groups of which they are not members. Ultimately, people, not countries, negotiate and sign peace treaties.' With this statement, Martin and Nakayama highlight the fundamental and instrumental point, namely that change has to start with the individual and that each person carries this responsibility in our increasingly globalized and interconnected world.

2.2 Conflict: definition and terminology

Although terms such as disagreement, dissent and conflict are often employed in a somewhat interchangeable manner, some clarification for the usage of these terms and their differentiation is required and of value to the discussion of conflict. I shall define a disagreement as an utterance that 'qualifies, questions or opposes a prior utterance' (Stadler, 2007: 18). As such, disagreements are not necessarily an act of aggression or a precursor to a falling-out of any kind. They are mere expressions of differences in opinions or views. In having said this, people can and do feel quite strongly about some of their opinions and can become quite defensive or aggressive about upholding their viewpoint. While disagreement can be viewed as a relatively neutral speech act, it has the potential to build up to conflict.

My use of the word dissent, on the other hand, is representative of a disagreement to which people have attached a negative emotional reaction. While dissent is a disagreement which is tainted by negative affect, arising from an incompatibility of objectives, I view conflict as the aftermaths of tensions resulting from such emotions, i.e. disagreement gone awry. Pološki Vokić and Sonton (2010) define conflict as an 'interactive process manifested in incompatibility, disagreement, or dissonance within or between social entities (i.e. individual, group, organization, etc.)' (p. 56). In a sense then, conflict can be viewed as the behavioural and linguistic manifestation of negatively affective dissent. While many researchers do not seem to distinguish between disagreement, dissent and conflict, I think this distinction is an important one, because interactional impact and outcome are quite different. Richmond and McCroskey (2010) also highlight the importance of this distinction. They see disagreement as a normal and essential aspect of everyday conversation, while they see conflict as an escalated form of personalized disagreement, stating that 'when disagreement is personalized it becomes verbal aggression and the interaction becomes conflict' (p. 361).

Jehn (1992) emphasizes the effect of subjective responses and of taking disagreements personally. He sees conflict as an interpretive behaviour that involves the perceived incompatibilities between parties of the views, wishes and desires they each hold. This aspect of conflict is a critically important one, because the subjective perception and reaction to a situation means that conflict can arise between individuals and in contexts where the same situation would not lead to conflict among other individuals. Consequently, there are no intrinsically and innately problematic situations or communication aspects to intercultural communication, but are made so only by the interactants themselves. On the flip side, this implies that there are no intrinsically safe behaviours either. Mortensen (1974) speaks of a pre-dispositional factor, i.e. an expectation for conflict to occur, which regulates the degree to which people prefer to avoid conflict. The notion here is that perceptions of how likely conflict is to occur precludes to what extent we are likely to engage in it or not. This is particularly true considering that conflict is not a factual matter, but a matter of perception, or as Borisoff and Victor (1989: 20) put it: conflict 'does not actually exist but instead is perceived as existing'. In other words, different cultures in no way perceive argumentativeness, disagreement and conflict in the same terms. Resultant behaviours can thus be expected to differ accordingly. However, according to Kim et al. (2001), the role of such communicative predispositions on actual manifestations and behaviours is 'virtually unknown' (p. 404).

According to Nicotera and Robinson (2010), it is the 'differences in beliefs about and predispositions for aggression that require the most attention, as it is these differences that most perplex and aggrieve interactants, thereby begging for explanation' (p. 100). Suzuki and Rancer (1994, 256) assert that in intercultural encounters 'conflict can often be caused by differences in communicative behaviours grounded in different contextual and interactional norms'. If we assume that conflict behaviours are rooted in cultural norms, beliefs, attitudes and practices, then it is paramount to understand how exactly they are interlinked. To fully comprehend what constitutes conflict, how gravely conflict is perceived and whether cultures perceive a need for conflict resolution requires a sound understanding of the influence cultural priming and cultural value systems exert on us.

2.3 Preference structure

Disagreement has essentially been construed as what linguists refer to as dispreferred speech act. A dispreferred action is defined by Pomerantz (1984: 63) as 'an initial assessment [that] may be so structured that it invites one next action over its alternative. A next action that is oriented to as invited will be called a preferred next action, its alternative, a dispreferred next action'. Disagreement, she claims, is a dispreferred next action, unless it is produced subsequent to self-deprecation. The notion is that disagreement is unpleasant and unwelcome and that people go out of their way (at least in terms of communicative effort) to either try to avoid it altogether or to present it as a dispreferred option and ameliorate its impact. According to Gardner (2000), we mostly aim for agreement and conflict-avoidance in interaction. Festinger (1957) presents this as a de facto conditioning of human behaviour. He speaks of dissonance as a psychologically uncomfortable condition that 'will motivate the person to reduce the dissonance and achieve consonance', just as the condition of 'hunger leads to activity oriented to hunger reduction' (p. 3). Because of this 'natural' tendency, disagreements are perceived as face-threatening, as they 'challenge the fundamental tendency in talk to cooperate and align' (p. 32). Disagreements are regarded as delicate matters and many researchers share Pomerantz's (1984) and Gardner's (2000) views, portraying disagreements as face-threatening (see e.g. Lüger, 1999), because, as an oppositional move, they establish an adversarial position and involve some measure of hostility (Vuchinich, 1984). As people do not wish to threaten their social bonds, conflict – or rather the avoidance thereof – is dictated by the need for solidarity maintenance or building (Georgakopoulou, 2001). For this reason and because, for the most part, our drive to maintain social bonds is stronger than our wish to voice our own opinions, we invest substantial conversational effort in minimizing the impact of our disagreements. Disagreements are therefore often phrased to look like agreement or are at least weakened, Gardner (2000) claims. These studies all portray disagreement as the dispreferred option under most circumstances. The sheer number of disagremement markers and cues to signal dispreference for disagreement seems to confirm this view.

There are, however, two fundamental flaws with this kind of research: (a) within an argumentative framework, different norms are operationalized which diverge from 'normal' conversational standards and procedures and (b) the bulk of this research stems from English-speaking contexts, thereby portraying a somewhat biased and one-sided view of conflict orientations.

The notion that disagreement is dispreferred is a de-contextualized observation that simply does not hold across certain social situations. A preference for disagreement has been found to be inherent in certain communicative genres. For interviews and talk shows, adversarial talk has been found to be a standard and expected speech feature (Blum-Kulka et al., 2002; Greatbach, 1992; Yeager-Dror, 2002; Günthner & Luckmann, 2001). According to Clayman (1992), interviewers typically make provocative statements to open a discussion in order to elicit disagreement and they intervene to avoid closure and thereby encourage further disagreement (Myers, 1998), because they want to achieve a controversial, lively and entertaining discussion (Greatbach, 1992), and impoliteness has an entertainment value (Bousfield, 2007; Culpeper, 2005). While this is a very context-specific phenomenon, the preference for disagreement in conflict talk is not restricted to the genre of interviews and talk-shows alone, but applies to conflict talk in general. Within an argumentative framework, disagreement is not dispreferred. According to Bilmes (1993) and Kakava (2002), preference organization does not seem to operate in conflict talk. Under such circumstances, the expectation is that assessments will be disagreed with (Vuchinich, 1984). The reason why the typical constraints and markers for dispreference do not seem to apply in such conditions is that within the arena of conflict 'the overriding aim is not affiliation and cooperation but disaffiliation and conflict' (Auer et al., 1999: 78). Hence, attitudes towards disagreement and conflict are to some extent context-specific. However, while context undeniably constitutes an important element that informs our behaviours in conflictual circumstances, the basic platform for whether disagreement is viewed as dispreferred act comes largely down to cultural priming.

An enormous problem with the portrayal of disagreement as a categorically dispreferred speech act stems from the source cultures where much of the research on speech acts has been carried out. The discussion of disagreement and conflict comes predominantly from English-speaking and Commonwealth cultures, mostly North America, Britain, Australia and New Zealand. A less pronounced but secondary strand of research on this issue stems from Asian cultures, especially Japan and Mainland China. This research has, perhaps unsurprisingly, yielded very similar findings. While the similarity in findings may be due to very different cultural factors, such as an enculturated notion of routine politeness in English-speaking cultures, and a strong face-consciousness in many Asian cultures, the outcomes are fairly uniform. The problem with this research focus is that it may well be representative of these particular cultural contexts, but it presents a very incomplete and fragmented overgeneralization that may not be representative across all cultural boundaries. Even the cultural comparisons across these cultural contexts, Nicotera and Robinson (2010) raise conceptual equivalence concerns, cautioning that methodological frameworks that function in one cultural context are not necessarily transferrable as a measuring tool for other cultures. Suzuki and Rancer (1994, p. 257) admonish that researchers should carefully examine cultural equivalence before applying measurement tools across contexts, cautioning that 'we cannot simply assume that the internal structures of the two constructs, the orthogonal relationship between the two and the construct validity of the scales, which have been tested and supported in the United States, are generalizable to another cultural context'. In recent years, an ever-increasing number of studies have challenged this assumption of disagreement as categorically dispreferred speech act and demonstrated that this view by no means holds on a global scale.

Although, in reality, the notion of preference or dispreference toward disagreement exists along a continuum, there appears to be a somewhat dichotomous trend. Intuitively, it might seem a little hard to imagine that there are cultures that prefer disagreement over agreement, but this seems indeed to be the case. In their study on Jewish traditions of dispute, Blum-Kulka et al. (2002, p. 1572) found a 'long folk history of Jewish argumentativeness'. Their study confirms Schiffrin's (1984) earlier findings on Jewish conversational styles. They argue that Jewish culture shows a strong preference for disagreement over agreement and, as a consequence, lack the disagreement markers hailed as typical for data from US or Commonwealth contexts; quite the opposite in fact. Jewish disagreements have been found to be unmitigated, unprefaced and lacking in dispreference marking. In other words, instead of minimizing disagreement, this culture has a tendency to foreground disagreement. Jewish culture is not an isolated case. A preference for a direct, confrontational disagreeing style has also been identified in Turkish culture (Doğançay-Aktuna & Kamışlı, 2001), Venezuelan culture (Edstrom, 2004), African American culture

(Goodwin, 1990), Polish culture (Ronowicz, 1995), Austrian culture (Gruber, 1993), German culture (House, 1986; Günthner, 1994; Günthner & Luckmann, 2001), Spanish culture (Fant, 1992), and Greek culture (Kakava, 2002). The preference for disagreement in these cultures should not be misinterpreted as a lack of politeness, consideration or face-concern, however (cf. Stadler, 2007). Rather, it has to do with whether a confrontational style is an acceptable or potentially even desirable attribute in a culture. While it has been argued that English-speaking and Asian cultures show a tendency to agree, cooperate and align, these mostly European, Middle Eastern and Latin cultures lean towards open, straightforward and unmitigated communication.

It may seem counter-intuitive that disagreement should be seen as something enjoyable. Yet, this phenomenon is fairly pervasive. In a study comparing the disagreeing behaviour of Germans and New Zealanders (Stadler, 2002), German participants commented that they enjoyed a 'good, heated debate'. The background to viewing disagreement as sociable is bi-fold. On the one hand, disagreement is seen as a willingness to interact and engage with others, along the lines of: 'if we all agree all the time what is there left to talk about'. Disagreement can foster and encourage interaction and in the genre of political television discussions, this phenomenon is deliberately exploited for viewership. This genre, as well as other genres, purposely invites discussants of opposing opinions (cf. e.g. Clayman, 2002; Greatbatch & Dingwall, 1997; Heritage, 2002; Jacobs, 2002). Agreement would make for very meagre entertainment. The German expression 'wie Suppe ohne Salz' ('like soup without salt') indicates that an interaction without disagreement would be considered rather bland and boring. On a trip to Borobudur temple in Java I overheard a German member of my tour group stating bluntly: 'Entweda mia diskutiern hier oda mia lass mas bleim' ('either we are having a discussion here or we leave it be altogether'). This exclamation very nicely demonstrates the German attitude that whatever a person has to say they should be able to say unimpededly – even if it ruffles a few feathers – or there is no point in talking to others at all. As a cultural construct, this attitude reaches far beyond genre-specific concerns and instead spans across most contexts and circumstances, as Günthner's (2008) research, among others, highlights. Günthner (2008, p. 208) confirms in her research on German–Chinese conversations that Germans assessed their conversational partners as 'just not interesting' and 'boring conversationalists' on the basis of their evasion of argumentative exchanges, something that she refers to as a rather typical expectation within German student culture. Although Richmond and McCroskey (2010) relate this discussion to individual personality traits rather than cultural trends, they highlight that people with a high propensity for argumentativeness enjoy arguing and debating, and that this form of argumentation is carried out as a form of recreation. Their view postulates that people have a different tolerance for disagreement and that this impacts on whether people engage or disengage from argumentative discussions. Although they do not mention culture, findings on cultures such as German, Jewish, Spanish or Greek culture seem to suggest that this is not merely a matter of personality, but that such personality traits are more prevalent in some cultural context than others, presumably because some cultures embrace and reward individual expression and action. If a culture celebrates debate and flamboyant discussion tactics, it makes sense that such a thing is also practised and adopted more widely. Ramirez et al. (2001, p. 314) liken aggressiveness to cultural values and norm sets, claiming that 'norms for aggression vary considerably among cultures'. In that sense then, tolerance for verbal aggression can indeed be regarded as a cultural trait, rather than merely as an idiosyncratic matter of personality.

In such cultures, argumentative behaviours are tied to the notion of face, though the motivations differ starkly to the face concerns that guide Asian conflict-avoidance. In German culture, it can be considered more face-threatening not to be able to defend one's opinion or not to stand up for oneself (Kotthoff, 1991) than to generate conflict in the process of arguing one's point. People may be considered as lacking 'backbone', wit or skill if they give in to disagreement too easily. Voicing one's opinion outright is not only considered acceptable, but also desirable (depending of course on the social, contextual and situational circumstances). Consequently, face is an important social construct that either prevents cultures from engaging in disagreement, because it could threaten the recipient's face, or propels cultures to engage in disagreement, because it could threaten the speaker's own face not to do so.

What happens when such divergent cultural preferences collide can be illustrated in the following example.

Case study: Preference clash

At an English language school in Cairns (Queensland, Australia), students were paired up and tasked with discussing recent movies they watched. I was paired up with a Japanese girl, and, as a starting point to the conversation, I inquired whether the Japanese girl liked a particular movie, to which she responded 'yes'. However, in the subsequent discussion, it became evident that she did not seem to like the movie. As a response, I asked her again. The Japanese girl's answer became more evasive this time, though she still upheld that she liked the movie. I then became frustrated with the less-than-concrete answer and retorted in an exasperated tone: 'well did you like it or not?', to which the Japanese girl eventually responded with 'not really'.

My expectation was clear, honest, straightforward communication embedded in an engaging discussion of opinions. The Japanese girl's expectation was polite, other-oriented communication. She probably did not want to offend my opinion, already knowing that I liked the movie. Her evasive behaviour was well-intended and face-saving. However, being unfamiliar with Japanese culture at this point, I interpreted this behaviour as intentionally deceitful, which I considered entirely unnecessary, especially given the trivial nature of the subject under discussion. The Japanese girl's

> reaction left no doubt that she considered my pressing for an answer and raised, exasperated tone of voice intimidating, pushy and most likely also more than just a little rude.

While no negative intent occurred on either side, communication broke down quickly, because of the misalignment in expectations on appropriate speaking conventions and a complete failure to understand the dynamics that informed the other's communicative choices. We both avoided each other after this incident and I have no doubt that this incident left the Japanese girl with equally negative impressions as it did me.

Günthner (2000) discusses another such example where cultural differences concerning the willingness to engage in argumentative exchanges led to a breakdown in communication. While Germans saw argumentative exchanges as a way to get to know someone and cherish the idea of having a good argumentative exchange, the Chinese exchange students did not. Günthner (2000, p. 218) reports the Chinese perceiving the German students as 'direct', 'aggressive' and 'rude', while the Chinese students were labelled by the German students as 'just not interesting', 'don't have opinions', and 'awkward'. With the resultant negative mutual perceptions, the desire to continue such intercultural exchanges was, understandably, not great, despite the fact that the German students were keen on meeting Chinese students, due to their interest in the culture.

Despite the intention to make communication work (and cooperation may not always be a given in intercultural communication), a misalignment for preferences for/against argumentative discourse can bring interactional exchanges to a halt. This can be sufficient to not only hamper communication, but also the relationship altogether.

2.4 Orientations and their impact

Differences in attitudes invariably also impact behaviour. Behavioural differences are therefore equally as different as people's perceptions and attitudes. However, the impact on behaviours is not the only concern. As the aforementioned example of my discussion with a Japanese girl has demonstrated, behavioural differences also exert a strong impact on mutual perceptions, and hold potential for more grave repercussions on relationships, business outcomes, etc.

In a contrastive study comparing German and New Zealand disagreeing behaviours (Stadler, 2007), Germans were found to use significantly more verbal, non-verbal and prosodic strengthening devices during disagreement, while at the same time producing only half as many mitigation devices. Hence, instead of ameliorating the impact of a disagreement, like English-speaking cultures have been found to do, they used upgraders to strengthen the force of disagreements – a clear indicator that this culture has no inclination towards conflict-avoidance. However, this type of stance towards open disagreement is not at all appreciated by members of other cultures. The same study reports that German disagreeing behaviour was perceived negatively by New Zealanders. Dunkel and Meierewert (2004) also report that Hungarian employees 'often see open critique expressed by their Austrian or German colleagues as impropriety and disrespect' (p. 162).

However, such effects have not only been observed of German and Austrian cultures. Ogiermann (2009) reports that imperatives, as a form of request, are more likely to be seen as polite by Polish and Russian interlocutors than by English speakers, where they are more likely to be perceived as face-threatening. Russians are reported to be more prone to see indirectness not as a form of politeness, but as a waste of the hearer's time (Zemskaja, 1997, cited in Ogiermann). Ogiermann (2009) further reports that Russians do not necessarily regard a request as imposition, nor does a refusal to a request involve the same degree of face-loss as it would in other cultures. This further evidences not only that attitudes towards face-threatening speech acts are culturally primed, but also that the consequences cultures accord to potential communication outcomes are quite different. If a speech act is not seen as particularly imposing in the first place, and if face-loss is not perceived to be as grave, then this allows for much more direct and straightforward communication. It is then unsurprising that she found that direct requests have a more central role in Polish and Russian cultures than in the already relatively direct German culture. Where other cultures would be far more likely to employ interrogative structures for requests, in Russian culture, imperatives are the most frequent and appropriate strategy (Rathmayr, 1994). A higher level of directness is also reported for Persian speakers by Jalilifar (2009). Hidalgo, Hidalgo and Downing (2014) also speak of directness as being closely associated with continental Spanish culture. The participants in their study were found to try to employ the model of indirectness found in English, but nevertheless ended up using a wider range and more direct types of strategies than native speakers, seeing as in their culture, disagreement is not a dispreferred act of speech. Hence, despite efforts of accommodation, the cultural tendency of speakers towards a more open engagement with disagreement is still observable.

This is in stark contrast to behavioural outputs that are associated with interlocutors from many Asian cultural contexts. According to Gao (1998), Chinese endorse conflict-avoidance and take more indirect approaches to conflict situations. In their observations on Chinese students, Walker et al. (1996) found that students seemed very reluctant to challenge each other and a lack of open conflict was very noticeable. While students reluctantly engaged in discussing differing opinions, they seemed to refrain from allowing disagreement to become heated or emotional. Walker et al. (1996) therefore conclude that verbal exchanges in Chinese culture are means of expressing affect and strengthening relationships, so argumentative and confrontational modes are seen as counter-productive to these goals. Miike (2006) refers to Asian communication style as responsive, cooperative and yielding, while he describes the speech style typical for many Western cultures as confronting, aggressive and assertive. Being assertive, however, is not valued in Chinese culture, but reflects ill character and threatens harmony and cohesion of interpersonal relationships (Gao, 1998), direct confrontation is thus deemed rude and consequently avoided (Tang & Ward, 2003). Conversely, an unwillingness to engage in an argumentative debate style is seen as a refusal to work on establishing an interesting, engaging and meaningful basis for a relationship in many Western contexts. The notion in such cultures is that, by making opinions, views and standpoints clear early in a relationship, it shows whether interactants have things in common. Personal views on general topics are able to tell us a lot about the person we are interacting with, hence, they provide an opportunity to establish whether there is common ground for a future relationship.

Given these discrepant viewpoints surrounding conflict situations, it is not hard to see why negative perceptions can arise across cultures. These clashes in both attitudes and behavioural practices incur mutually unfavourable impressions, and thereby impact to no small degree on intercultural relations. Attitudes are therefore much more than mere differences in opinion. They lay the foundation for dislike and distrust, when overlooked or ignored.

2.5 Summary

This chapter has addressed the notion that our attitudes towards conflict, and our approach to resolving it, is to a substantial degree influenced by the preference structures and orientations of our cultural backgrounds. The findings of this discussion are indicative of the fact that cultures exist along a continuum of conflict-related comfort levels. While some cultures are accepting of disagreement, or even of stronger, more aggravated forms of dissent, other cultures tend to shy away from disagreement, or the mere expression of opinions, even in the early and relatively more neutral stages of interactional development. Preferential differences can lead to negative impressions of the interactional partners at best, or even a complete fall-out resulting from a misinterpretation of the other's intentions. If we attribute another person's stance towards conflict as a character flaw, ill-will, uncooperative behaviour, aggressive nature, or as an unwillingness to align and compromise, then it will severely impact on the relationship with this person, and as a consequence, on interactional and transactional outcomes. Shachaf (2008) reports that the harmony-oriented Japanese style, which is focused on maintaining relationships, was perceived by Americans as creating conflict and intensifying existing misunderstandings. A conflict-avoidant style can therefore become the impetus for conflict itself. A better understanding of such interactional mechanisms can facilitate intercultural attitudes and foster more accurate interpretations of other people's behaviours and their intentions. Hence, by understanding how others view disagreement and dissent, we may well be able to avoid conflict from arising.

References

Addison, T. & Murshed, S.M. (2001). From conflict to reconstruction: Reviving the social contract. UNU/WIDER Discussion Paper No. 48. Helsinki: UNU/WIDER. (Available from: www.wider.unu.edu/research).

Aguilar, J.L. (1981). Insider research: An ethnography of a debate. In D.A. Messerschmidt (ed.), *Anthropologists at Home in North America* (pp. 15–26). Cambridge: Cambridge University Press.

Auer, P., Couper-Kuhlen, E. & Müller, F. (1999). On the prosody and syntax of turn-continuation. In E. Couper-Kuhlen & M. Selting (eds.), *Prosody in Conversation* (pp. 57–100). Cambridge: Cambridge University Press.

Benet-Martínez, V. & Oishi, S. (2008). Culture and personality. In O.P. John, R.W. Robins & L.A. Pervin (eds.), *Handbook of Personality: Theory and Research* (pp. 542–567). New York:Guilford Press.

Bilmes, J. (1993). Ethnomethodology, culture, and implicature: Toward an empirical pragmatics. *Pragmatics* 3(4), 387–411.

Blum-Kulka, S., Blondheim, M. & Hacohen, G. (2002). Traditions of dispute: From negotiations of Talmudic texts to the arena of political discourse in the media. *Journal of Pragmatics* 34(10–11), 1569–1594.

Borisoff, D. & Victor, D. (1989). *Conflict Management: A Communication Skills Approach.* Englewood Cliffs, NJ: Prentice-Hall.

Bousfield, D. (2007). Impoliteness, preference organization and conductivity. *Multilingua* 26(3), 1–34.

Burleson, E. (2017). Dakota access to justice and pipeline politics: Tribal consultation, environmental justice and rules of engagement. In W.H. Rogers & E. Burleson (eds,), *Environmental Law Treatise.* Toronto: Thomson Reuters.

Carasik, L. (2016). Dakota pipeline protest is a harbinger of many more. (Available from: http://digitalcommons.law.wne.edu/cgi/viewcontent.cgi?article=1133&context=media).

Clayman, S.E. (1992). Footing in the achievement of neutrality: The case of news-interview discourse. InP. Drew & J. Heritage (eds.), *Talk at Work: Interaction in Institutional Settings* (pp. 163–198). Cambridge: Cambridge University Press.

Clayman, S.E. (2002). Disagreements and third parties: Dilemmas of neutralism in panel news interviews. *Journal of Pragmatics* 34(10–11), 317–328.

Cuesta, J. & Murshed, M. (2008). The mircro-foundations of social contracts, civil conflicts and international peace-making. MICROCON Research Working Paper 8. Brighton: MICROCON.

Culpeper, J. (2005). Impoliteness and entertainment in the television quiz show: The Weakest Link. *Journal of Politeness Research* 1(1), 35–72.

Doğançay-Aktuna, S. & Kamışlı, S. (2001). Linguistics of power and politeness in Turkish: Revelations from speech acts. In A. Bayraktaroğlu \ M. Sifianou (eds.), *Linguistic Politeness across Boundaries: The Case of Greek and Turkish* (pp. 75–104). Amsterdam: John Benjamins.

Dunkel, A. & Meierewert, S. (2004). Culture standards and their impact on teamwork: An empirical analysis of Austrian, German, Hungarian and Spanish culture differences. *Journal for East European Management Studies* 9(2), 147–174.

Edstrom, A. (2004). Expressions of disagreement by Venezuelans in conversation: Reconsidering the influence of culture. *Journal of Pragmatics* 36(8), 1499–1518.

Fant, L. (1992). Scandinavians and Spaniards in negotiation. In I.A. Sjogren & L. Janson (eds.), *Culture and Management in the Field of Ethnology and Business Administration* (pp. 125–153). Stockholm: Stockholm School of Economics and the Swedish Immigration Institute and Museum.

Festinger, L. (1957). *A Theory of Cognitive Dissonance*. Evanston, IL: Row, Peterson & Co.

Fraser, B. (1990). Perspectives on politeness. *Journal of Pragmatics* 14(2), 219–236.

Fraser, B. & Nolen, W. (1981). The association of deference with linguistic form. *International Journal of the Sociology of Language* 27, 93–109.

Gagné, N. (2008). On the ethnicisation of New Zealand politics: The foreshore and seabed controversy in context. *The Asia Pacific Journal of Anthropology* 9(2), 123–140.

Gao, G. (1998). Don't take my word for it: Understanding Chinese speaking practices. *International Journal of Intercultural Relations* 22(2), 163–186.

Gardner, R. (2000). Resources for delicate manoeuvres: Learning to disagree. *Australian Review of Applied Linguistics* 16, 32–47.

Georgakopoulou, A. (2001). Arguing about the future: On indirect disagreements in conversation. *Journal of Pragmatics* 33(12), 1881–1900.

Goodwin, M.H. (1990). *He-Said-She-Said: Talk as Social Organization among Black Children*. Bloomington, IN: Indiana University Press.

Greatbatch, D. (1992). On the mangaement of disagreement between news interviewees. In P. Drew & J. Heritage (eds.), *Talk at Work: Interaction in Institutional Settings* (pp. 268–301). Cambridge: Cambridge University Press.

Greatbatch, D. & Dingwall, R. (1997). Argumentative talk in divorce mediation sessions. *American Sociological Review* 62, 151–170.

Grice, H.P. (1975). Logic and conversation. In P. Cole & J.L. Morgan (eds.), *Syntax and Semantics 3: Speech Acts* (pp. 41–58). New York:Academic Press.

Gruber, H. (1993). Öffentlicher Dissens. *Wiener Linguistische Gazette* 47(4), 1–27.

Günthner, S. (1994). 'Also moment so seh ich das nicht'. Informelle Diskussionen im interkulturellen Kontext. *Zeitschrift für Literaturwissenschaft und Linguistik* 24(3), 97–122.

Günthner, S. (2000). Argumentation and resulting problems in the negotiation of rapport in a German-Chinese conversation. InH.Spencer-Oatey (ed.), *Culturally Speaking*. London: Continuum.

Günthner, S. (2008). Negotiating rapport and German-Chinese conversation. In H. Spencer-Oatey (ed.), *Culturally Speaking* (pp. 207–226). London: Continuum.

Günthner, S. & Luckmann, T. (2001). Asymmetries of knowledge in intercultural communication: The relevance of cultural repertoires of communicative genres. In A. Di Luzio, S. Günthner & F. Orletti (eds.), *Culture in Communication: Analyses of intercultural situations* (pp. 55–85). Amsterdam: John Benjamins.

Hallsworth, M., List, J., Metcalfe, R. & Vlaev, I. (2017). The behavioralist as tax collector: Using natural field experiments to enhance tax compliance. *Journal of Public Economics* 148, 14–31.

Heritage, J. (2002). The limits of questioning: Negative interrogatives and hostile question content. *Journal of Pragmatics* 34(10–11), 1427–1446.

Hidalgo, L., Hidalgo, R. & Downing (2014). Strategies of (in)directness in Spanish speakers' production of complaints and disagreements in English and Spanish. InM. de los Ángeles Gómez González, F. Ruiz de Mendoza Ibáñez, F. Gonzálvez García

& A. Downing (eds.), *The Functional Perspective on Language and Discourse* (pp. 261–284). Amsterdam: John Benjamins.

House, J. (1986). Cross-cultural pragmatics and foreign language teaching. In Seminar für Sprachlehrforschung der Ruhr-Universität Bochum (ed.), *Probleme und Perspektiven der Sprachlehrforschung. Bochumer Beiträge zum Fremdsprachenunterricht in Forschung und Lehre* (pp. 281–295). Frankfurt: Scriptor.

Jacobs, S. (2002). Maintaining neutrality in dispute mediation: Managing disagreement while managing not to disagree. *Journal of Pragmatics* 34(10–11), 1403–1426.

Jalilifar, A. (2009). Request strategies: Cross-sectional study of Iranian EFL learners and Australian native speakers. *English Language Teaching* 2(1), 46–61.

Jehn, K.A. (1992). The impact of intragroup conflict on group effectiveness: A multi-method examination of the benefits and detriments of conflict. Doctoral Dissertation, North Western University.

Kakava, C. (2002). Opposition in modern Greek discourse: Cultural and contextual constraints. *Journal of Pragmatics* 34(10–11), 1537–1568.

Kim, M.S., Aune, K.S., Hunter, J., Kim, H. & Kim, J. (2001). The effect of culture and self-construals on predisposition toward verbal communication. *Human Communication Research* 27(3), 382–408.

Kluwe, J. & Krumpe, E.E. (2003). Interpersonal and societal aspects of use conflicts. *International Journal of Wilderness* 9(3), 28–33.

Kotthoff, H. (1991). Zugeständnisse und Dissens in deutschen, anglo-amerikanischen und in nativ-nichtnativen Gesprächen. *Linguistische Berichte* 135, 375–397.

Lakoff, R. (1973). The logic of politeness: Or, minding your p's and q's. In *Papers from the Ninth Regional Meeting of the Chicago Linguistic Society* (pp. 292–305). Chicago: Chicago Linguistic Society.

Lüger, H.H. (1999). A propos de la politesse verbale: Aspects descriptifs et didactique. *Französisch Heute 2*, 132–143.

Mackett, R.L., Achuthan, K. & Titheridge, H. (2007). Conflicts between macro level policy and micro level implementation – the case of social exclusion. *Social Research in Transport Clearninghouse.* (Available from: ///C:/Users/s.stadler/Downloads/view content.cgi.pdf).

Martin, J.N. & Nakayama, T.K. (2011). *Experiencing Intercultural Communication.* New York:McGraw-Hill.

Matsumoto, D. (1993). Ethnic differences in affect intensity, emotion judgments, display rule attitudes, and self-reported emotional expression in an American sample. *Motivation and Emotion* 17(2), 107–123.

Miike, Y. (2006). Non-Western theory in Western research? An Asiacentric agenda for Asian communication studies. *The Review of Communication* 6(1–2), 4–31.

Mortensen, C. (1974). A transactional paradigm of verbalized social conflict. In G. Miller & H. Simons (eds.), *Perspectives on Communication in Social Conflict* (pp. 90–124). Englewood Cliffs, NJ: Prentice-Hall.

Myers, G. (1998). Displaying opinions: Topics and disagreements in focus groups. *Language in Society* 27(1), 85–111.

Nicotera, A.M. & Robinson, N.M. (2010). Culture and aggressive communication. In T.A. Avtgis & A.S. Rancer (eds.), *Arguments, Aggression and Conflict.* New York: Routledge.

Ogiermann, E. (2009). Politeness and in-directness across cultures: A comparison of English, German, Polish and Russian requests. *Journal of Politeness Research* 5, 189–216.

Parker, R.S., Haytko, D.L. & Hermans, C.M. (2009). Individualism and collectivism: Reconsidering old assumptions. *Journal of International Business Research* 8(1), 127–139.

Pološki Vokić, N. & Sonton, S. (2010). The relationship between individual characteristics and conflict handling styles: The case of Croatia. *Problems and Perspective in Management* 8(3), 56–67.

Pomerantz, A. (1984). Agreeing and disagreeing with assessments: Some features of preferred/dispreferred turn shapes. In M. Atkinson & J. Heritage (eds.), *Structures of Social Action: Studies in Conversation Analysis* (pp. 57–101). Cambridge: Cambridge University Press.

Ramirez, J.M., Andreu, J.M. & Fujihara, T. (2001). Cultural and sex differences in aggression: A comparison between Japanese and Spanish students using two different inventories. *Aggressive Behaviour* 27(4), 313–322.

Rathmayr, R. (1994). Pragmatische und sprachlich konzeptualisierte Charakteristika russischer direktiver Sprechakte. In H.R. Mehling (ed), *Slavistische Linguistik 1993* (pp. 251–277). Munich: Otto Sagner.

Richmond, V.P. & McCroskey, J.C. (2010). Tolerance for disagreement. In T. Avtgis & A. Rancer (eds.), *Arguments, Aggression, and Conflict: New Directions in Theory and Research* (pp. 359–371). London: Sage.

Ronowicz, E.A. (1995). Aussies are friendly and Poles aren't rude: Some remarks on overcoming problems in intercultural communication. *Papers and Studies in Contrastive Linguistics* 30, 31–44.

Schiffrin, D. (1984). Jewish argument as sociability. *Language in Society* 13(3), 311–335.

Shachaf, P. (2008). Cultural diversity and information and communication technology impacts on global virtual teams: An exploratory study. *Information and Management* 45(2), 131–142.

Stadler, S.A. (2002). Learning to disagree in German: The case of New Zealand University students. Unpublished MA Thesis, Victoria University of Wellington.

Stadler, S.A. (2007). *Multimodal (Im)Politeness: The Verbal, Prosodic and Non-Verbal Realization of Disagreement in German and New Zealand English*. Hamburg: Verlag Dr. Kovač.

Suzuki, S. & Rancer, A.S. (1994). Argumentativeness and verbal aggressiveness: Testing for conceptual and measurement equivalence across cultures. *Communication Monographs* 61(3), 256–279.

Tang, J. & Ward, A. (2003). *The Changing Face of Chinese Management*. London: Routledge.

Vuchinich, S. (1984). Sequencing and social structure in family conflict. *Social Psychology Quarterly* 47(3), 217–234.

Walker, A., Bridges, E. & Chan, B. (1996). Wisdom gained, wisdom given: Instituting PBL in a Chinese culture. *Journal of Educational Administration* 34(5), 12–31.

Yaeger-Dror, M. (2002). Register and prosodic variation, a cross-language comparison. *Journal of Pragmatics* 34(10–11), 1495–1536.

Yule, G. (1996). *Pragmatics*. Oxford: Oxford University Press.

Zemskaja, E.A. (1997). Kategorija vežlivosti: Obšie voprosy – nacional'no-kul – turnaja specifika russkogo jazyka. *Zeitschrift für Slavische Philologie* 5, 271–301.

Chapter 3

Conversational style

Drake (1995) refers to style as a multidimensional construct relating to patterned responses or predispositions to utilize particular groups of interrelated behaviours over others in specific contexts.

Of particular interest is her notion of multidimensionality, since style can indeed comprise of a vast array of culture-specific preferences, including communication styles (such as argumentation, negotiation and persuasion styles), writing styles, intellectual styles and presentation styles, to name only some of the most pervasive language/communication related aspects. Communication styles vary enormously across cultures, contributing to what Hooker (2008) refers to as a staggering variety of styles.

3.1 Stylistic preferences and their impact on conflict

While style might seem to constitute a minor cultural difference with relatively modest repercussions, it probably has become clear by now that nothing in intercultural communication is too minor to cause issues and potentially lead to conflict, or at the very least, unfavourable attitudes towards others. Viewing the concept of style through the eyes of Count de Buffon (cited by Dournon, 1994, p. 394), who claimed that 'le style est l'homme même' ('style is the person him/herself'), it becomes much more clear why style can become problematic. If style is seen as an extension of a person, then any negative attitudes towards a particular style or disregard for someone's stylistic preferences can be taken rather personal, as indeed Faure (1999) states of violating Chinese negotiation preferences and principles. Consequently, stylistic differences matter, as they can assert a substantial impact on impression management and interpersonal relations.

3.1.1 Information density and presentation style

Culture has been known to affect us on largely subconscious levels across a multitude of domains (see e.g. Stadler, 2007; Zaharna, 1995). This includes even design-related and aesthetic sensibilities. According to Lavie and Tractinsky (2004), culture has an effect on user perception of aesthetics and usability. Marcus and

Baumgartner (2004) observed culturally diverse preferences of user interfaces on websites, including different preferences for graphical layouts. One of the most eye-opening and memorable instances of working on the eChina-UK project was when one of the participants commented on the Chinese Powerpoint presentation style.

Case Study: Powerpoint

The 'busyness' of Chinese websites ... is also apparent in Powerpoint presentations. We see a few brief bullet points as a more effective communication medium than the 'kitchen sink' style of the Chinese Powerpoint. I always thought that was because the Chinese just didn't understand Powerpoint - now I know that it was me not understanding the Chinese. (Reid, Stadler & Spencer-Oatey, 2009, p. 21)

The insight the participant gained, i.e. that it was his inability to correctly interpret Chinese motivations for this particular presentation style that led to his negative perceptions is indeed correct. Schmid-Isler (2000) found that Chinese websites are often more complex, while Western websites tend to be organized around one focal point. According to Reinecke, Schenkel and Bernstein (2010), Eastern cultures often opt for user interfaces with high information density, whereas Westerners prefer lower information density with greater structure. Finns, for example, have been found to lean towards simplicity and functionality (Karvonen, 2000). People unconsciously integrate their cultural values into functionalities and aesthetics (Reinecke, Schenkel & Bernstein, 2010). The same dynamics of course apply to the perceiver, who also brings his own expectations and preferences to the table, be it in web-based user interfaces, Powerpoint presentations, academic seminars or business meetings.

As this example demonstrates, even simple design choices can become catalysts for negative impressions of others' levels of competence, as neither the designation 'kitchen sink', nor the notion that the Chinese do not understand how to use a standard presentation tool are very favourable. Yet, it is not a simple matter to identify what constitutes a stylistic preference. Zaharna (1995, p. 242) cites Daniels (1975) as stating that 'when differences aren't perceived as differences, they are perceived as right and wrong'. According to Hooker (2008), American presentation slides typically contain flashy visuals with catchphrases that were perceived by Germans as childish. What this implies is that we are much more prone to denounce someone else's preferences than to question the influences that inform them, even when it pertains to something as minor as visual aesthetics.

3.1.2 Formality style

Another, somewhat more grave difference can be found in stylistic preferences regarding formality levels, as they are inadvertently tied to notions of politeness, hierarchy and respect. Different cultures emphasize either more formal or more casual ways of interacting, both in informal settings and professional contexts. It is not surprising that a culture, such as Japan, that emphasizes vertical interpersonal relationships (Nishiyama, 2000) and a hierarchical workplace structure (Wingate, 2011) gravitate more towards a formal tone in interaction. This is especially important when even minor age gaps impact on seniority and resultant rights, even in informal settings. More egalitarian cultures are prone to adopt fairly informal interactional styles, on the other hand.

Shachaf (2008) distinguishes between contextual and personal styles, the former being formal and reflecting social and organizational differences between people, the latter assuming similarity and equality. Shachaf's (2008) findings indicate that German and Japanese participants felt uncomfortable with the more personal (informal) communication style of the English, as it did not allow them to maintain the social structure. They reported experiencing this as frustrating. Eastern cultures are also linked to a generally very formal style, where informality is not well received (Guirdham, 1999).

Case Study: 'Workshop'

During a visit of the British participants of a collaborative project to China, a range of workshops were organized by the hosts. While the British intended to discuss the progress of the joint project, they were met with a formal event that consisted exclusively of speeches, allowing no room for informal interactions, though some allowance for this was made due to the British requesting some time be set aside for discussions. Despite the venue clearly indicating the tone of the event as highly formal (formal, large room, large, solid tables, formal speaker podium, formal attire of the hosts, flower arrangements, introductory addresses), some of the British participants failed to adapt to this style. The following acknowledgement speeches clearly indicate this discrepancy in stylistic preference:

Translations of one of the Chinese speakers:

And last, Professor X would like to take the opportunity to express his heartfelt appreciation for the support from different parts. First, appreciation to Mrs Y and Mr Z from MoE of China. Second from Dr. A and also other colleagues from HEFCE. And third from colleagues of [name of British university] and [name of British university]. Thank you very much for your support and collaboration. Thank you.

British speaker:
    Ok, I look forward to speaking to you more about these materials tomorrow,
    but that's all folks. Thank you.
                                            (Stadler & Spencer-Oatey, 2009, p. 10)

The tone of these two thank-you speeches could hardly be more contrastive. While there is nothing wrong with either style per se, if an event is
organized in a way where every aspect communicates formality, some form
of accommodation would arguably have been preferable. According to
Guirdham (1999), formal language, titles and deference are expected in
Asian cultures. A failure to do so can come at a cost to relationships, which
require careful nurturing in a culture, such as the Chinese. Hooker (2008)
speaks of humour suggesting a casualness that might translate into an ill-
considered undertaking; I believe this extends to casualness in general. In
cultures where formality denotes respect, professional attitudes and expected
etiquette, informality can convey a lack of respect for hierarchical stratification and come across as unprofessional. While a correlation between
formal behaviour and professionalism is perceptual rather than factual, many
people confuse seriousness with professionalism (Yates, 2001). Despite the
fact that being serious is not actually tied to being professional, the
humorous and casual style of Americans was deemed inappropriate by
Germans (Hooker, 2008). In intercultural communication, intentions
unfortunately do not matter much; interpretations have the far more salient
impact. And these have a tendency to be negative when confronted with
something that is viewed as non-normative according to one's own cultural
viewpoints.

3.1.3 Writing style

Even writing styles can differ substantially and lead to negative mutual perceptions. Clyne (1987) speaks of Germanic discourse patterns when writing in
English, such as more variable text structure and a larger number of markers of
logical relationships (Hutz, 1997). According to Siepmann (2006), English and
French are writer responsible (reader is assumed to have less subject knowledge
than writer), while German is reader responsible (reader is assumed to share
writer's subject knowledge). English is 'point early', French is predominantly
'point early', while German is 'point late'.
    One of the more prominent aspects of German writing style are what Göp-
ferich (2007, p. 414) refers to as 'Textkondensate' ('condensed text'). One such
element is the so-called 'Hypotaxe', the subordinate order of ancillary sentences
into a long and complex sentence structure, in which information is extremely
condensed. Fabricius-Hansen (1996, p. 558) explains that German packs 'much

information into each sentence and/or clause by way of compex syntactic structure', which results in 'high informational density'. According to Bisiada (2016), German is said to prefer this hierarchical, hypotactic style. Kęsicka (2017, p. 34) relates this to a desire for 'sprachliche Ökonomie' ('linguistic economy').

The result is typically that German texts become so convoluted and inaccessible that a mentor of mine told me that she read Freud in its English translation, because she deemed the German original too tedious to read. This is probably linked to Siepmann's (2006) findings in that a writer-responsible style emphasizes writing in a way that makes a text as accessible and understandable as possible to another person, who might not share the same content knowledge, while the reader-responsible attitude in German writing exudes the attitude that the reader should be intelligent enough to digest the content.

Norwegian, like English, on the other hand demonstrates a preference for an incremental, paratactic style (Fabricius-Hansen, 1996). Even though all three languages are of Germanic origin, they differ in their preferred style choices. It would appear then that even writing styles are closely tied to cultural values and preferences. Siepmann (2006) and Galtung (1981) argue the culture-specificity of cognitive and textual structures. Like other stylistic considerations, writing style can also exert a negative influence on intercultural communication. Vrij and Winkel's (1994) research revealed that speech style can have a negative influence on impression formation on members of other cultures. Though there is scarcely any literature examining the impact of written communication on impression formation, Vignovic and Thompson (2010) uncovered that, in computer-mediated communication, participants formed negative perceptions of the sender of an email containing technical language violations and deviations from etiquette norms. Their findings are indicative that differences in writing style have a similarly unfavourable impact as other stylistic differences.

3.1.4 Expressiveness style

Emotional expressions are prime communication channels (Dunsmore & Halberstadt, 1997). However, according to Langford (2000), culture shapes how expressive we are allowed to be. Consedine et al. (2002) point out that most of the factors involved in emotion processes show cultural variation and suggest that cultures assert influence over expressive styles as well.

The emotional expressiveness of the family environment we grow up in has a primary role to play in our future behaviours (Halberstadt, 1986). This relates to frequency, intensity and duration of positive and negative emotional expressiveness in a family (Halberstadt, Crisp & Eaton, 1999). Saarni (1992) speaks of learned cultural display rules. Dunsmore and Halberstadt (1997, p. 58) indicate that 'the Uktu and Javanese do not emphasize emotional or expressive control' in early childhood, while 'the Gusii and the Americans begin emotional socialization early in infancy'. Rodrigues et al. (2000) also identified cultural differences with regard to emotion expression in the Netherlands and Spain. Culture, thus, plays a central role in how emotionally expressive we are.

Thomas Mann, in his literary work *Mario und der Zauberer*, describes the Mediterranean interaction style with the following words: 'Unter Südländern ist die Sprache ein Ingredienz der Lebensfreude ... Man spricht mit Vergnügen, man hört mit Vernügen – und man hört mit Urteil' ('Among Southerners, language is an ingredient of the joy for life. One speaks with enjoyment, one listens with enjoyment – and one listens with judgment.') What Mann essentially describes is what is known as high involvement style, typical for Southern European interactional styles. Pennebaker et al.'s (1996) research does in fact point to a North–South distinction, with Northerners on the less emotionally expressive spectrum and Southerners on the more expressive end. Hooker (2008) also denotes French and Italians as animated and emotional in business meetings.

Tannen (1984) describes high involvement style as a preference for expressive paralinguistic behaviour. This is not restricted to prosodic cues, but denotes an overall affective disposition, which – in addition to a colourful speech prosody – also involves emotional involvement and thus a more affective style (Selting, 1994). Benet-Martínez's (1999) study on culture-personality correlation, for example, revealed that, in Spanish culture, a culture-specific human personality dimension exists that is tied to associations of the notion of passion, such as impulsive, intense and passionate. These emotional expressions are fostered and encouraged in Spanish culture. Casiglia, Lo Coco and Zappulla (1998) even argue that in Sicilian culture, aggression is viewed as being akin to leadership by peers.

On the other end of the spectrum, Japanese culture is defined by a preference for emotional restraint. Japanese people tend to 'subdue their emotional expressions so as to maintain harmonious relationships and not impose their personal feelings on others' (Ruby et al., 2012, p. 1206). For this reason, public displays of emotion tend to be discouraged in Japanese culture, including even laughter and smiling (Tanaka et al., 2010; Oda, 2006). Japanese people have traditionally been expected not to show their emotions and refraining from laughter has been considered a virtue in Japan (Oda, 2006).

Demonstration of emotions, however, is somewhat selective and compartmentalized (Milner Davis, 2006). While Japanese people may be somewhat more emotionally expressive among close friends in private settings, this does not apply to professional contexts. Japanese business culture is dominated by a strong and definitive hierarchy (Adachi, 1997). Japanese people therefore restrain themselves in professional situations and around authority figures, as showing too much feeling can violate Japanese codes of business (Marsh, 1988). Even when Japanese people adopt a more relaxed attitude, they will do this with a great deal of consideration for their interlocutors.

Emotional moderation is generally seen as consistent with traditional Asian values (Markus & Kitayama, 1991; Russell & Yik, 1996). In Chinese culture, for example, shy, reticent and quiet behaviour is encouraged (Ho, 1986). By contrast, Soto et al. (2011) describe emotional moderation as less consistent with European American values. Rubin (1998) speaks of explicit endorsement of assertive and competitive behaviour in North America and Western Europe. While there might be a general trend, there are also exceptions to this comparative contrast.

Emotional restraint was also observed in Finnish culture, which is said to favour a calm, controlled, non-expressive way of dealing with emotions (Greenglass & Julkunen, 1991). Tixier (1996) purports that modesty and harmony are valued in Finland and that importance is attached to hierarchy. In this respect, Finnish culture shows several parallels to Japanese culture. Catanzariti (2005) describes Finns as being wary of passion and emotion. According to her, Finns do not raise their voice and their conversations are even and measured. Even disagreement or perplexity is expressed through silence rather than by raising the tone (Tixier, 1996). Catanzariti (2005) explains that in other cultures, such as Australia, just-contained anger serves as an effective tactic in hostile negotiations. This, she cautions, does not work in Finnish culture, where anger, passion and emotion are equivalent to a loss of control and result in a loss of authority and credibility. Showing strong negative emotions is considered bad manners, is seen as unprofessional and can lead to a loss of face, which she claims can be devastating in a small country like Finland. This seems to apply more widely to emotional display in general, since Järvi (2015) observes that it is not part of Finnish culture to show emotions in public. A good example for this stems from the sports' sector.

Case Study: Ski jump

Although Janne Ahonen, a Finnish ski jumper, is one of the most successful ski jumpers of all time, one would rarely see him smile, even on the podium. He has been known for his apparent lack of emotion, which earned him the nickname 'The man with the mask'. The Teamusa (2010) website calls him one of the most stoic athletes on the circuit and speaks of a trademark lack of emotion. When asked about it, he allegedly responded with: 'We came here to jump and not to smile.'

This leads to Finns sometimes being viewed as cold, distant and reserved by outsiders, though apparently this is changing somewhat among younger generations, who are no longer quite as reserved and taciturn (Järvi, 2015). However, interruptions, as are commonplace in high involvement cultures and characteristic for emotional involvement, are nevertheless poorly tolerated and considered to be really bad manners (Finland Promotion Boards, 2015). It is not too hard to imagine the negative repercussions springing from such kind of transgression, especially in a culture where silence is seen as a part of the communication process and forms an integral part of cultural identity (Järvi, 2015). Finns, apparently, are only prone to react when a piece of information proves false (Tixier, 1996). In this respect, Finnish culture appears to be similar to German culture, where perceived (or real) violations of honesty lead to strong reactions (refer to Case Study: Overcharging in Chapter 1), as trust and honesty are important in Finland (Järvi, 2015).

A discrepancy in emotional expressivity also tends to lead to negative perceptions of others. Holmes (2003) found that Finns use backchannels (nonverbal and vocal feedback while another person is speaking) infrequently, which is perceived by Pākehā (New Zealanders of European descent) as a lack of interest. Fant (1992) arrived at a similar conclusion comparing Swedish and Spanish communication behaviours, stating that Swedes have an unspoken rule of 'no more than one speaker at a time' (p. 138), while the Spaniards' rule is 'no less than one speaker at a time' (p. 139), resulting in Spaniards being perceived as aggressive and pushy by the Swedes, while the Swedes were perceived as inhibited by the Spaniards. A culture's typical speech style can thus be an affront to members of a culture with a different style, without any intention to offend (Kamışlı & Doğançay-Aktuna, 1996; Stadler, 2007).

3.1.5 Negotiation style

Drake (1995, p. 75) describes negotiation as a 'bargaining process wherein two or more parties attempt to agree' on 'what each shall give and take or perform and receive in a transaction between them' (Putnam & Wilson, 1989, p. 121). Negotiations range from peace negotiations on a macro level to individual damage settlements on a micro level (Pillar, 1983). The importance of considering cultural trends in negotiation style is due to the fact that 'bargainers bring with them variations in prior experience, background and outlook that may affect the manner and effectiveness with which they interact', as Rubin and Brown (1975, p. 157) assert. Van (2009) established that people have certain perceptions about their negotiating partners before they go into it. Mintu-Wimsatt (2002, p. 729) speaks of 'predictive powers'. Negotiation style is essentially a repertoire upon which we build assumptions about the negotiator's likely future behaviour (Drake, 1995), as it consists of tactics and strategies negotiators consistently employ (Lewicki & Litterer, 1985). As with more or less any aspect of intercultural communication, pre-formed assumptions and expectations often clash with the actual realities of transactions. The predictive mechanisms we typically apply within our own cultural domains will no longer be equally effective.

Graham, Mintu and Rodgers (1994) have argued that cultural context helps shape negotiation norms and activities. According to Parnell and Kedia (1996), attitudes, values and traditions embedded in the cultural context of negotiators impact on the bargaining process. Just like different influences have created different cultures over time, different practices relating to international business and negotiation processes have developed (Tu, Lin & Chang, 2011), as different cultures can generate distinct negotiation styles and perception (Gulbro &

Herbig, 1994). These differences originate from the fact that every society places different degrees of importance on relationships, negotiation strategies, decision making processes, spatial and temporal orientations, contracting practices and other behaviours (Acuff, 1997; Tu, Lin & Chang, 2011). These are not singular observations, but are supported by a myriad of researchers who work on negotiation styles. Salacuse (1998) also confirms that culture affects the range of strategies that negotiators develop, while Faure (1999) and Sebenius (2002) agree that identifying central cultural values and norms helps in understanding how these values and norms influence negotiating practices. Salacuse (1999, p. 217) highlights that 'culture profoundly influences how people think, communicate and behave'. Van (2009), therefore, stresses the importance of considering cultural contexts in this domain. This is all the more critical as Faure (1999, p. 190) describes differences across cultures as 'quite complex'. Cultural factors constitute a complicated interplay of a wide variety of cultural values, combined with a variety of norms and expectations that lead to strongly divergent characteristics even across cultures that are close in physical proximity as well as religious influences. Even cultures, such as Mainland China and South Korea that are not only situated in close proximity but also strongly influenced by Confucian principles and ideals are very different in outlooks, orientations, values and behaviours.

American negotiation style is typically described as competitive and confrontational (LePoole, 1989; Leung, 1987; Morris et al., 1998), as deal-oriented (Salacuse, 1999), as independent, persistent and authoritative (Harris & Moran, 1991), or as informal (Hall & Hall, 1990). This latter, for example, stands in contrast to the formal German negotiation style (Hall & Hall, 1990). American negotiation style is further defined by what Graham and Herberger (1983, p. 160) labelled the 'John Wayne style of negotiations', a team with a supreme leader who has complete decision-making authority, a style that is conducive to making commitments and decisions more quickly. This, again, is contrasted to the Germans, who are slow to negotiate and make decisions (Hall & Hall, 1990).

China and Korea are characterized by a high orientation to problem-solving (Graham, Mintu & Rodgers, 1994). Many Asian countries, according to Church and Katigbak (2000), prefer harmony-enhancing procedures, such as cooperative problem-solving. The Vietnamese negotiation style is based on a concentration on long-term single source arrangements and, as such, negotiation styles are strongly relationship-oriented (Van, 2009). This is characteristic also for the Japanese, Chinese and other Asian styles, of which Pye (1982) says that the goal of a negotiation is not a signed contract but the creation of a relationship. This relationship-orientation tends to come with other implications and stipulations on negotiation styles, such as indirect communication preferences and strong face-considerations (for a more detailed exploration of the interplay between relationships and negotiation styles, please refer to Chapters 6 and 7).

Most studies discussing negotiation styles attempt to attribute negotiation style preferences to generic cultural trends, such as individualistic versus collectivistic cultures, East versus West. However, those generalizations are problematic. As the juxtaposition of American and German negotiation styles clearly demonstrates, there is no such thing as one single 'Western' style. There is nearly as much variation within Western or Eastern cultures as there is between them. What is more, many so-called collectivistic cultures experience increasing pressure for individual success and achievement. Singapore, for example, has grown into a meritocratic society that is characterized by encouragement to excel on an individual level, while at the same time upholding Confucian ideals of filial piety, harmony and in-group cohesion. Tan (2008) refers to meritocracy as a key principle of Singapore governance and speaks of an ideological shift within its society. With a society such as Singapore, it is nearly impossible to say which outweighs which, collectivistic or individualistic considerations. Even Mainland China, which can be regarded as the epitome of a collectivist culture, has experienced a drastic shift since the one-child generation of 'little emperors' have grown into adulthood and with them, self-centred concerns have begun to override collectivistic orientations in many a situation (Wang & Fong, 2009). Parker, Haytko & Hermans (2009) thus encourage us to reconsider the validity of old assumptions about individualism and collectivism, stating that while these assumptions may have been supported in the past, this may no longer be applicable now. They mention China's rapid economic growth and progress as an industrialized nation as a factor for reorientation to more individualistic practices. Conversely, Lalonde and Cameron (1993) explain that the influx of immigration into Western cultures may lead to the reverse effect in so-called individualistic countries. Lumping cultures together under umbrella-terms is therefore somewhat counter-productive, all the more so because cultures are dynamic entities that shift, change, develop and adapt over time. Cultural variations in terms of stylistic preferences therefore always have to be approached with socio-economic, political and individual developments in mind. This is not so say, however, that cultural tendencies should be ignored.

Stylistics are more than mere preferential structures upon which to draw during negotiations. They have the potential to aggravate negotiations and to destroy relationships. Faure (1999, p. 209) describes Chinese negotiations as particularly treacherous affairs. A combination of the 'Middle Kingdom Syndrome' (Kissinger, 1979, p. 735) and 'Chinese sensitiveness' means that something as simple as a suggestion supported by an argument (as he describes as being characteristic for the American negotiation style) is not merely counter-productive but can be felt as a blow to the Chinese identity on the whole. While Faure's (1999) description may appear somewhat extreme, Spencer-Oatey and Xing (2008) paint a similarly dire picture, where even seating arrangements for the negotiation (though well-intended by the British), speaking turns during the negotiation, and the absence of a certain team member, due to family issues, caused a collapse in the relationship between Chinese and British trade partners, who felt offended and disrespected by the actions of the British. Cross-cultural negotiations are simply more complex than mono-cultural negotiations, because many negotiators lack understanding of the cultural differences that inform them, resulting in unsuccessful outcomes (Tu, Lin & Chang, 2011). The propensity for difficulties in terms of stylistic preferences should therefore not be underestimated.

Salacuse (1999) claims that differences in culture can obstruct negotiations in many ways, not least due to misunderstandings in communication and impasses in the interpretation of actions. Successful negotiation requires a sound understanding of the context of the negotiation and similarities and differences of each culture by both parties (Korobkin, 2000; Gannon, 2001). Gulbro and Herbig (1999) mention a flexible and adaptable approach in order to meet the other party's style.

3.1.6 Persuasion style

Persuasive styles, like other stylistic considerations, are determined by culture (Johnstone, 1989). 'Although a person has access to multiple persuasive tactics, culture forces a particular group of persuading behaviours to become routinized in our approach to persuasive situations' (Drake, 1995, p. 74). Argument styles, like persuasive styles, are determined by cultural logics (Walker, 1990). Persuasive communications transmit and reflect the values of a culture (Han & Shavitt, 1994).

Glenn et al. (1977), for example, point to an American preference for persuasion style based on inductive reasoning, while Soviets lean more towards deductive logic and axiomatic principles, and Arab cultures tend to rely on affective and intuitive persuasion styles. Drake (1995, p. 74) asserts that while Western cultures emphasize what she calls a 'quasilogical' style, composed of rational argument-making, neutrality, conditional clauses and argument, Eastern cultures emphasize 'analogical' styles, including poetry, repetition, paraphrase, metaphor, emotion and parable. While her dichotomous East–West portrayal downplays complexities and is therefore somewhat problematic, her argument is nevertheless useful in that it illustrates culture-specific preferences and outlooks.

Such predispositions and preferences can be shaped by a variety of factors, with cultural value systems constituting one of the most central and pivotal. Onyekwere (1989), who observed about Nigeria that people best respond to a coercive persuasion style, argues that in Nigerian culture, beside socio-cultural factors, Nigerian folklore, the country's history and environmental factors also play a central part in this style preference. This is very much in line with Glenn et al.'s (1977, p. 53) argument that people tend to rely on approaches 'consistent with their own past experiences', which of course are deeply impacted by a culture's past and its resultant outlooks. Aaker (2000) offers a similar perspective, namely that differences in culturally based traditions, religions and histories impact on differences in persuasion styles. For effective persuasion, it is necessary to not only understand trends, but the roots, development and perspectives of a society at large.

3.2 Summary

Stylistic considerations denote cultural differences in preferences for communication style (spoken or written). While not necessarily exerting a major or catastrophic effect, they do contribute considerably to impression formation. Rozin and Royzman (2001) investigated the effects of impression formation and observed that negative events are more salient, potent, dominant and efficacious than positive events. This is known as negativity bias. Pratto and John (1991) explain that people assign more value, importance and weight to negative than positive events. What this means for style differences is that if we encounter unfamiliar stylistic preferences that do not conform to our own outlook, our ethnocentric tendencies make us prone to judging them negatively. Once negative impressions are formed, they are very hard to undo or eradicate with subsequent positive experiences. First impressions often manifest in lasting negative perceptions and attitudes. In other words, negative impressions linger and are as long-lived as they are persistent. Rozin and Royzman (2001, p. 296) refer to a Russian saying that 'a spoonful of tar can spoil a barrel of honey, but a spoonful of honey does nothing for a barrel of tar'. In other words, some small faux pas can outdo a lot of socio-culturally appropriate behaviours, since we do not notice behaviour that we consider to be normal; however, we do notice deviations. Schoppenhauer (1995, p. 575) explains this in a very accessible manner: 'We feel pain, but not painlessness'. Hence, we are pre-dispositioned to only notice the negative. It is perhaps fair to say then that negative affective responses can cause irreparable damage to relationships and, as such, they do contribute to no small degree to conflict formation. They should not be taken lightly and should be given careful thought and consideration just like considerations of other pragma-linguistic and demographic variables should.

References

Aaker, J.L. (2000). Accessibility or diagnosticity? Disentangling the influence of culture on persuasion processes and attitudes. *Journal of Consumer Research* 26(4), 340–357.
Acuff, F.L. (1997). *How to Negotiate Anything with Anyone Anywhere around the World.* New York: AMACOM.
Adachi, Y. (1997). Business negotiations between the Americans and the Japanese. *GlobalBusiness Language* 2(4), 19–30.
Benet-Martínez, V. (1999). Exploring indigenous Spanish personality constructs with a combined emic-etic approach. In J.C. Lasry, J.G. Adair & K.L. Dion (eds.), *Latest Contributions to Cross-Cultural Psychology* (pp. 151–175). Lisse: Swets and Zeitlinge.

Bisiada, M. (2016). 'Lösen Sie Schachtelsätze möglichst auf': The impact of editorial guidelines on sentence splitting in German business article translations. *Applied Linguistics* 37(3), 354–376.

Casiglia, A.C., Lo Coco, A. & Zappulla, C. (1998). Aspects of social reputation and peer relationships in Italian children: A cross-cultural perspective. *Developmental Psychology* 34(4), 723–730.

Catanzariti, T. (2005). Finnish silence and other cultural minefields. Crikey. (Available from: https://www.crikey.com.au/2005/08/09/finnish-silence-and-other-cultural-m inefields/).

Church, T. & Katigbak, M. (2000). Trait psychology in the Philippines. *American Behavioral Scientist* 44(1), 73–95.

Clyne, M. (1987). Cultural differences in the organization of academic texts. English and German. *Journal of Pragmatics* 11(2), 211–247.

Consedine, N.S., Magai, C., Cohen, C.I. & Gillespie, M. (2002). Ethnic variation in the impact of negative affect and emotion inhibition on the health of older adults. *Psychological Sciences* 57B(5), 396–408.

Daniels, N. (1975). *The Cultural Barrier: Problems in the Exchange of Ideas*. Edinburgh: Edinburgh University Press.

Dournon, F. (1994). *Dictionnaire des Mots ef Formules Célèbres*. Paris: Le Robert.

Drake, L.E. (1995). Negotiation styles in intercultural communication. *International Journal of Conflict Management* 6(1), 72–90.

Dunsmore, J.C. & Halberstadt, A.G. (1997). How does family emotional expressiveness affect children's Schemas? *New Directions for Child Development* 77, 45–68.

Fabricius-Hansen, C. (1996). Informational density: A problem for translation and translation theory. *Linguistics* 34(3), 521–566.

Fant, L. (1992). Scandinavians and Spaniards in negotiation. In I.A. Sjogren & L. Janson (eds.), *Culture and Management in the Field of Ethnology and Business Administration* (pp. 125–153). Stockholm: Stockholm School of Economics.

Faure, G.O. (1999). The cultural dimension of negotiation: The Chinese case. *Group Decision and Negotiation* 8(3), 187–215.

Finland Promotion Board. (2015). This is Finland- Things You Should and Shouldn't Know. (Available from: http://finland.fi/Public/default.aspx?).

Galtung, J. (1981). Structure, Culture and Intellectual Style. *Social Science Formation* 20, 817–856.

Gannon, M.J. (2001). *Understanding Global Cultures*. Newbury Park, CA: Sage.

Glenn, E.S., Witmeyer, D. & Stevenson, K.A. (1977). Cultural styles of persuasion. *International Journal of Intercultural Relations* 3, 52–65.

Göpferich, S. (2007). Kürze als Prinzip fachsprachlicher Kommunikation. In J.A. Bär, T. Roelcke & A. Steinhauer (eds.), *Sprachliche Kürze. Konzeptuelle strukturelle and pragmatische Aspekte* (pp. 412–434). Berlin: de Gruyter.

Graham, J.L. & Herberger, R.A. (1983). Negotiators abroad – don't shoot from the hip: Cross cultural business negotiations. *Harvard Business Review* 61, 160–183.

Graham, J., Mintu, A. & Rodgers, W. (1994). Explorations of negotiation behaviors in ten cultures using a model developed in the United States. *Management Science* 40(1), 72–95.

Greenglass, E.R. & Julkunen, J. (1991). Cook-Meddley hostility, anger, and Human Kinetics. Type A behavior pattern in Finland. *Psychology Report* 68, 1059–1066.

Guirdham, M. (1999). *Communicating across Cultures*. Lafayette, IN: Ichor.

Gulbro, R.D. & Herbig, P. (1994). The effect of external influences in the cross-cultural negotiation process. *Journal of Strategic Change* 3(6), 329–340.

Gulbro, R.D. & Herbig, P. (1999). Cultural differences encountered by firms when negotiating internationally. *Industrial Management and Data Systems* 99(2), 47–53.

Halberstadt, A.G. (1986). Family socialization of emotional expression and nonverbal communication styles and skills. *Journal of Personality and Social Psychology* 51(4), 827–836.

Halberstadt, A.G., Crisp, V.W. & Eaton, K.L. (1999). Family expressiveness. In P. Philippot, R.S. Feldman & E.J. Coats (eds.), *The Social Context of Nonverbal Behavior* (pp. 109–155). Cambridge: Cambridge University Press.

Hall, E.T. & Hall, M.R. (1990). *Understanding Cultural Differences*. Yarmouth: Intercultural Press.

Han, S.P. & Shavitt, S. (1994). Persuasions and culture: Advertising appeals in individualistic and collectivistic societies. *Journal of Experimental Social Psychology* 30(4), 326–350.

Harris, P.R. & Moran, R.T. (1991). *Managing Cultural Differences: High-Performance Strategies for a New World of Business*. Houston, TX: Gulf Publishing.

Ho, D.Y.F. (1986). Chinese patterns of socialization: A critical review. In M.H. Bond (ed.), *The Psychology of Chinese People* (pp. 1–35). New York:Oxford University Press.

Holmes, J. (2003). 'I couldn't follow her story …'. Ethnic differences in New Zealand narratives. In J. House, G. Kasper & S. Ross (eds.), *Misunderstanding in Social Life* (pp. 173–198). London: Pearson.

Hooker, J. (2008). Cultural differences in business communication. (Available from: http://web.tepper.cmu.edu/jnh/businessCommunication.pdf).

Hutz, M. (1997). *Kontrastive Fachtextlinguistik für den fachbezogenen Fremdsprachenunterricht: Fachzeitschriftenartikel der Psychologie im interlingualen Vergleich*. Trier: WVT.

Järvi, P.M.A.C. (2015). Emotion regulation methods of Finnish IT leaders. Master's Dissertation. (Available from: https://brage.bibsys.no/xmlui/bitstream/handle/11250/301349/jarvi_piamaria.pdf?sequence=1).

Johnstone, B. (1989). Linguistic strategies and cultural styles for persuasive discourse. In S. Ting-Toomey & F. Korzenny (eds.), *Language, Communication, and Culture* (pp. 139–156.). Newbury Park, CA: Sage.

Kamışlı, S. & Doğançay-Aktuna, S. (1996). Effects of social power on language use across speech communities. *International Journal of Applied Linguistics* 6(2), 199–222.

Karvonen, K. (2000). *The Beauty of Simplicity: Proceedings of the ACM Conference on Universal Usability*. Arlington, VA: The Association of Computing Machinery.

Kęsicka, K. (2017). Zwischen Sprach- und Rezeptionsökonomie. Zu Verweisungen als Mittel der Textverdichtung an Beispielen aus dem Deutschen STGB. *Comparative Legilinguistics* 29, 31–48.

Kissinger, H. (1979). *White House Years*. Boston, MA: Little, Brown.

Korobkin, R. (2000). A positive theory of legal negotiation. *George Law Journal* 88(6), 1789–1831.

Lalonde, R.N. & Cameron, J.E. (1993). An intergroup perspective on immigrant acculturation with a focus on collective strategies. *International Journal of Psychology* 28(1), 57–74.

Langford, D. (2000) The influence of culture on internationalisation of construction. In A.B. Ngowi & J. Segawa (eds.), *Challenges Facing the Construction Industry in Developing*

Countries: Proceedings of the Second International Conference of CIB TG29 (pp. 12–21). Gaborone, Botswana.

Lavie, T. & Tractinsky, N. (2004). Assessing dimensions of perceived visual aesthetics of web sites … International Journal of Human-Computer Studies 60, 269–298.

LePoole, S. (1989). John Wayne goes to Brussels. In R.J. Lewicki, J.A. Litterer, D.M. Saunders & J.W. Minton (eds.), Negotiation (pp. 553–557). Burr Ridge, IL: Irwin.

Leung, K. (1987). Some determinants of reactions to procedural models for conflict resolution: A cross-national study. Journal of Personality and Social Psychology 53(5), 898–908.

Lewicki, R.J. & Litterer, J.A. (1985). Negotiation. Burr Ridge, IL: Irwin.

Marcus, A. & Baumgartner, V.J. (2004). A visible language analysis of user interface design components and culture dimensions. Visible Language 38, 252–261.

Markus, H.R. & Kitayama, S. (1991). Culture and the self: Implications for cognition, emotion, and motivation. Psychological Review 98, 224–253.

Marsh, R. (1988). The Japanese Negotiator. Tokyo: Kodansha.

Milner Davis, J. (2006). Introduction. In J. Milner Davis (ed.), Understanding Humour in Japan (pp. 1–14). Detroit, MI: Wayne State University Press.

Mintu-Wimsatt, A. (2002). Personality and negotiation style: The moderating effects of cultural context. Thunderbird International Business Review 44(6), 729–748.

Morris, M., Williams, K., Leung, K., Larrick, R., Mendoza, M., Bhatnagar, D.et al. (1998). Conflict management style: Accounting for cross-national differences. Journal of International Business Studies 29(4), 729–748.

Nishiyama, K. (2000). Doing Business with Japan. Honolulu, HI: University of Hawai'i Press.

Oda, S. (2006). Laughter and the traditional Japanese smile. In J. Milner Davis (ed.), Understanding Humour in Japan (pp. 15–26). Detroit, MI: Wayne State University Press.

Onyekwere, E.C.O. (1989). Culture, persuasion and the management of environmental attitudes. Africa Media Review 3(2), 16–25.

Parker, R.S., Haytko, D.L. & Hermans, C.M. (2009). Individualism and collectivism: Reconsidering old assumptions. Journal of International Business Research 8(1), 127–139.

Parnell, J. & Kedia, B. (1996). The impact of national culture on negotiating behavior across borders. International Journal of Value-Based Management 9(1), 45–61.

Pennebaker, J.W., Rimeé, B. & Blankenship, V.E. (1996). Stereotypes of emotional expressiveness of Northerners and Southerners: A cross-cultural test of Montesquieu's hypotheses. Journal of Personality and Social Psychology 70(2), 372–380.

Pillar, P.R. (1983). Negotiating Peace: War Termination as a Bargaining Process. Princeton, NJ: Princeton University Press.

Pratto, F. & John, O.P. (1991). Automatic vigilance: The attention-grabbing power of negative social information. Journal of Personality and Social Psychology 61(3), 380–391.

Putnam, L.L. & Wilson, S.R. (1989). Argumentation and bargaining strategies as discriminators of integrative outcomes. In M.A. Rahim (ed.), Managing Conflict: An Interdisciplinary Approach (pp. 121–141). New York:Praeger.

Pye, L. (1982). Chinese Negotiating Style. Cambridge, MA: Oelgeschlager, Gunn and Hain.

Reid, S., Stadler, S. & Spencer-Oatey, H. (2009). The Global People Landscaping Study: Intercultural Effectiveness in Global Education Partnerships. Warwick Occasional Papers in

Applied Linguistics 1. (Available from: https://warwick.ac.uk/fac/cross_fac/globalp eople/resourcebank/gppublications/).

Reinecke, K., Schenkel, S. & Bernstein, A. (2010). Modeling a user's culture. In E.G. Blanchard & A. Allard (eds.), *The Handbook of Research in Culturally-Aware Information Technology: Perspectives and Models* (pp. 242–264). Hershey, PA: ICI Global.

Rodriguez, P.M., Manstead, A.S. & Fisher, A.H. (2000). The role of honor-related values in the elicitation, experience and communication of pride, shame, and anger: Spain and the Netherlands compared. *Personality and Social Psychology Bulletin* 26(7), 833–844.

Rozin, P. & Royzman, E.B. (2001). Negativity bias, negative dominance, and contagion. *Personality and Social Psychology Review* 5(4), 296–320.

Rubin, J. & Brown, B. (1975). *The Social Psychology of Bargaining and Negotiating.* New York: Academic Press.

Rubin, K.H. (1998). Social and emotional development from a cultural perspective. *Developmental Psychology* 34(4), 611–615.

Ruby, M.B., Falk, C.F., Heine, S.J., Villa, C., and Silberstein, O. (2012). Not all collectivisms are equal: Opposing preferences for ideal affect between East Asians and Mexicans. *Emotion* 12(6), 1206–1209.

Russel, J.A. & Yik, M.S.M. (1996). Emotion among the Chinese. In M.H. Bond (ed.), *The Handbook of Chinese Psychology* (pp. 166–188). New York:Oxford University.

Saarni, C. (1992). Children's emotional-expressive behaviors as regulators of others' happy and sad emotional states. In N. Eisenberg & R.A. Fabes (eds.), *Emotion and its Regulation in Early Development* (pp. 91–106). San Francisco, CA: Jossey-Bass.

Salacuse, J.W. (1998). Ten ways that culture affects negotiating style. *Negotiation Journal* 14(3), 221–240.

Salacuse, J.W. (1999). Intercultural Negotiation in International Business. *Group Decision and Negotiation* 8(3), 217–236.

Schmid-Isler, S. (2000). *The Language of Digital Genres: A Semiotic Investigation of Style and Iconology on the World Wide Web. Proceedings of the 33rd Hawai'i International Conference on System Sciences.* (Available from: https://www.alexandria.unisg.ch/11938/1/HICSS %202000.pdf).

Schoppenhauer, A. (1995). *The World as Will and Representation* (Vol. II). New York: Dover.

Sebenius, J.K. (2002). The hidden challenge of cross-border negotiations. *Harvard Business Review* 80(3), 76–85.

Selting, M. (1994). Emphatic speech style: With special focus on the prosodic signaling of heightened emotive involvement in conversation. *Journal of Pragmatics* 22(3/4), 375–408.

Shachaf, P. (2008). Cultural diversity and information and communication technology impacts on global virtual teams: An exploratory study. *Information and Management* 45(2), 131–142.

Siepmann, D. (2006). Academic writing and culture: An overview of differences between English, French and German. *Meta* 51(1), 131–150.

Soto, J.A., Perez, C.R., Kim, Y.H., Lee, E.A. & Minnick, M.R. (2011). Is expressive suppression always associated with poorer psychological functioning? A cross-cultural comparison between European Americans and Hong Kong Chinese. *Emotion* 11(6), 1450–1455.

Spencer-Oatey, H. & Xing, J. (2008). Issues of face in a Chinese business visit to Britain. In H. Spencer-Oatey (ed.), *Culturally Speaking* (pp. 258–273). London: Continuum.

Stadler, S. A. (2007). *Multimodal (Im)Politeness: The Verbal, Prosodic and Non-Verbal Realization of Disagreement in German and New Zealand English*. Hamburg: Verlag Dr. Kovač.

Stadler, S. & Spencer-Oatey, H. (2009). *Sino-British Interactions in Professional Contexts*. Warwick Occasional Papers in Applied Linguistics #6. (Available from: https://warwick.ac.uk/fac/cross_fac/globalpeople/resourcebank/gppublications/).

Tan, K.P. (2008). Meritocracy and elitism in a global city: Ideological shifts in Singapore. *International Political Science Review* 29(1), 7–27.

Tanaka, A., Koizumi, A., Imai, H., Hiramatsu, S., Hiramoto, E. & de Gelder, B. (2010). I feel your voice: Cultural differences in the multisensory perception of emotion. *Psychological Science* 21(9), 1259–1262.

Tannen, D. (1984). *Conversational Style*. Norwood, NJ: Ablex.

Teamusa. (2010). Ahonen back for one last shot at Olympic medal. (Available from https://www.teamusa.org/News/2010/January/29/Ahonen-back-for-one-last-shot-at-Olympic-medal).

Tixier, M. (1996). Cultural adjustments required by expatriate managers working in the Nordic countries. *International Journal of Manpower* 17(6/7), 19–42.

Tu, Y.T., Lin, S.Y., & Chang, Y.Y. (2011). A cross-cultural comparison by individualism/collectivism among Brazil, Russia, India and China. *International Business Research* 4(2), 175–182.

Van, D.T.T. (2009). A comparative study of Vietnamese and American customers' behavior in negotiation style and implications for global pricing strategy. *Journal of Global Business Issues* 3(2), 25–32.

Vignovic, J.A. & Thompson, L.F. (2010). Computer-mediated cross-cultural collaboration: Attributing communication errors to the person versus the situation. *Journal of Applied Psychology* 95(2), 265–276.

Vrij, A. & Winkel, F.W. (1994). Perceptual distortions in cross-cultural interrogations: The impact of skin color, accent, speech style and spoken fluency on impression formation. *Journal of Cross-Cultural Psychology* 25(2), 284–295.

Walker, G.B. (1990). Cultural orientation of argument in international disputes: Negotiating the law of the sea. In F. Korzenny & S. Ting-Toomey (eds.), *Communicating for Peace: Diplomacy and Negotiation* (pp. 96–117). Newbury Park, CA: Sage.

Wang, Y., & Fong, V.L. (2009). Little emperors and the 4:2:1 generation: China's singletons. *Journal of American Academic Child Adolescence Psychiatry* 48(12), 1137–1139.

Wingate, K. (2011). Japanese salarymen: On the way to extinction? *Undergraduate Journal of Global Citizenship* 1(1), 1–31.

Yates, S. (2001). Finding your funny bone: Incorporating humour into medical practice. *Australian Family Physician* 30(1), 22–24.

Zaharna, R.S. (1995). Understanding cultural preferences of Arab communication patterns. *Public Relations Review* 21(3), 241–255.

Chapter 4

Conflict markers

In interpersonal interaction, we typically do not ambush our interactants with unpleasant behaviours (if we consider them unpleasant that is – a cultural and idiosyncratic construct in and of itself). Instead, we draw on signals that function much like road signs, such as windy road signs, deer crossings, or upcoming speed bumps, that warn us that potential dangers and hazards await. Like road signs, we employ markers that indicate our upcoming speaking intent, particularly where hazardous speech acts, such as conflict, are concerned.

4.1 Conflict markers as early warning signs

People have a way of signalling their speaking intentions by way of verbal, prosodic or non-verbal cues. These are typically referred to as markers. They serve as indicators for whether an upcoming contribution aligns with preference structures. The idea behind preference marking is that some speech acts are inherently either preferred or dispreferred. Disagreement has generally been construed as dispreferred and we thus try to avoid it or at least construe our responses as such. The idea is not that we never bring forth a dispreferred next move, but that we position it in a way so that it is clear to our interlocutors that we are hesitant in coming forth with an unpleasant and disliked next move. How this is achieved is through so-called disagreement markers or opposition markers.

Holtgraves (1992) identifies three strategies that cater to a disagreement's dispreferred status: seek agreement (by choosing a safe topic or by agreeing), avoid disagreement (by producing token agreement, mitigation or expressing distaste) and seek common ground (by markers such as 'you know'). Such markers include, but are not limited to, elaborate wording (as people may feel the need to provide a justification and/or 'beat around the bush' before coming to their point), indirectness (as explicit disagreement can be more offensive), delay (pauses and hesitation), prefacing (typically by an initial agreement, such as 'yes, but …'), mitigation (lexical softening devices, modal verbs and hedges, such as 'not *quite* right', 'could', 'I think'), concessions, accounts or apologies (cf. Rees-Miller, 2000; Ronowicz, 1995; Bardovi-Harlig & Salsbury, 2004;

Ford et al., 2004; Kuo, 1994; Pomerantz, 1978; Pomerantz, 1984; Sacks, 1987; Sacks & Schegloff, 1979; Schegloff, 2007).

While these markers are tied to disagreements and not to conflict on a wider scale, it is necessary to address how conflict is marked and what can serve as early warning signs for potential conflict. The reason I do not speak of disagreement markers or opposition markers is that they seem to be fairly formulaic in nature. Kuo (1992), for example, speaks of their formulaic characteristic. However, conflict marking does not seem to fall into the same category. Conflict talk can range from disagreements to argumentative stances, i.e. from relatively minor disruptions and inconsistencies to a complete fallout and disintegration of relationships. Due to its wider scope, signalling conflict comes in a wider range of markings. Leung (2002) denotes conflict talk as a common, but complex phenomenon and highlights the problems in delineating scope and exact definition. On the whole, Leung (2002) seems to follow Jacobs and Jackson's (1981) conceptualization of conflict being a form of argumentation that is structurally an extension of disagreement and functionally a means of managing disagreement. Because of its wider scope, it may be less straightforward to identify markers of conflict than markers of disagreement, but that does not mean that there are no markers if one knows what to look for. They tend to be there, albeit somewhat less formulaic in nature than disagreement markers. What makes them even more difficult to define and identify across cultures is the fact that some cultures are categorically more prone to rely on formulaic language than others (Stadler, 2007; House, 1986; 2005), meaning that in some cultures more linguistic variation exists irrespective of the particular speech event in question. Despite their variability within and across cultures, it is possible to detect and identify conflict markers.

Because minor irritations can manifest into conflict, it pays to learn to read indicators for problems early on. Nipping a problem in the bud before it solidifies is very much advisable, as problems are easiest to resolve before negative affect gets involved. Reactions to interactional problems are closely tied to personal feelings and emotions. The more personal someone takes something, the stronger the reactions, and once negative emotions come into play, it becomes much harder to prevent problems from escalating into conflict. Research has demonstrated that some cultures are more prone to interpret milder forms of conflict (e.g. disagreement) as pre-cursor to more severe forms of conflict, while other cultures are less inclined to view mild forms of conflict as serious or problematic (Stadler, 2002; Suzuki & Rancer, 1994). The level to which cultures view these as independent or interdependent variables will invariably impact on their reactions. The ability to detect early warning signs can therefore be a vital tool in conflict prevention.

Conflict can be marked in almost any way and through a multitude of more or less direct means (see Stadler, 2013 for a more thorough discussion of this example). While the following instance does not flag conflict per se, it is an indication for problematic aspects during the communication process. Here, the

Table 4.1 Case study: Teachers as authors

BM	Can I just ask one question? xxxxxx If I understood you, xxxxxxxxxxxx you were talking about
CM	m
BM	the aspirations for teachers, xxxxxx and x I think you used the word their knowledge of
CM	mhm
NV	[-nod-]
BM	design. xxxxxx. Does that imply
CM	mhmmm
NV	[pronounced nod]
BM	that you see the role of teachers as authoring and creating their own materials
CM	
NV	[————————two very slow nods————————]
BM	xxx for use in computer based learning? xxxxxxxxxxxxxxxxxxxx
CM	mhmmm mhm
V	[emphatic] [-reluctant-]
NV	[-hesitant nod-] [-repeated minimal nods-]
BM	Should I read that into what you say? xx oh maybe I'm not clear. (followed by explanation)
CM	
NV	

BM=British Male; CM=Chinese Male; V=Vocal (Prosodic); NV=Non-verbal; x=pause

Chinese Male speaker (CM) provides consistent and regular backchannels (i.e. feedback) for the speaker, signalling listenership and possibly agreement, thereby encouraging the British Male (BM) to continue. These backchannels occur at nearly every transition relevant point (TRP). TRPs are points where it is legitimate for another speaker to take the speaking turn. TRPs are instances where the speaker's voice drops partially or fully, signalling the end of a phrase or sentence. They do not necessarily indicate that the speaker is finished with his/her turn, but offer a valid entry point for another speaker. At practically every phrase-final point, CM provides a backchannel. At first, these are only of a verbal nature (m; mhm), then they are additionally accompanied by non-verbal cues (nods), which become increasingly emphatic in nature, both vocally and non-verbally. This continues until the important point, when BM asks whether he indeed understood the Chinese's intentions correctly, where feedback is indispensable. At this point, all feedback is suddenly withheld. However, the warning sign occurs one TRP earlier already, where the feedback is going from emphatic to hesitant. At this point, it should be clear to an observant interlocutor that there is an interactional problem of sorts, either content-based or understanding-based. Indeed, BM is able to conclude immediately that there is a problem in understanding and goes on to try to elaborate on his earlier explanation.

While the British Male speaker in this example does pay attention to the hesitation in the Chinese Male speaker's sudden withholding of positive and emphatic backchannels, only a few turns later he ignores the same kind of warning signs and this turns into a conflict of interest at a later point during the collaboration. Though such small warning signs may seem inconspicuous, even the most minor transgressions can have extremely serious consequences.

4.2 Diversity of markers and cultural preferences

That disagreement is not necessarily dispreferred has been amply established by now. The extent to which a culture deems disagreement to be something that is to be avoided or engaged in, obviously has strong implications for the explicitness and strength of the markers with which problems are flagged. Both the frequency and types of markers are tied to cultural preference structures. Their frequency appears to be closely linked to a society or culture's attitude towards disagreement. New Zealanders, for example, employ significantly more mitigation devices (i.e. attempts at ameliorating the impact of possible conflict) and use significantly less strengthening devices in their disagreements than German speakers (Stadler, 2007). Clearly, Germans do not shy away from conflict to the extent New Zealanders do and see less of a need to preserve outwardly polite appearances during stances of dissent. The types of markers also differ, with Germans favouring verbal strategies, while New Zealanders seem to resort to other linguistic, prosodic and non-verbal means.

Besides preferences for particular linguistic strategies, cultures also differ with regard to their interpretation of the contextual factors that surround a given conflict situation. While it is true that some cultures shy away from conflict if possible and others embrace it as entertaining or as cement to social bonds, the situation determines largely how people will react, irrespective of how welcome or unwelcome conflict is to the interactants otherwise. These social, contextual and situational factors can therefore not be ignored.

Status, for example, has a strong bearing on how entitled people feel to object and voice opinions freely. Those at the top have far fewer repercussions to fear and, as such, can employ more direct interactional means. According to Debyser (1980), disagreeing is strongly linked to status and authority. Those at the top end of the scale may disagree frequently, while those at the bottom end are not expected to disagree with people of higher status. Status restricts and regulates both the frequency of disagreements and their force. Doğançay-Aktuna and Kamışlı (2001) and Kuo (1994) found that downward disagreements (disagreements from a person of high status and authority to a person of lower status and authority) can be very direct, while upward disagreements (disagreements from a person of lower status directed to a person of higher status) are much more polite. The freedom to disagree in a direct manner is based, in part, on the fact that a person of higher authority does not have to fear retribution for his/her actions (Doğançay-Aktuna & Kamışlı, 2001). This, in turn, of course, also impacts on the amount and type of markers required to flag upcoming content. The lower the status position of the contributor, the more hesitant the unfavourable contribution will typically be, resulting in an increase of the number and types of markers.

I previously mentioned genre as an important factor, with some genres lending themselves to disagreement, argumentation and conflict. In fact, some genres seem to exist for this very reason. Adversarial talk was deemed an inherent feature of interviews and talk shows, for example (Blum-Kulka et al., 2002; Gardner, 2000; Greatbach, 1992; Yaeger-Dror, 2002). Since genres guide expectations of what will be said (Günthner & Luckmann, 2001), adversarial talk will be expected in these situations. According to Greatbach (1992), within this genre's framework, it is agreement that is avoided in interviews, because agreeing with critical questions gives a negative impression, according to Birkner and Kern (2000). Generally speaking, within an argumentative framework, disagreement is not dispreferred and therefore different parameters operate during conflict talk (Bilmes, 1993; Kakava, 2002). The typical dispreference markers no longer operate in such interactional circumstances. The typical rhythmical delay that signals upcoming disagreement and shows its dispreferred status (Auer et al., 1999) is no longer applicable. Within an argumentative framework, the expectation is that assessments will be disagreed with (Vuchinich, 1984), and disagreements, therefore, tend to be immediate and unmitigated (Blum-Kulka et al., 2002; Goodwin, 1983). Delay, on the other hand, comes across as a sign of weakness during conflict talk and can be threatening to one's own face (Kotthoff, 1991), while immediate disagreement is seen as self-defence (Auer et al., 1999). A strong counter reaction constitutes a form of self-repair, as it allows the interlocutor to state his point of view (Birkner & Kern, 2000), and forms an important tool for expressing one's autonomy and freedom (Debyser, 1980).

Kuo (1992) argues for situation-specific reactions and behaviours regarding the use of opposition markers. In Chinese culture, formal and especially hierarchically structured interactions, are typically reticent and constrained (Young, 1982). On the other hand, the informal, casual, private exchanges between status equals, that Kuo (1992) observed, showed that interactants communicate freely without suppressing spontaneous feelings and without being constrained by considerations of impression management. In such settings, interactants can be observed drawing on the most direct and aggravated opposition makers.

Consequently, even within a single culture, one cannot speak of a stable unified system of appropriate reactions to conflict situations, as a multitude of factors will impact on our reactions and behaviours. Given the complexity of conflict as a research construct, combined with the complexity of *intra*cultural variation, conflict markers should be regarded as less static, formulaic and predefined as disagreement markers typically are.

This then, of course, raises the question how one can define conflict markers at all if they are to be viewed as variable, permeable and changeable. In several ways, the detection of conflict markers borrows from the intercultural competence constructs of being attuned to one's interlocutor (Spencer-Oatey & Stadler, 2009) and forensic stylometry, the notion that each person has an individualized, but fairly consistent style of speaking.

4.3 Idiosyncratic marking styles

As previously discussed, conflict can stem from a wide spectrum of origins and is less easily definable than disagreement. Due to its wider scope, the markings to signal conflict, or more generally problems in interaction, are therefore also somewhat less tangible.

What my data across different cultures reveals is that marking conflict seems somewhat more idiosyncratic in nature. Earlier, I have demonstrated that a simple withholding of backchannels can have the effect of signalling problems in conversation. However, there were a multitude of behaviours that people exhibited both during informal conversations with friends, as well as in the professional domain. What became evident across these data sets was that these behaviours seemed relatively consistent within speakers, but not across speakers. There appear to be ties between generally more conflict-avoidant cultures and more implicit means of flagging problems, and ties between more conflict-embracing cultures and more explicit conflict markers, however, the choice of specific markers seems to be tied to individual preferences more than to culturally shared preferences.

I would like to pick up Hellström's (2001) notion of 'conflict culture', which she describes as an organization's propensity to escalate disagreement into conflict (even violent conflict) to have their needs met, as well as ways in which they go about dealing with conflict. Her observations are important here for two reasons. She establishes that cultural differences exist, and identifies these differences to be situated on the individual, organizational level more than the national cultural level. In this way, conflict works quite differently to disagreement, which is employed fairly consistently in line with national cultural standards and expectations.

Her observations are not entirely isolated, however. In the forensic linguistic sector, there have long been debates concerning the possible existence of idiolectal fingerprints (see Juola, 2006; van Halteren et al., 2005), i.e. the notion that, while we all have the same language repertoire at our disposal, we have fairly unique ways of using language (Iqbal, 2010); Stamatatos, 2009). Baayen et al. (2002, p. 35) speak of 'considerable authorial structure'. It may be debatable whether language use is indeed so individualized in nature that it makes a person uniquely identifiable, but there clearly are consistent patterns within individual language usage. According to Grant (2013) and Coulthard (2004, 2013), at least in the realm of text messaging, where people are more inclined to make up their own writing rules, individual writers and their preference patterns can be identified successfully, especially when dealing with only a handful of suspects or potential alternative writers. This has been proven to be the case in kidnapping and murder cases they analysed. Bhargava et al. (2013) report a 95.16% accuracy rate in identifying individual writers through short messages. Similarly, the single term 'cool-headed logician' led a brother to correctly identify the Unabomber, and put an end to two decades of lethal assaults (Coulthard, 2004). Clearly then, there is something to be said for the identifiability of individualized patterns and for within-speaker consistency in language usage.

The following examples from my data demonstrate that the use of conflict marking is rather speaker-specific in nature, but highly consistent within a speaker's repertoire. In the subsequent example, a group of friends, from a diverse range of backgrounds, who all spent the summer studying at a Japanese language school in Tokyo, is discussing where to have lunch. While some of them are just fooling around initially, Ken makes a suggestion. However, his contribution is being ignored entirely. His reaction, instead of aggressive verbal tactics, just consists of repeating his contribution, despite the fact that it keeps on getting ignored.

Although Nadja eventually picks up on Ken's contribution, the very next interjection diverts away from Ken's suggestion again. A post-recording interview with him revealed that Ken perceived the interaction as problematic. While he regarded all participants of this interaction as friends, he did not think people participated in the interaction on even par and voiced some frustration over this fact.

Table 4.2 Case study: Noodles or rice

	Olle	It's up to you Malte. You decide now.
	Malte	I decide?
	Nadja	[Ya.]
	Monika	[Ya.]
	Olle	[Ya.] Where to eat.
	Nadja	Ya.
→	Ken	Noodles or [rice.]
	Nadja	[What] to-
	Monika	(It goes) by the [maj]ority.]
	Malte	[Poo]
	Olle	[Poo.][Awesome]
	Nadja	[Poo? Poo?]
	Monika	Poo?
	Olle	Free poo- ((high pitched))
	Ingrid	What's funny about that.
→	Ken	Noodles or rice.
	Nadja	Poo? No:. ((facing Malte))
→	Ken	What do you think. Noodles or rice.
	Ingrid	En:
	Olle	Poo?
	Nadja	noodles. ((facing Ken))
	Monika	(sushi)
	Ingrid	I don't want sushi.
	Olle	You don't want (a shoe)?

As a very indirect means of disagreement, assertion by way of repetition is also visible in my Balinese data set. In this example, a German business woman is in negotiation with a local hotel in the Munduk area of Northern/Central Bali. Her expectation is to bring tourists there for Balinese cooking classes. While she wishes to take the tour participants to the local village market in order to first view what fresh local ingredients are on offer and then make up a menu on the fly, based on the ingredients available, the hotel manager pushes her towards the existing programme of cooking classes based on a pre-set menu. He smiles the entire time and never directly disagrees with her, but the discussion, which continued for over an hour, is always steered back to the existing cooking classes through continuous repetition.

Wayan keeps responding to Manu's suggestions favourably, with repeated 'yah' and 'yeah' interjections as well as assertions, such as 'of course we are'. He also tries to be helpful by making sure he understands, with the prompt 'the other way round', and by clarifying that her approach will require a modification of the menu. However, throughout, he keeps referring to the existing menu, and, in the end, keeps pointing her back to the food they normally cook. This pattern continues for quite some time, with the manager explaining afterwards that the cook is not a proper chef and that, while the cook is knowledgeable, he will not be able to explain all the ingredients. Thus, he subversively keeps steering her back towards the existing menu. Subsequently, other, unrelated issues, ensue, where the same pattern is observable.

Table 4.3 Case study: Balinese cooking class

	Manu	I would like to have this cook also come with us to the morning market with the translator, and then at the morning market we decide what to cook.
→	Wayan	Ahhhh, on that case yah. But basically, you chose from this one (referring to their menu). Yeah, because this is the small market, not big market so what you see here might not be available there.
	Manu	Which is why, see this is why we should go there first, see what is available and then decide what to cook. Makes more sense.
	Wayan	Yeah. The other way round,
	Manu	The other way round.
	Wayan	Also if there is, yeah, pick there (referring to market) not is in here (pointing to pre-set cooking menu), then we have to modify
	Manu	Doesn't matter. I am flexible. As long as you are flexible,
	Wayan	Yeah, of course we are.
	Manu	Ok, then it's fine.
→	Wayan	Then the the, this is the type of food that normally we cook.

While the manager tries to accommodate verbally, he does not budge from pre-set patterns, which eventually leads the German business woman to conclude that she needs to find another establishment for her cooking classes. A meeting with the cook the following day made it abundantly clear that (a) the hotel refuses to buy ingredients from the local market and only wants to use the vegetables they have already available at the hotel and (b) that the cook is incapable of suggesting recipes ad hoc, based on the availability of local ingredients, and is only capable of cooking from the pre-set menu. After this, all further negotiations with the hotel end, as Manu concludes that this is not a viable option for her business.

Case study: The video

Fay	But we don't have the video yet–
Al	And I don't think I think spoken it through last time also with (Name of CEO) that it's gonna take too long to get the video.
Fay	So we might not do the video anymore? Ok.
Al	But no no we will do the video but we gotta get this. If we stop and wait for the video it's gonna take us time.
Sue	What we want to do is to push this out.
Al	I really wanna do the video,
Sue	Ya.
Fay	So do we want to do the video or not?
Sue	We can do the video. But for the next round.
Fay	What's the next round?

Al	We are going -
Sue	July.
Fay	You mean the next batch of attendees?
Sue	Yes.
Fay	Okay.
Al	We need to push this forward.
Fay	Right right-
Al	With much haste-

While Taiwanese and Balinese conflict management styles are subversive and indirect in nature, a range of conflict styles can be viewed in a business meeting involving participants from diverse backgrounds. In the following excerpts, three participants discuss a training programme and the materials to be used. Fay, a Filipina, joined the team relatively recently and was tasked with developing a training video for the programme. Sue, a Singaporean and Al, an Australian, explain during

Case study: Client brief

Fay	So - okay, you are looping me into this whole exercise, so that I can provide you with a client brief?
Sue	No it's not a client brief, it's a case study.
Fay	No. Let's be clear what a case study is. An Effie's entry is a case study.

the meeting that there is insufficient time to get the video done in time for the next training programme. As a result, Fay is becoming increasingly irritated about getting roped into the project and spending a considerable amount of time and effort on this video, which seems to have been wasted. She is clearly not pleased and the discussion concerning the implementation of a training video constitutes the beginning of a string of altercations. This occurs approximately half-way through the one-hour-long meeting. Subsequent to this excerpt, communication

Case study: Busy people

Fay	Ok, just give me the brief. What do you want me to do? Ok basically we are all busy people right? We are all doing all sorts of stuff, you guys are not the only busy people in this office. And I also put in time for this so can you just tell me now very clearly, because we are talking about giving instructions or briefing people, so what exactly in black and white do you need me to work on. What sort of inputs do you want.

starts to disintegrate increasingly and the meeting eventually comes to a break-down after Fay vents her exasperation. None of the issues get resolved and they simply abandon the meeting due to the breakdown.

Despite the fact that Al and Sue are trying to deflect from Fay's complaints with vague promises of future action, Fay keeps pushing for answers and keeps complaining about the situation.

Eventually, Fay starts to get rather aggressive and makes it clear that she is not prepared to waste any more of her time unless she gets concrete answers.

In response to this, Al becomes rather exasperated over the situation himself, and instead of addressing Fay's justified complaints about her efforts and time commitment going to waste, he starts to vent his own frustration.

Case study: Reinventing wheels

Al	Here here. I have done a lot of work here already and it's – it's –
Sue	I'm trying – let's not reinvent wheels um because I really want to push this out and that's what John is – I'm getting very impatient because I've been talking about this for months.
Al	For months. And we are coming back and it looks to me like there is a significant amount of rewrite that you are proposing.
Sue	Yes.
Fay	It's –
Al	And who's gonna do it? Cos I'm not. Cos I've spent my time – a lot of time on this already and I'm not going back and rewrite it.
Fay	Okay – so –
Al	And I've done a lot of thinking about the structure of the exercises and everything so –

Even within the short space of these few excerpts, Fay produces six instances of 'so', six instances of 'okay', two instances of 'right', and one instance of 'no'. Fay clearly employs conflict markers very consistently. Despite the high level of within-speaker consistency, the other interactants fail to respond to the markings that clearly indicate trouble. Beyond vague promises of the possibility that her efforts may or may not be used at an uncertain future point, no real effort is made to resolve the situation. Certainly, no effort had been made initially to ensure that Fay's time would be used productively and Al and Sue seem to make it worse instead of better, as they all eventually blow their lid and the situation escalates until it comes to a complete breakdown. The early warning signs certainly had not been taken into account, even though the problems were already visible during the meeting early on.

Table 4.4 Case study: Resal

Resal	Na! Des sagad I aa ned ei. No! I wouldn't accept that either. Na! Do kennadsd mi ned. No! Not me. Na! De legad I aa ned o. No! I wouldn't wear that either. Ja mei! Dafuer is aa an andane qualitaet; (untranslatable expression of opposition. 'ja' is pronounced in a clipped way and does not indicate yes, like the German 'ja:', but rather an opposing stance. 'Mei' further reinforces the 'ja' and adds an air of exasperation). But it's a different quality. Ja mei do is ja olle stund a andare drin. (opposition expression). There's another one in there every hour. Ja Zenz. De han jo krank. (opposition marker) + address term. They are ('jo' serves as either opposition marker or reinforcement; here it is a mixture of both) sick. Ah! Des glangt jo nimma. No! That's definitely not enough. Ja! Des moan I aa! (opposition marker). That's what I think should be done as well! Naja, is jo klar Bruni; Yeah well, of course + address term. Naja, d'Michi de buid eams hoid aa ei. A so muass I sogn. Yeah well, name, she imagines that (reinforcement marker) too. I have to say.

Table 4.5 Case study: Bruni

Bruni	Mei des Resal! Jesus, this Resal! Oiso woasst wos da I sog, oba dann tring ma mir vorher an Kaffee. (opposition marker) you know what I tell you, but then we will drink coffee beforehand. Oiso bis hoibe 3 wart I oba dann mog I an Kaffee, des woasst scha. (opposition marker) I will wait until 2.30pm, but then I want a coffee, I tell you. Ja etz horch a moi. (opposition marker) now listen to me. Ja oba wenns da Michi scha so geht; Yes but if even Michi has this problem; Ja, oiso de Carmen de is- de is im Kopf scho a weng krank. Well, (attention seeker/opposition marker) this this Carmen, she is – she is a bit sick in the head.

Although, in the subsequent extracts from German data, there is no communication breakdown, there are some clashes and argumentations about differences in viewpoints. Opinions on a range of topics are split and while some
of the topics are of a more trivial nature, the topic of care-taking of the husband has been an ongoing point of argumentation between participants for
years and draws strong reactions from the interactants.

The subsequent interjections make it clear that the German interactants
approach conflict and problem situations in rather confrontational ways, with
unmitigated, direct and somewhat sarcastic reactions being the norm.

Although they are equally as direct, forceful and confrontational, Bruni
draws on a slightly different range of preferred markings.

Though there is some overlap due to their shared family background (Resal
and Bruni are sisters) and the frequency of their interactions, there is also a clear
difference in the use of preferred markers. In other words, not only individuals
from different cultures will draw on a different range of markers, but interactants from the same cultural background will also employ a somewhat individualized preference system. Within-speaker consistency is, in line with
forensic stylometry, far more consistent than across speaker consistency even
within the constraints of the same cultural context.

4.4 Cultural inclinations for conflict markers

While I made the case for individualized preferences for marking problems in
conversation, it is important to highlight how and in what way cultural orientations operate alongside individualized preferences. Those cultures that are
generally deemed to be more conflict-avoidant cultures, such as Taiwanese and
Singaporean cultures, can be seen to employ rather indirect means of flagging
issues and reacting with withdrawal rather than escalation (though it is arguable
whether ignoring conflict does not have more lasting and scarring impacts on
relationships than escalation and resolution of conflict (refer to Chapter 8 for
details)). In a sense then, coming back to the earlier example of road signs as
warning mechanism, individual choices should be seen as situated in the wider
socio-cultural context in which they occur. Just as the dogsled crossing road
signs that can be found in Illulisat, Greenland, would make little sense in Australia's Northern Territory, Australian Koala crossing signs make no sense outside Australia. Likewise, highly aggressive markers make little sense for
individuals operating in harmony-oriented cultures. After all, individual choices
are still situated within the general concerns for social cohesion prevalent in a
given cultural context.

Ken did not voice his frustration openly among the group of friends, but
rather provides feedback individually and in written form retrospectively.
Instead of trying to resolve his impression that members of the group are not
given equal consideration, he prefers to restrain his emotions and face-needs for
harmony's sake. His behaviour seems reflective of Taiwanese conflict style,

Table 4.6 Idiosyncratic strategies

Speaker	Nationality	Communicative Channel	Strategy
CM	Chinese	Non-verbal/Prosodic	Withholding of backchannels, withdrawing of emphatic markers
Ken	Taiwanese	Paralinguistic & Pragmatic	Repetition
Sue	Singaporean	Non-verbal	Eye-rolling, exaggerated expression of disbelief/surprise, rejection by passing back pen and paper
Wayan	Balinese	Verbal	Explanation, repetition
Al	Australian	Prosodic	Mocking laughter, tone of voice (increasingly assertive and exasperated), increased volume
Fay	Filipina	Verbal	Ok, so, right, no
Resal	German	Verbal & Prosodic	Ja mei; na; naja; ah; oba Raised voice
Bruni	German	Verbal	Von wegen; oiso (woasst); wos moanst; mei; (ja) etz; ja oba

which Trubisky, Ting-Toomey and Lin (1991, p. 65) describe as 'obliging' and 'avoidant'. Similar behaviours can be observed from the Singaporean's reactions. As a more established and more senior member of the team, she obviously feels more entitled to show how she feels about Fay's attitude and failure to take notes, but she does so predominantly non-verbally (refer to Chapter 5 for an example of this). Her verbal reactions are not aggressive and attempt to pacify rather than exacerbate the situation. Eventually, when outright conflict becomes unavoidable, Sue reacts with calling off the meeting under the pretence of having other engagements, thereby sidestepping the issue rather than engaging in conflict.

Australian culture is defined both by a more outspoken attitude, but an overall tendency to avoid full conflict. Kim et al. (1994) describe Australian society as one where feelings are expressed openly, though there is nevertheless also a great emphasis on doing so politely (Ronowicz, 1995). Barraja-Rohan (2003) asserts that Australians may sometimes be perceived as direct, but, in actual fact, are characterized by the use of euphemisms and understatements. Bello et al. (2006) describe Australian culture in this respect as rather complex. This can be viewed in Al's orientation of not shying away from conflict per se, visible in his sarcastic reactions or some snide comments, but abandoning conflict when it becomes too aggravated.

Filipino culture, with its heavy Spanish colonial influence and later American colonial influence, on the other hand, does not shy away from conflict easily.

Hechanova, Alampay and Franco (2006) speak of a mixture of Eastern and Western influences. Though they assert that Filipino culture is defined by a collectivistic outlook and hierarchical workplace structure, they state that 'American management … practices are the basis for how most Filipino organizations are run' (p. 73). Filipinos, they claim, value direct participation and power-sharing. Boonkongsaen (2013) also identifies Filipino culture as more assertive, compared to other Asian cultures, stating that Filipinos value equality and were seen to employ direct strategies more frequently and were 'more straightforward in saying no' (p. 33). Fay's reactions can therefore be observed to be oriented more towards conflict resolution, even if it means openly addressing unpleasant situations and circumstances.

In the German data, it is visible that Resal and Bruni show individual preferences for certain types of markings that they rely on predominantly. However, it is also visible that there is some overlap in commonly used markers in Bavarian language that they share as well. The marking then appears to be a mixture between overuse of specific, personally favoured language items, while also drawing on other, shared, markings with lesser frequency.

These individuals all exhibit repeated patterns of marking conversational conflict, but show very little consistency across speakers. Parallels can be found between Resal and Bruni, probably because they are sisters and communicate with each other frequently. However, even across these two speakers, there is more diversity than similarity, though they are very consistent in their pattern in their individual language usage.

These excerpts, in fact, behave precisely as findings on text messaging in forensic linguistic analysis suggests. Coulthard (2011) and Grant (2010) found in their forensic investigations that between speaker variation is greater than within-speaker variation, and that messages from associated pairs (i.e. people who speak/write to each other) are more similar than independent pairs. What their data further highlights is that only a very small number of turns/messages are required in order to identify patterns of usage. MacLeod and Grant (2012) found that even single messages can be discriminated from other authors' messages with reasonable accuracy.

Transferred to the concept of conflict marking then, this suggests that, though speakers do not use markers uniquely, they do have preferences that can be identified within a relatively short space. In other words, if listeners are attuned to their interlocutors, they should be able to successfully identify how an individual flags conflict within a short space of time, irrespective of how diverse the range of conflict indicators might be.

4.5 Summary

Conflict markers are neither easy to detect nor define. However, if approached with a degree of sensitivity and perceptiveness, it is possible to identify individual conflict marking preferences, as they are fairly consistent and relatively limited within the same speaker's repertoire. Overall, cultural preference patterns and trends can indicate what types of markers individual speakers may rely on more and therefore assist in identifying individualized use of conflict makers. A combined approach that considers both cultural tendencies with individual usage can aid in not only identifying interactional problems, but may constitute a valuable tool in conflict prevention.

References

Auer, P., Couper-Kuhlen, E. & Müller, F. (1999). *Language in Time: The Rhythm and Tempo of Spoken Interaction*. Oxford: Oxford University Press.

Baayen, R., van Halteren, H., Nejit, A. & Tweedie, F. (2002). An experiment in authorship attribution. In *Proceedings of JADT 2002: Sixth International Conference on Textual Data Statistical Analysis* (pp. 29–37). St Malo: JADT.

Bardovi-Harlig, K. & Salsbury, T. (2004). The organization of turns in the disagreements of L2 learners: A longitudinal perspective. In D. Boxer & A. Cohen (eds.), *Studying Speaking to Inform Second Language Learning* (pp. 199–227). Clevedon: Multilingual Matters.

Barraja-Rohan, A.M. (2003). How can we make Australian English meaningful to ESL learners? In J. loBianco & C. Crozet (eds.), *Teaching Invisible Culture: Classroom Practice and Theory* (pp. 101–108). Melbourne: Language Australia.

Bello, R., Ragsdale, J.D., Brandau-Brown, F.E. & Thibodeaux, T. (2006). Cultural perceptions of equivocation and directness II: A replication and extension of the dimensional hypothesis. *Intercultural Communication Studies* 15(2), 23–32.

Bhargava, M., Mehndiratta, P. & Asawa, K. (2013). Stylometric analysis for authorship attribution on twitter. In V. Bhatnagar & S. Srinivasa (eds.), *Big Data Analytics* (pp. 37–47). Cham: Springer.

Bilmes, J. (1993). Ethnomethodology, culture, and implicature. Toward an empirical pragmatics. *Pragmatics* 3(4), 387–411.

Birkner, K. & Kern, F. (2000). Impression management in East and West German job interviews. In H. Spencer-Oatey (ed.), *Culturally Speaking* (pp. 255–271). London: Continuum.

Blum-Kulka, S., Blondheim, M. & Hacohen, G. (2002). Traditions of dispute: From negotiations of Talmudic texts to the arena of political discourse in the media. *Journal of Pragmatics* 34(10–11), 1569–1594.

Boonkongsaen, N. (2013). Filipinos and Thais saying 'no' in English. *Manusya: Journal of Humanities Regular* 16(1), 23–40.

Coulthard, M. (2004). Author Identification, idiolect, and linguistic uniqueness. *Applied Linguistics* 25(4), 431–447.

Coulthard, M. (2011). The linguist as detective and expert witness. Inaugural lecture. (Available from: http://streaming.aston.ac.uk/communications_ram/Inaugral_).

Debyser, F. (1980). 'Expressing disagreement (exprimer son desaccord)'. *Studies in Second Language Acquisition* 3(1), 42–56.

Doğançay-Aktuna, S. & Kamışlı, S. (2001). Linguistics of power and politeness in Turkish: Revelations from speech acts. In A. Bayraktaroğlu & M. Sifianou (eds.), *Linguistic Politeness across Boundaries: The Case of Greek and Turkish* (pp. 75–104). Amsterdam: John Benjamins.

Ford, C. E., Fox, B.A. & Hellermann, J. (2004). Getting past 'no'. In E. Couper-Kuhlen & C.E. Ford (eds.), *Sound Patterns in Interaction* (pp. 233–269). Amsterdam: John Benjamins.

Gardner, R. (2000). Resources for delicate manoeuvres: Learning to disagree. *Australian Review of Applied Linguistics* 16, 32–47.

Goodwin, M.H. (1983). Aggravated correction and disagreement in children's conversations. *Journal ofPragmatics* 7(6), 657–677.

Grant, T. (2010). Text messaging forensics: txt 4n6: Idiolect free authorship analysis? In M. Coulthard & A. Johnson (eds.), *The Routledge Handbook of Forensic Linguistics* (pp. 508–522). London: Routledge.

Grant, T. (2013). TXT 4N6: Method, consistency, and distinctiveness of the analysis of text messages. *Journal of Law and Policy* 21(2), 467–494.

Greatbach, D. (1992). On the management of disagreement between news interviewees. In P. Drew & J. Heritage (eds.), *Talk at Work: Interaction in Institutional Settings* (pp. 268–301). Cambridge: Cambridge University Press.

Günthner, S. & Luckmann, T. (2001). Asymmetries of knowledge in intercultural communication: The relevance of cultural repertoires of communicative genres. In A. Di Luzio, S. Günthner & F. Orletti (eds.), *Culture in Communication: Analyses of Intercultural Situations* (pp. 55–85). Amsterdam: John Benjamins.

Hechanova, R.M., Alampay, R.B.A., & Franco, E.P. (2006). Psychological empowerment, job satisfaction and performance among Filipino service workers. *Asian Journal of Social Psychology* 9(1), 72–78.

Hellström, E. (2001). *Conflict Cultures - Qualitative Comparative Analysis of Environmental Conflicts in forestry.* Silva Fennica Monographs 2 (pp. 1–109). Helsinki: The Finnish Society of For Sci/The Finnish For Res Institute.

Holtgraves, T. (1992). Yes, but … positive politeness in conversation arguments. *Journal of Language and Social Psychology* 16(2), 222–239.

House, J. (1986). Cross-cultural pragmatics and foreign language teaching. In Seminar für Sprachlehrforschung der Ruhr-Universität Bochum (ed.), *Probleme und Perspektiven der Sprachlehrforschung. Bochumer Beiträge zum Fremdsprachenunterricht in Forschung und Lehre* (pp. 281–295). Frankfurt: Scriptor.

House, J. (2005). Politeness in Germany: Politeness in Germany? In L. Hickey & M. Stewart (eds.), *Politeness in Europe* (pp. 12–28). Clevedon: Multilingual Matters.

Iqbal, F., Binsalleeh, H., Fung, B.C.M. & Debbabi, M. (2010). Mining writeprints from anonymous e-mails for forensic investigation. *Digital Investigation* 7(1–2), 56–64.

Jacobs, S. & Jackson, S. (1981). Argument as natural category: The routine grounds for arguing conversation. *The Western Journal of Speech Communication* 45(2), 118–132.

Juola, P. (2006). Authorship attribution. *Foundation and Trends in Information Retrieval* 1 (3), 233–334.

Kakava, C. (2002). Opposition in modern Greek discourse: Cultural and contextual constraints. *Journal of Pragmatics* 34(10–11), 1537–1568.

Kim, U., Triandis, H.C., Kagitcibasi, C., Choi, S.C., & Yoon, G. (1994). *Individualism and Collectivism: Theory, Method, and Applications.* Thousand Oaks, CA: Sage.

Kotthoff, H. (1991). Zugeständnisse und Dissens in deutschen, anglo-amerikanischen und in nativ-nichtnativen Gesprächen. *Linguistische Berichte* 135, 375–397.

Kuo, S.H. (1992). Formulaic opposition markers in Chinese conflict talk. In J.E. Alatis (ed.), *Georgetown University Roundtable on Languages and Linguistics 1992* (pp. 388–402). Washington, D.C.: Georgetown University Press.

Kuo, S.H. (1994). Agreement and disagreement strategies in a radio conversation. *Research on Language and Social Interaction* 27(2), 95–121.

Leung, S. (2002). Conflict talk: A discourse analytical approach. *Working papers in TESOL and Applied Lingustics* 2(3), 1–19.

MacLeod, N. & Grant, T. (2012). Whose tweet? Authorship analysis of micro-blogs and other short form messages. In S. Tomblin, N. MacLeod, R. Sousa-Silva & M. Coulthard (eds.), *Proceedings of the International Association of Forensic Linguists' Tenth Biennial Conference* (pp. 210–224). Birmingham: Centre of Forensic Linguistics.

Pomerantz, A. (1978). Compliment responses: Notes on the co-operation of multiple constraints. In J. Schenkein (ed.), *Studies in the Organization of Conversational Interaction* (pp. 79–112). New York: Academic.

Pomerantz, A. (1984). Agreeing and disagreeing with assessments: Some features of preferred/dispreferred turn shapes. In M. Atkinson & J. Heritage (eds.), *Structures of Social Action: Studies in Conversation Analysis* (pp. 57–101). Cambridge: Cambridge University Press.

Rees-Miller, J. (2000). Power, severity and context in disagreement. *Journal of Pragmatics* 32(8), 1087–1111.

Ronowicz, E.A. (1995). Aussies are friendly and Poles aren't rude: Some remarks on overcoming problems in intercultural communication. *Papers and Studies in Contrastive Linguistics* 30, 31–44.

Sacks, H. (1987). On the preferences for agreement and contiguity in sequences in conversation. In G. Button & J.R.E. Lee (eds.), *Talk and Social Organisation* (pp. 54–69). Clevedon: Multilingual Matters.

Sacks, H. & Schegloff, E.A. (1979). Two preferences in the organization of reference to persons and their interaction. In G. Psathas (ed.), *Everyday Language: Studies in Ethnomethodology* (pp. 15–21). New York: Irvington Press.

Schegloff, E.A. (2007). *Sequence Organization in Interaction: A Primer in Conversation Analysis, Volume 1*. Cambridge: Cambridge University Press.

Spencer-Oatey, H. & Stadler, S. (2009). *The Global People Competency Framework: Competencies for Effective Intercultural Interaction*. Warwick Occasional papers in Applied Linguistics #3. (Available from: https://warwick.ac.uk/fac/cross_fac/globalpeople/resourcebank/gppublications/).

Stadler, S. (2002). Learning to disagree in German: The case of New Zealand University students. Unpublished MA Thesis, Victoria University of Wellington.

Stadler, S. (2007). *Multimodal (Im)Politeness: The Verbal, Prosodic and Non-Verbal Realization of Disagreement in German and New Zealand English*. Hamburg: Verlag Dr. Kovač.

Stadler, S. (2013). Why intercultural interaction demands a dual role-relationship. *Language and Dialogue* 3(2), 167–185.

Stamatatos, E. (2009). A survey of modern authorship attribution methods. *Journal of the American Society for Information Science and Technology* 60(3), 538–556.

Suzuki, S. & Rancer, A.S. (2009). Argumentativeness and verbal aggressiveness: Testing for conceptual and measurement equivalence across cultures. *Communication Monographs* 61(3), 256–279.

Trubisky, P., Ting-Toomey, S. & Lin, S.L. (1991). The influence of individualism-collectivism and self-monitoring on conflict styles. *International Journal of Intercultural Relations* 15(1), 65–84.

van Halteren, H., Baayen, R.H., Tweedie, F., Haverkort, M. & Neijt, A. (2005) New machine learning methods demonstrate the existence of a human stylome. *Journal of Quantitative Linguistics* 12(1), 65–77.

Vuchinich, S. (1984). Sequencing and social structure in family conflict. *Social Psychology Quarterly* 47(3), 217–234.

Yaeger-Dror, M. (2002). Register and prosodic variation, a cross-language comparison. *Journal of Pragmatics* 34(10–11), 1495–1536.

Young, L.W. (1982). Inscrutability revisited. In J.J. Gumperz (ed.), *Language and Social Identity* (pp. 72–84). Cambridge: Cambridge University Press.

Chapter 5

Multimodality and conflict

In Chapter 4, I addressed the fact that people have individualized preferences for the use of certain types of markers. Despite the idiosyncratic nature of conflict markers, the channels and levels of explicitness through which conflict is communicated seems to be linked to cultural orientations to conflict. More direct cultures, with a low tendency for conflict avoidance, tend to prefer clear and direct verbal strategies, strong and explicit prosodic cues (such as raising one's voice, expressions of exasperation etc.), and more aggressive kinds of non-verbal cues. Cultures more prone to avoiding conflict, on the other hand, tend to draw on somewhat less direct means, typically showing a preference for prosodic and non-verbal marking. Such subversive types of markers make it sufficiently clear that the speaker is not aligned with the other's opinion, without having to actually verbalize conflicting views. This type of usage is of a more passive-aggressive nature. On the far end of the spectrum is the kind of marking that only hints at problems without expressing overt disagreement or argument at all. However, not only the level of directness of the various modalities of communication differs across cultures. Differences in the preferences and use of various modalities are capable of creating conflict in and of themselves.

5.1 Cultural differences and their role in the escalation of conflict

Gabbott and Hogg (2001) assert that during the interaction process, a multitude of non-verbal exchanges happen, intentional or unintentional, that exert 'a central effect upon participants' perceptions of an 'event' (p. 6). Argyle, Alkema and Gilmour's (1971) findings suggest that non-verbal cues exert a far greater effect on interlocutors than verbal cues did in hostile conditions. Yammiyavar et al. (2008) assert that non-verbal communication practices are culture-specific and these cultural differences impact on the quality of our interactions. Von Raffler-Engel (1980) even claimed that all of our movements, from infancy on, are culturally conditioned. Subtle though they may seem, cultural differences in the use of multimodal communication patterns can be responsible for creating conflict.

Collett (1971) regards non-verbal behaviour as a source of misunderstanding. Hurn (2014) and Sharma (2011) list a whole range of different practices that cause issues, ranging from personal space, eye contact, and touch, to differences in the use of gestures, facial expressions and behavioural practices. Hurn (2014, p. 188) therefore cautions that

> different cultures have their own cultural conventions and those who live and work in the international environment need to be fully aware of these differences. We can make great efforts to try to learn a foreign language, but often we may ruin the effect of speaking the foreign language by using culturally inappropriate body language. Mistakes can adversely affect success in business negotiations and in building relationships.

This phenomenon is not limited to non-verbal communication alone, but extends to other communicative channels. Wichmann (2004) affirms that 'all speech is said with prosody, but how something is said rather than what is said is an intrinsic, but often neglected, dimension of what speakers say and hearers hear' (p. 1525). In some instances though, the how is even more important than the what (Couper-Kuhlen, 1986; Crystal, 2012), because prosodic cues play a major role in giving meaning to an utterance (Linell, 2002). The distinction between truthful and sarcastic remarks, for example, is nearly exclusively in the prosody of the utterance. Prosody also carries a great deal of emotional information (Bolinger, 1986; Crystal, 1995) and can convey negative information, e.g. in the form of low(ered) pitch register (Bolinger, 1978; Perrin et al., 2003). Bolinger (1964) and Ohala (1984) have also linked low or falling pitch to authority, threat and aggression, while Huron, Kinney and Precoda (2006) discuss links between aggression and loudness. According to Popkova (2015), the role of intonation in interactive communication should not be underestimated, as it determines the overall impact of an utterance.

Even relatively minor differences in speech prosody can lead to negative evaluations. Bolinger (1989) and Zellner Keller (2004; 2005) established that people form impressions based on intonation and other prosodic cues. Stadler (2007), for example, found that during disagreements, Germans spoke faster and louder than New Zealanders did. By testing the effect of these differences, the study uncovered that Germans were perceived negatively as a result of these differences. This is likely due to the fact that speech intensity often correlates with anger (Pittam & Scherer, 1993), while increased speech rate conveys increased emotional involvement and is thus equated with arousal, excitement or anger (Kehrein, 2002; Chafe, 2002). Gu, Zhand and Fujisaki (2011) also uncovered a correlation between fast speech and hostile attitude. The New Zealanders may well have interpreted anger and hostility instead of engagement and excitement. German participants self-report enjoying interesting discussions and a good heated debate (Stadler, 2007), which leads to high involvement, as expressed through their speech. Seeing as louder speech has been linked to perceptions of higher levels of competence (Ray, 1986), the louder disagreeing behaviour of Germans is likely the result of seeking to assume more authority for one's arguments and opinions – seeing as being able to defend one's opinions is viewed as positive in German culture (Kotthoff, 1991). Within an argumentative cultural framework this is unproblematic, but in conflict avoidant cultures this comes across as aggressive and argumentative; a phenomenon also documented by Günthner (2000) in her study on German–Chinese interactions. It is therefore unsurprising that New Zealanders would also interpret the disagreeing behaviour of Germans negatively. Ratner's (2000) findings indicate that this is not an uncommon occurrence, stating that emotions are not always interpreted correctly due to cultural differences.

Though there is evidence that, for the most part, people can correctly identify emotions in other languages (cf. e.g. Scherer et al., 2001; Thompson & Balkwill, 2006), there is also evidence of an in-group processing advantage (Pell et al., 2009; Pell & Skorup, 2008; Elfenbein & Ambady, 2002), that enables greater accuracy in identifying emotions of speakers from one's own cultural and linguistic background. Pell et al. (2009) report that for English speaking samples, surprise was often confused with happiness, in German, fear was confused with sadness, and in Hindi, neutrality was confused with sadness. It appears then that where clear-cut expressions, such as hot anger, are concerned, people are able to correctly identify emotions, but people are prone to misjudging less distinct emotional expressions across cultures. According to Mentcher (1979) and Grover et al. (1987), where intonation contour is wrongly applied across cultures, it likely causes misunderstanding of attitude or intent. Popkova (2015) found that neutral statements in Russian sound to English native speaker ears emotional and annoyed. Hellmuth (2010) mentions that the type of accenting of words in Egyptian Arabic (EA) is perceived as 'overemphasis' in other cultures. He refers to anecdotal evidence that speakers of phrase-level accent distribution languages, like English, may perceive speakers of word-level accent distribution languages, such as EA, to be speaking in an angry or aggressive manner. This association can be explained by the insights Arndt and Janney (1985) offer, that all forms of emphatic behaviour in negative utterances are susceptible to aggressive or hostile interpretations.

Case study: Bavarian to Brazilian ears

While a Brazilian friend visited me in Auckland, I received a phone call from my family. After the conversation ended, my friend inquired if I had had an argument, because I sounded angry and irritated. What was but a neutral conversation to me, came across as harsh and aggressive to her.

Speech prosody is judged on the basis of the sounds we are familiar with. If these differ from our own language, they may well lead to misjudgements of, for example, aggression, where none was intended, with potentially pernicious repercussions. Hurn (2014) ascertains that a misinterpretation of multimodal cues is particularly detrimental in the early stages of doing business, when first impressions are critically important and one is trying to build a solid working relationship.

The issue of intentionality that Gabbott and Hogg (2001) raise forms an important aspect in the affronting effect of multimodal cues. The role multimodal cues play in the creation of conflict is twofold then; they can be employed deliberately or they can cause conflict unintentionally. Either way, their impact is forceful and repercussions can be great.

5.2 Intentional conflict incitement

As previously outlined, sometimes people have motivations for exacerbating rather than deferring conflict, even in generally conflict avoidant cultures, depending on situational and contextual factors. Shying away from conflict is therefore not always the goal. Where people have reason to engage in conflict, they may purposely incite it. Multimodal cues constitute an effective means for doing so.

Camras (1977) says of conflict encounters that they are one form of social interaction where non-verbal cues play an important role. They can serve as signals of covert conflict (D'Errico et al., 2015), including facial and bodily expressions of acidity (D'Errico & Poggi 2014), or threatening stares (Owens et al., 2002). Camras (1977) reports that even Kindergarten-age children employ aggressive facial expressions to deter other children from accessing disputed objects – successfully so. Underwood (2004, p. 371), in her study on girls' interactions, examines the power and impact of non-verbal social aggression among girls, of 'nasty faces and gestures deployed to hurt and exclude'. In another study, Paquette and Underwood (1999) and Malove (2014) uncovered that non-verbal aggression is even more prevalent than verbal aggression, yet just as hurtful. Underwood (2004) explains that non-verbal aggression is a particularly suitable means for girls to vent, because they are socialized into being overly nice and conciliatory for fear of social exclusion (Brown & Gilligan, 1993; Zahn-Waxler, 2000) and because, historically, aggression was deemed unacceptable behaviour for girls (Baker Miller, 1976). Non-verbal means are ideal ways of expressing aggression for them, because they are fleeting, with few social consequences, yet highly effective, Underwood (2004) explains. Even in cultures where overt forms of opposition are not possible, people find ways to express their disalignment in more subtle non-verbal ways. Magwaza (2001) explores how Zulu women, in a society where they have been given minimal or marginal opportunity to express their views, draw on symbolism and dress code to express a multitude of cultural and social functions, including silent social protest.

A powerful linguistic tool in conflict talk comes in the form of turn control. In political and judicial debates, turn overlapping and interruptions occur frequently during conflict talk (Pesarin et al. 2012; Navarretta 2013), as interruptions have been linked to asserting dominance and power (cf. e.g. San-chez-Cortes at al., 2010). According to Goldberg (1990), interruptions have tra-ditionally been viewed as indicators of interactional dominance. Interruptions can be indicative of aggressiveness and hostility (West, 1979), as they can be interac-tional strategies for exerting and overtly displaying power or control over both the discourse and the interlocutor (Orcutt & Harvey, 1985). While Goldberg (1990) emphasizes that not all interruptions are power-displays, she establishes that there is a correlation between interruptions and conversational control.

Facial and gestural expressions can further serve to discredit, and as a means of derision against the opponent (Poggi et al. 2012; D'Errico, Poggi & Vincze, 2013). Underwood (2004) further mentions glares of contempt and eye-rolls of disgust. Lewis (2006) and van Heugten (2010) mention loud sighs and eye-rolling as means to express disdain and intolerance. Hutchinson (2013) men-tions derisive tone of voice as form of non-verbal intimidation, and Stadler (2007) discusses examples where eye-rolling or saying the opponent's name in an exasperated tone of voice were sufficient means to serve this purpose, even without additional verbal expressions of derision. Simmons (2002, p. 47) refers to such non-verbal means as 'the ultimate undercover aggression'. The fol-lowing case study demonstrates this point.

Case study: Note-taking

In a meeting involving a Singaporean, an Australian and a Filipina, the Filipina, who only recently joined the company, is tasked with taking minutes during the meeting. Halfway through the hour-long meeting she admits that she does not know how to take minutes, and that her notes consist of nothing but scribbles and drawings. In response, the Singaporean opens her mouth wide and raises her eyebrows in an exaggerated expression of disbelief. The Australian then asks the Singaporean if she is skilled at note-taking, to which she gives an emphatically affirmative response. The Filipina passes her the writing equipment. However, prior to starting the note-taking, she pushes pen and paper away.

Despite the fact that the Singaporean interactant does not utter a single word, it is very clear that she is unimpressed with the Filipina, that she ridicules her lack of skill, and that she is displeased with this late announcement of her incapacity to take notes. She responds with another signal of discontent to the note-taking invitation, indicating clearly (and later verbalizing this) that she is unwilling to take on the role of secretary and that she considers this beneath her level as a manager. These non-verbal gestures constitute very deliberate and unmistakable signs of refusal.

What the case study further highlights is an unwillingness to cooperate. For the most part, I would argue that we approach communication with the notion that interactants wish to make it work and seek to cooperate and align. In fact, several researchers have proposed models for what it means to be polite, considerate interactional partners, such as Lakoff (1973) and Leech (1983) in their attempts at unveiling conversational maxims. Perhaps even more prominent are Grice's (1975) Cooperative Principles, which discuss how to be a maximally cooperative interactional partner. However, this notion that we actually wish to be cooperative in communication with others is by no means always a given. House (2000) discusses uncooperativeness as an interactional issue. Her insights are not isolated. Margić (2017) also mentions interactants' uncooperativeness as a cause for miscommunication in intercultural interactions. Piskorska (2017, p. 3) alludes to 'manifestly uncooperative speakers', and Lytle and Willaby (2006) mention that in intercultural negotiations, cooperation may not always be the primary goal. Some negotiators, they claim, are more strongly motivated by personal goals, by their desire to be more competitive, or by simply placing their own benefits first. Cooperation and a wish to align can therefore not be taken for granted in intercultural interactions, and this resistance is oftentimes expressed more non-verbally than verbally. Even silence can be an expression of uncooperativeness, disengagement, unresponsiveness or resistance (Knapp, 2000). Non-vocalization, Knapp (2000) says, can be viewed as *somebody's* silence. In this way, uncooperativeness and resistance in interaction are truly multimodal communicative tools.

However, just because they are not verbalized does not mean they lack in effect. Chollet et al. (2014) found that people are very adept at identifying expressions of negative affect. Participants were able to identify correctly dominance and hostility displays even from virtual graphical models. Even children of five years of age are able to recognize emotions such as anger correctly (Camras, 1977). Loveland et al. (1997) even found that children with autism are nearly as apt at emotion recognition as non-autistic children. What is more, they tended to rely on non-verbal information even more strongly than on verbal information, exemplifying all the more the importance of non-verbal cues in the communication of affective stances. The very real harm that non-verbal aggression can cause has been addressed in studies on the effect of bullying through this form of subversive aggression (cf. e.g. Malove, 2014; Cleary et al., 2009).

I have said much about the way in which non-verbal and prosodic markers can cause conflict and harm when used intentionally. However, I would argue that for the most part, conflict arises from vocal and non-verbal cues as a result of misalignment in intention and interpretation of messages.

5.3 Unintentionality and bias

While there is some awareness that communication differs across cultures, somehow we do not seem to extend these insights to vocal, non-verbal and behavioural differences. One of the root causes for this is that we are far less aware of such behaviours and the far-reaching impact that culture exerts on these subversive communicative means. Researchers have long been discussing the unconscious or subconscious nature of culture and its impact on us (Sheldon, 1951; Hall, 1976). The notion of unconscious processes goes back to Freudian and Jungian theories, as Ekstrom (2004) explains. The idea behind it is that beyond our cognitive processes lies an element of the unconscious, which influences our actions and interactions.

Uleman et al. (2008) claim that people make social inferences without intentions, awareness or effort – spontaneously, that is. Ekman and Friesen (1969) refer to them as involuntary habits. Mohammadi and Vinciarelli (2012) assert that this phenomenon is so pervasive that it even extends to impersonal encounters, i.e. when we see people in pictures, videos or listen to them in audio-recordings. They explain that 'our behavior is not driven by the actual personality of the people we have around, but by the traits we spontaneously perceive and attribute to them' (p. 1).

This unconscious and all-pervasive impression-formation tendency plays a central role in intercultural encounters. According to Schein (2004), organizational culture is made up of deep assumptions that drive behaviour at the subconscious level, i.e. values that influence day to day work. Though Schein (2004) speaks only of organizational culture, this applies to culture in all of its incarnations and variants. Ting-Toomey (2012, p. 199) asserts of intercultural communication practices that 'individuals often practice ethnocentric behaviours and biased attributions without a high degree of awareness'.

Weaver (1986) likened culture to an iceberg, with only 10% of its substance showing above the water, i.e. within our awareness, while the danger lies in the 90% hidden out of sight, and out of our conscious awareness. This applies to culture on the whole, though it appears that prosodic and non-verbal behaviours fall nearly entirely in the hidden domain. Lakoff and Johnson (1999) distinguish between two areas of the unconscious. One of them is responsible for all our automatic cognitive operations, such as visual and auditory processing and motor operations. The other relates to implicit knowledge that resides 'in the cognitive unconscious' (p. 13). Their differentiation would explain, to an extent, why prosodic and non-verbal channels are even further out of reach of our immediate conscious awareness, because they are nearly entirely automated and we do not give much thought to them. Kelly (2011) explains that we are sensitive to vocal and non-verbal cues, but mostly on a subconscious level. It is hardly surprising then that multimodal differences lend themselves to inciting conflict where none was intended. Argyle (2013) refers to cultural differences in non-verbal communication as a major source of friction.

The problem, in part, lies in the fact that non-verbal communication and affective reactions are closely interlinked. This applies both to setting the tone of the interaction and communicating emotion content alike. Arndt and Janney (1985) explain that non-verbal cues play a central role in establishing the emotive contexts in which utterances are interpreted, while Gabbott and Hogg (2001, p. 7) speak of non-verbal signals as 'salient indicators of thoughts and attitudes'. Mehrabian (1972), in his influential work, even claimed that emotion is communicated nearly entirely through non-verbal and prosodic communication. Non-verbal cues impact on both the sending and the receiving of messages. Bias gets communicated and interpreted, whether thus intended or not. This forms an ongoing continuous process during communication. Gabbott and Hogg (2001, p. 7) speak of the continuous exchange of non-verbal messages as 'a second level of conversation'. A misinterpretation of such messages then regularly causes communication breakdown, they claim. As our framework for interpretation is culturally primed, we are not very apt at interpreting such messages across cultural contexts (Yammiyavar et al., 2008). What is more, negative affect spreads across members of a group. Consequently, what may have started as the negative subjective experiences of one individual may end up impacting entire groups. Cheshin et al. (2011) refer to this phenomenon as emotion contagion, a process they describe as 'powerful and fundamentally unconscious' (p. 2).

Seeing as affect also lies outside our conscious awareness (Shouse, 2005; Deleuze & Guttari, 1980), as do the cognitive processes underlying biased reasoning (Dawson et al., 2002), we have no more control over our reactions to perceived transgressions than the transgressors have in committing them. I speak of perceived transgressions, because we do not judge actual intentions – which we cannot possibly know – but only perceptions and interpretations of speaker intentions. This explains why people are usually willing to make allowances for non-native speakers for things they perceive as learner mistakes, but because vocal and non-verbal aspects lie outside our conscious awareness, this is not something people are willing to forgive or overlook, since they are not interpreted as mistakes, but as negative intent (cf. Vishnevskaya, 2012). The reactions of the Chinese pertaining to hotel arrangements, seating arrangements, speaking rights, hosting practices, etc., as described by Spencer-Oatey and Xing (2000), are therefore equally unintentional and not based on a refusal to cooperate, but form a purely natural response to a perceived violation of expected behaviours and etiquette. Seeing as cultural norms and learned behaviours play an extremely large part in the interpretation of non-verbal communication (Gabbott & Hogg, 2001), a misalignment in message intent and interpretation constitutes an unavoidable presence in communication. The resulting reactions are thus rooted in a failure to fully comprehend constraints and customs of other cultures.

Pronin et al. (2004) explain that people are often confronted with instances in which others respond to events differently from the way they themselves are responding. This discrepancy in response – especially when it violates one's expectation that reasonable people will respond similarly to oneself – is liable for much of the attributional work people do (Pyszczynski & Greenberg, 1981; Wong & Weiner, 1981). This attribution then typically behaves as described by Ichheiser (1949), where we assume superior interpretation skills for ourselves compared to others:

> We tend to resolve our perplexity arising out of the experience that other people see the world differently than we see it ourselves by declaring that those others, in consequence of some basic intellectual and moral defect, are unable to see the things "as they really are" and to react to them "in a normal way". We thus imply, of course, that things are in fact as we see them and that our ways are the normal ways. (Ichheiser, 1949, p. 39)

In any given scenario then, where people behave in different ways to what we expect, we tend to respond negatively and, what is worse, all too often attribute negative intentions to divergent behaviours.

Unfortunately, the problem with cultural differences in these communication aspects is that intention does not seem to matter. Of course, we can never know a speaker's intentions, so at best we can guess. Whereas the actor's knowledge of his or her own intentions is 'direct', the observer's knowledge of those intentions is 'indirect, usually quite inferior, and highly subject to error' (Jones & Nisbett, 1972, p. 84). Argyle (2013) speaks of the perception of non-verbal communication as subjective experiences. Just how subjective impression formation is has been documented by Biesanz and West (2000), who found that agreement between assessors is low, i.e. people form very inconsistent impressions of others. The most well-intended behaviours may therefore result in conflict nonetheless, because we are far too used to interpreting behaviours based on our own cultural frameworks for interpretation. Cultural frameworks are just that, culture-specific and highly subjective viewpoints of what constitutes appropriate behaviour in certain situations and contexts, though ethnocentrism makes us prone to perceiving our own cultures as objective and normative.

We all have the ethnocentric predisposition to perceive in-group members more positively. In the third-person perceptual effect, as it is known, social distance constitutes an important corollary. The greater the social distance of an out-group, the more we are inclined to associate negative attributes with them. Scharrer (2002, p. 696) explains that 'those less socially or psychologically close attain an impersonal quality that allows individuals to assign them negative outcomes'. Scharrer (2002), in her study on media influence, for example, documents that people perceive themselves as being less influenced by media than outgroups, especially those with greater social distance to their own culture, where negative media influence is concerned. Duck, Terry and Hogg (1995), on the other hand, found that people perceived their in-group to be more affected by the media where positive effects of media exposure was concerned. Pronin et al. (2004) made similar observations, stating that people are prone to perceiving others as being more easily influenced by negative behaviours than themselves. Because we draw our social identity to a large extent through the group membership we belong to (Brewer & Gardner, 1996), we all have a tendency to make 'intergroup comparisons that favour the ingroup' (Duck et al., 1999, p. 1882). Scharrer (2002) calls this the self-serving bias.

'People have a need to view themselves positively. This is easily the most common and consensually endorsed assumption in research on the self' (Heine et al., 1999, p. 766). Allport (1937, p. 48) refers to this form of bias as 'nature's oldest law'. Apparently this need to view ourselves positively is so strong that it virtually overrides reality. Mezulis et al. (2004, p. 711) assert that 'people seek a positive image of themselves and their environments with such vigor that reality is at times selectively interpreted and at other times patently ignored'. This bias is responsible not only for seeking to attribute positive traits with the self but also for dismissing negative events as attributable to other causes (Mezulis et al., 2004). While the self-serving bias may serve a positive function to the self, it of course comes with the downside, that we are prone not only to attribute negative events to other causes but also often to other people. The greater the social distance, the more we are prone to negative attributions. This causes a propensity to interpret behaviours of others as ill-will rather than as culturally divergent practices. This is also known as fundamental attribution error, a sort of 'victim-blaming', where one underestimates the degree to which behaviour is externally caused, and instead attributes it to internal traits, i.e. personality dispositions (Sabini et al., 2001). Nisbett and Ross (1991) established that people go wrong in their predictions and understandings because they have a general tendency to attribute behaviour to dispositions rather than to situations. Hughes (2008), for example found that non–native speaker intonation contours are not perceived as linguistic differences but 'as directly revealing personality traits or at least emotional or attitudinal states' (p. 38). We do this because we lack knowledge and understanding of the behavioural choices of unfamiliar cultures. Fiske and Taylor (2013) explain that with increasing information about another person we start to look more towards situational factors to explain their actions and reactions. This constitutes a very strong reason why intercultural sensitivity, knowledge of and experience with other cultures are hugely important in intercultural communication, especially where unconscious non-verbal communication is concerned. The inability to identify and interpret non-verbal communication as intended can have unpleasant or downright serious consequences.

5.4 multimodal communication practices as conflict triggers

'A pause in the wrong place, an intonation misunderstood, and a whole conversation went awry' (Forster, 1924, p. 305). With these words, Forster (1924) underscores that – where multimodality is concerned – it really does not take much for conflict to arise. According to Haynes (2004, p. 1) 'very few gestures are universally understood and interpreted'. The unconscious nature of non-verbal cues, their ever-present existence, combined with our predisposition to interpret them subjectively/culturally make them somewhat of a minefield. At best, discrepancies lead to unfavourable perceptions of others, but consequences can get far more severe. Misinterpretation can lead to offence, conflict, or even physical violence. In a discussion exercise, one student reported the following incident from his travels to the Tessin region (the Italian-speaking part of Switzerland).

Case study: Landlord

The student and his friend had arrived at their accommodation, but after settling in, the owner of the hostel came to talk to them about something, though he did not speak much English and the student and his friend did not speak any Italian. Somewhat perplexed by the Italian address and a little embarrassed by the situation, the student reported stroking his beard while trying to figure out what was going on. As a response to this, the owner started yelling at them and arguing with them. They later found out that the motion of the beard stroking was interpreted as an insult by the owner.

According to Black (2011), in Southern Italy, a chin flick – i.e. a tilting back of the head while flicking the fingers from under the chin forward in an arching motion – is a sign of negation. Ren (2014) translates the meaning as 'get lost'. According to Marchetti (2015), it means 'I couldn't care less'. Darthorso (2014), however, regards the meaning of 'I couldn't care less' as a polite translation, stating that the actual meaning is more along the lines of 'I don't give a f***'. According to a blogger from Sicily the gesture means 'non mi frega niente', which she translates into 'f*** off'. Though the translations vary somewhat, the common theme is a rudely expressed disinterest in the situation. It is not hard to see why this would be taken negatively by the owner of the hostel, as it indicates a refusal to comply as well as a lack of regard for the house rules, and for him as a person. The fact that this was in no way intended by the student did not matter at all.

Another incident where intention and interpretation were entirely misaligned was reported to me by a friend in New Zealand, based on a newspaper report.

Case study: Beckoning

On the street, two men bumped into each other, one a New Zealander, the other of Asian origin. The Asian man lost his balance and fell down. The New Zealander wanted to help the man up and beckoned him (palm facing up) in what was intended as a 'come on, I'll help you up' gesture. In response to this, the Asian man jumped up and started punching the New Zealander, which resulted in a fist-fight between the two and ended at a police station.

Though my friend did not recall the nationality of the Asian man, he may have been of Filipino origin. Forbes (2015) explains that in the Philippines, using your hand to make a 'come here' gesture is one of the most offensive things you can do. It is considered an insult (Ginting & Kleiner, 2000). Apparently, in the Philippines, this gesture is used only for dogs. To use it with a person is derogatory as it implies that one regards the other as subservient and inferior (Merritt, 2010; Kaur, 2013). Forbes (2015) and Kaur (2013) assert that it is deemed so bad that one can get arrested for it in the Philippines. In the light of this meaning, it is quite understandable that the man reacted in such an aggressive manner. Not only did the collision result in him falling, but the hand gesture communicated to him that he was blamed for the incident and subsequently insulted and challenged. Unbeknownst to the New Zealander, he invited a fight with what was intended as a friendly and considerate gesture of redress.

This case study demonstrates not only a misinterpretation of the intention of the New Zealander but also demonstrates that such misunderstandings can come with rather serious consequences. Ekman (1975) considers the repercussions of misalignment in the understanding of non-verbal communication aspects as so severe that he stated that 'a person could get confused, and sometimes killed, by doing the wrong thing in the wrong place' (p. 35).

How real the consequences of misinterpretation can be is also exemplified in some court cases. Meissner and Kassin (2002) describe a military trial case (U.S. v. PFC Timothy Bickel), where a confession to rape was extracted from a defendant, against whom there was no hard evidence, through persistent and aggressive interviewing techniques. When one of his investigators was asked why he pursued the defendant so aggressively, he answered:

> We gathered that he was not telling us the whole truth. Some examples of body language is that he tried to remain calm, but you could tell that he was nervous and every time we tried to ask him a question his eyes would roam and he would not make direct contact, and at times he would act pretty sporadic and he started to cry at one time.
>
> (p. 470).

Exhibiting signs of stress, which is – arguably – fairly normal, given the circumstances of an aggressive police interrogation and the accusations at hand, were essentially construed as signs of guilt.

Meissner and Kassin (2002, p. 471) describe a further case, where investigators accused the defendant, Tom Sawyer, of sexual assault and murder, after extracting a confession (likely to have been false and suppressed by the trial judge) after 16 hours of interrogation and threats. The reason he became the prime suspect in the first place was 'because his face blushed and he became embarrassed' during an initial interview, which was interpreted as deceitful behaviour. In actual fact, they were signs of a social anxiety disorder Sawyer suffered from, which caused him to 'sweat profusely and blush in evalutive situations'.

Investigator bias, as this phenomenon is known as, is responsible for a much wider variety of wrongdoings in the court system, but these two cases exemplify how normal, involuntary non-verbal reactions to situations can potentially get a person sentenced for murder. Though the non-verbal cues displayed in both cases are relatively minor, their consequences can potentially be grave.

5.5 Multimodal cues: cause versus effect

While this discussion regards non-verbal cues as the cause for miscommunication, there is another investigative stream that treats multimodal cues as the effect rather than cause of conflict. Greenbaum and Greenbaum (1983) and Ogbu (1982) see conflict as a result of non-verbal misunderstandings. They regard incommensurate systems of non-verbal communication as the effect of cross-cultural conflict. They discuss schooling systems in Pacific Island and Native American cultures (Greenbaum & Greenbaum, 1983) and East and West African cultures (Ogbu, 1982), and came to the conclusion that the introduction of schooling systems into foreign cultures without any contextual adaptation leads to a rejection by the pupils. The same is true for the inclusion of immigrant children into the school curriculum without any understanding on the part of teachers of fundamentally different values and core beliefs of their pupils, which also results in misalignment and rejection. While this side of multimodal misalignment is rarely addressed, it makes perfect sense within the framework of communication accommodation theory (CAT), which holds that we converge to the speaking behaviours of those we like and wish to be close to, but diverge if we want to build distance or exert resistance (cf. e.g. Ayoko et al., 2002). This divergence can manifest in a number of communicative features such as accent, speech rate, pauses, or non-vocal behaviours (Jones et al., 1999). This can occur in situations where strong power, role or status differences exist and individuals wish to maintain their social distance from one another (Street, 1991). If these school systems provide no inclusion for the pupils, it is not hard to see why the pupils themselves will also choose to diverge and therefore reinforce existing gaps. Given their low status, non-verbal and prosodic disalignment may well be the only tool at their disposal to achieve this.

Another form of non-verbal divergence has been documented by Matoesian (2008), in his observations of witness questioning in the courtroom. Witnesses, he noticed exert witness resistance through multimodal cues and manipulate the question-answer format to reframe participant structure and recalibrate institutional order, when they resent the control the strict questioning format exerts over the veracity of their statements.

This theory, that accommodation in communication can be the result of non-verbal prompts is further enhanced by Kleinfeld's (1974) research insights. He investigated the reverse side of it and found the same effect for convergence. In his study on Alaska Native classrooms, teachers' non-verbal warmth was found to result in stronger academic performance. In essence then, non-verbal alignment or misalignment can be seen as the aftermath of the way we approach people in the first place. Negative predispositions, stereotypes, attitudes, or an unwillingness to be open-minded vis-à-vis culturally diverse behaviours lead to conflict-inducing non-verbal behaviours as a result. Positive predisposition and inclusive non-verbal behaviours, on the other hand, can enhance in-group cohesion as well as individual effort and performance. Or as the age-old German adage goes: Wie man in den Wald hineinruft so schallt es heraus (How you yell into the forest is the echo you get back in return).

5.6 Summary

Non-verbal and prosodic cues are a normal by-product of our interpersonal interactions. Though we are largely unaware of producing and reacting to them, they exert a substantial and important influence on us. This affects our perceptions, interpretations, judgement-making, communicational alignment and bias. Due to the fact that we are far better equipped at interpreting such cues if they are consistent with our own cultural practices, there is a substantial margin for error in interpreting them across cultural divides. Though non-verbal cues and prosodic information seem rather inconspicuous and are often underestimated, they can potentially impact in serious and, at times, detrimental ways on intercultural communication, business outcomes and relationships.

However, non-verbal misalignment in communication is also the link between predispositions to interlocutors and resultant attitudinal and behavioural responses. In this way, non-verbal cues can enhance and foster positive non-verbal alignment and either ameliorate conflict and relationships, or exacerbate conflict and increase the gap between interactants. They also have the potential to create and exacerbate conflict when used deliberately as strategic means of communication management.

With their intricate interlinkage to communication outcomes, multimodal communication cues play a central role in the creation or resolution of conflict in both intentional and unintentional ways.

References

Allport, G.W. (1937). *Personality: A Psychological Interpretation*. New York:Holt.
Argyle, M. (2013). *Bodily Communication*. London: Routledge.
Argyle, M., Alkema, F. & Gilmour, R. (1971). The communication of friendly and hostile attitudes by verbal and non-verbal signals. *Journal of Social Psychology* 1(3), 285–402.
Arndt, H. & Janney, R. (1985). Improving emotive communication: Verbal, prosodic and kinesic conflict-avoidance techniques. *Per Linguam* 1(1), 21–33.
Ayoko, O.B., Härtel, C.E.J. & Callan, V.J. (2002). Resolving the puzzle of productive and destructive conflict in culturally heterogenous workgroups: A communication

accommodation theory approach. *International Journal of Conflict Management* 13(2), 165–195.

Baker Miller, J. (1976). *Toward a New Psychology of Women*. Boston: Boston Press.

Biesanz, J. & West, S. (2000). Personality coherence: Moderating self– other profile agreement and profile consensus. *Journal of Personality and Social Psychology* 79(3), 425–437

Black, R. (2011). Cultural considerations of hand use. *Journal of Hand Therapy* 24(2), 104–111.

Bolinger, D. (1964). Intonation across languages. In J.H. Greenberg, C.A. Ferguson & E.A. Moravcsik (eds.), *Universals of Human Language*, Vol. 2: *Phonology* (pp. 471–524). Stanford, CA: Stanford University Press.

Bolinger, D. (1978). Intonation across languages. In J.H. Greenberg (ed.), *Universals of Human Language* (pp. 471–524). Stanford: Stanford University Press.

Bolinger, D. (1986). *Intonation and its Parts: Melody in Spoken English*. Stanford: Stanford University Press.

Bolinger, D. (1989). *Intonation and its Uses*. Stanford: Stanford University Press.

Brewer, M.B., & Gardner, W. (1996). Who is this 'we'? Levels of collective identity and self-representations. *Journal of Personality and Social Psychology* 71(1), 83–93.

Brown, L.M. & Gilligan, C. (1993). Meeting at the crossroads: Women's psychology and girls' development. *Feminism & Psychology* 3(1), 11–35.

Camras, L.A. (1977). Facial expressions used by children in a conflict situation. *Child-Development* 48(4), 1431–1435.

Chafe, W. (2002). Prosody and emotion in a sample of real speech. In P.H. Fries, M. Cummings, D. Lockwood & W. Spruiell (eds.), *Relations and Functions within and around Language* (pp. 277–315). London: Continuum.

Cheshin, A., Rafaeli, A., & Bos, N. (2011). Anger and happiness in virtual teams: Emotional influences of text and behavior on others' affect in the absence of non-verbal cues. *Organizational Behavior and Human Decision Processes* 116(1), 2–16.

Chollet, M., Ochs, M. & Pelachaud, C. (2014). From non-verbal signals sequence mining to bayesian networks for interpersonal attitudes expression. *International Conference on Intelligent Virtual Agents* (pp. 120–133). New York:Springer.

Cleary, M., Hunt, G.E., Walter, G. & Robertson, M. (2009). Dealing with bullying in the workplace: Toward zero tolerance. *Journal of Psychosocial Nursing and Mental Health Services* 47(12), 34–41.

Collett, P. (1971). Training Englishmen in the non-verbal behavior of Arabs. *InternationalJournal of Psychology* 6(3), 209–215.

Couper-Kuhlen, E. (1986). *An Introduction to English Prosody*. London: Edward Arnold.

Crystal, D. (1995). *Encyclopedia of the English Language*. Cambridge: Cambridge University Press.

Crystal, D. (2012). *The Cambridge Encyclopedia of the English Language*. Cambridge: Cambridge University Press.

Darthoso, F. (2014). Understanding Italian gestures. (Available from: https://www.instructables.com/id/Understanding-Italian-Gestures/).

Dawson, E., Gilovich, T., & Regan, D.T. (2002). Motivated reasoning and the Wason selection task. *Personality and Social Psychology Bulletin* 28(10), 1379–1387.

Deleuze, G. & Guattari, F. (1980). *A Thousand Plateaus* (B. Massumi, Trans.). Minneapolis: University of Minnesota Press.

D'ErricoF., Poggi, I. (2014). Acidity the hidden face of conflictual and stressful situations. *Cognitive Computation* 6(2), 661–676.

D'Errico, F., Poggi, I., Vinciarelli, A. & Vincze, L. (2015). *Conflict and Multimodal Communication*. Cham: Springer.

D'ErricoF., Poggi, I., & Vincze, L. (2013). Discrediting body. A multimodal strategy to spoil the other's image. In I. Poggi, F. D'Erricoet al. (eds.), *Multimodal Communication in Political Speech Shaping Minds and Social Action*, Vol. 7688 (pp. 181–206). Cham: Springer.

Duck, J.M., Hogg, M.A., & Terry, D.J. (1999). Social identity and perceptions of media persuasion: Are we always less influenced than others? *Journal of Applied Social Psychology* 29(9), 1879–1899.

Duck, J.M., Terry, D.J., & Hogg, M.A. (1995). The perceived influence of AIDS advertising: Third-person effects in the context of positive media content. *Basic and Applied Social Psychology* 17(3), 305–325.

Ekman, P. (1975). Face muscles talk every language. *Psychology Today* 9(4), 35–39.

Ekman, P. & Friesen, W.V. (1969). The repertoire of nonverbal behavior: Categories, origins, usage, and coding. *Semiotica* 1, 49–98.

Ekstrom, S.R. (2004). The mind beyond our immediate awareness: Freudian, Jungian, and cognitive models of the unconscious. *Journal of Analytical Psychology* 49(5), 657–682.

Elfenbein, H., & Ambady, N. (2002). On the universality and cultural specificity of emotion recognition: A meta-analysis. *Psychological Bulletin* 128(2), 203–235.

Fiske, S.T. & Taylor, S.E. (2013). *Social Cognition: From Brains to Culture*. Los Angeles, CA: Sage.

Forbes, S. (2015). 18 gestures that can get you in trouble outside the US. (Available from: https://nypost.com/2015/03/24/18-gestures-that-can-get-you-in-trouble-out side-the-us/).

Forster, E.M. (1924). *A Passage to India*. New York:Harcourt, Brace and Co.

Gabbott, M. & Hogg, G. (2001). The role of non-verbal communication in service encounters: A conceptual framework. *Journal of Marketing Management* 17(1–2), 5–26.

Ginting, E. & Kleiner, B.H. (2000). Conducting business effectively in the Philippines. *Management Research News* 23(7/8), 107–110.

Goldberg, J.A. (1990). Interrupting the discourse on interruptions. *Journal of Pragmatics* 14(6), 883–903.

Greenbaum, P.E. & Greenbaum, S.D. (1983). Cultural differences, nonverbal regula- tion, and classroom interaction: Sociolinguistic interference in American Indian edu- cation. *Peabody Journal of Education* 61(1), 16–33.

Grice, H.P. (1975). Logic and conversation. In P. Cole & J.L. Morgan (eds.), *Syntax and Semantics*, Vol. 3: *Speech Acts* (pp. 41–58). New York: Academic Press.

Grover, C.Jamieson, D.G. & Dobrovolsky, M.B. (1987). Intonation in English, French and German: Perception and production. *Language Speech* 30(3), 277–295.

Gu, W., Zhang, T. & Fujisaki, H., (2011). Prosodic Analysis and Perception of Man- darin Utterances Conveying Attitudes. *Proceedings of Interspeech* (pp. 1069–2011). Firenze: Italy.

Günthner, S. (2000). Argumentation and resulting problems in the negotiation of rap- port in a German-Chinese conversation. In H. Spencer-Oatey (ed.), *Culturally Speaking*. London: Continuum.

Hall, E.T. (1976). *Beyond Culture*. Garden City, NY: Doubleday.

Haynes, J. (2004). Communicating with gestures. (Available from: www.everythingesl. net/inservices/body_language.php).

Heine, S.J., Lehman, D.R., Markus, H.R. & Kitayama, S. (1999). Is there a universal need for positive self-regard? *Psychological Review* 106(4), 766–794.

Hellmuth, S. (2010). The contribution of accent distribution to foreign accentedness: Causes and implications. In K. Dziubalska-Kolaczyk, M. Wrembel, & M. Kul (eds.), *Proceedings of the 6th International Symposium on the Acquisition of Second Language Speech, New Sounds 2010* (pp. 191–196). Poznan, Poland: Adam Mickiewicz University.

House, J. (2000). Understanding misunderstanding: A pragmatic-discourse approach to analyzing mismanaged rapport in talk across cultures. In H. Spencer-Oatey (ed.), *Culturally Speaking* (pp. 145–164). London: Continuum.

Hughes, R. (2008). *Spoken English, TESOL, and Applied Linguistics: Challenges for Theory and Practice*. New York:Palgrave Macmillan.

Hurn, B.J. (2014). Body language: A minefield for international business people. *Industrialand Commercial Training* 46(4), 188–193.

Huron, D., Kinney, D. & Precoda, K. (2006). Influence of pitch height on the perception of submissiveness and threat in musical passages. *Empirical Musicology Review* 1(3), 170–177.

Hutchinson, M. (2013). Bullying as workgroup manipulation: A model for understanding patterns of victimization and contagion within the workgroup. *Journal of Nursing Management* 21(3), 563–571.

Ichheiser, G. (1949). Misunderstandings in human relations: A study in false social perception. *American Journal of Sociology* 55(2), 1–70.

Jones, E., Gallois, C., Callan, V. & Baker, M. (1999). Strategies of accommodation: Development of a coding system for conversational interaction. *Journal of Language and Social Psychology* 18(2), 123–152.

Jones, E.E. & Nisbett, R.E. (1972). The actor and the observer: Divergent perceptions of the cause of behavior. In E.E. Jones, D.E. Kanouse, H.H. Kelley, R.E. Nisbett, S. Valins & B. Weiner (eds.), *Attribution: Perceiving the Causes of Behavior* (pp. 79–94). Morristown, NJ: General Learning Press.

Kaur, L. (2013). Communicating across cultures in the globalized context. *Journal of Research in Marketing* 1(2), 50–54.

Kehrein, R. (2002). The prosody of authentic emotions. In B. Bel & I. Marlien (eds.), *Proceedings of the Speech Prosody Conference* (pp. 423–426). Aix-en-Provence: SProSIG.

Kelly, G. (2011). *How to Teach Pronunciation*. Harlow: Longman.

Kleinfeld, J.S. (1974). Effects of nonverbal warmth on the learning of Eskimo white students. *The Journal of Social Psychology* 92(1), 3–9.

Knapp, K. (2000). Metaphorical and interactional uses of silence. (Available from: http://www.ph-erfurt.de/~neumann/eese/artic20/knapp/7_2000.html).

Kotthoff, H. (1991). Zugeständnisse und Dissens in deutschen, anglo-amerikanischen und in nativ-nichtnativen Gesprächen. *Linguistische Berichte* 135, 375–397.

Lakoff, G. & Johnson, M. (1999). *Philosophy in the Flesh: The Embodied Mind and Its Challenge to Western Thought*. New York:Basic Books.

Lakoff, R. (1973). The logic of politeness: or, minding your p's and q's. In C. Corum *et al.*, (eds.), *Papers from the ninth regional meeting of the Chicago Linguistic Society* (pp. 292–305). Chicago: Chicago Linguistic Society.

Lakoff, R. (1990). *Talking Power: The Politics of Language*. New York: Basic Books.

Leech, G. (1983). *Principles of Pragmatics*. London: Longman.

Lewis, M. (2006). Nurse buying: Organisational considerations in the maintenance and perpetration of health care bullying cultures. *Journal of Nursing Management* 14(1), 52–58.

Linell, P. (2002). Perspectives, implicitness and recontextualization. In C.F. Graumann & W. Kallmeyer (eds.), *Perspective and Perspectivation in Discourse* (pp. 25–39). Amsterdam: John Benjamins.

Loveland, K.A., Tunali-Kotoski, B., Chen, Y.R., Ortegon, J., Pearson, D.A., Brelsford, K.A. & Gibbs, M.C. (1997). Emotion recognition in autism: Verbal and nonverbal information. *Development and Psychopathology* 9, 579–593.

Lytle, A.L. and Willaby, H.W. (2006). Intracultural and Intercultural Negotiations. IACM 2006 Meetings Paper. (Available from: https://ssrn.com/abstract=905462).

Magwaza, T. (2001). Private transgressions: The visual voice of Zulu women. *Agenda* 16 (49), 25–32.

Malove, S.C. (2014). Using relational theory to treat adolescent girls victimized by social aggression. *Clinical Social Work Journal* 42(1), 1–12.

Marchetti, S. (2015). Italian hand gestures everyone should know. (Available from: https://edition.cnn.com/travel/article/experts-guide-to-italian-hand-gestures/index.html).

Margić, B. (2017). Communication courtesy or condescension?: Linguistic accommodation of native to non-native speakers of English. *Journal of English as a Lingua Franca* 6(1), 29–55.

MatoesianG.M. (2008). You might win the battle but lose the war: Multimodal, interactive, and extralinguistic aspects of witness resistance. *Journal of English Linguistics* 36 (3), 195–219.

Mehrabian, A. (1972). *Nonverbal Communication*. Chicago, IL: Aldine-Atherton.

Meissner, C.A. & Kassin, S.M. (2002). 'He's guilty!': Investigator bias in judgments of truth and deception. *Law and Human Behaviour* 26(5), 469–480.

Mentcher, E. (1979). Teaching English to Russian students. *ELT Journal* 34(1), 47–52.

Merritt, A. (2010). 10 common gestures easily misunderstood abroad. (Available from: https://matadornetwork.com/abroad/10-common-gestures-easily-misunderstood-abroad/).

Mezulis, A.H., Abramson, L.Y., Hyde, J.S. & Hankin, B.L. (2004). Is there a universal positivity bias in attributions? A meta-analytical review of individual, developmental, and cultural differences in the self-serving attributional bias. *Psychological Bulletin* 130(5), 711–747.

Mohammadi, G. & Vinciarelli, A. (2012). Automatic personality perception: Prediction of trait attribution based on prosodic features. *Affective Computing, IEEE Transactions* 3 (3), 273–284.

Navarretta, C. (2013). Predicting speech overlaps from speech tokens and co-occurring body behaviours in dyadic conversations. *Proceedings of the 15th ACM International Conference on Multimodal Interaction* (pp. 157–163). Sydney: Association for Computational Machinery.

Nisbett, R. & Ross, L. (1991). *The Person and the Situation*. New York:McGraw-Hill.

Ogbu, J.U. (1982). Cultural discontinuities and schooling. *Anthropology and Education Quarterly* 13(4), 290–307.

Ohala, J. (1984). An ethological perspective on common cross-language utilization of F0 in voice. *Phonetica* 41, 1–16.

Orcutt, J.D. & Harvey, L.K. (1985). Deviance, rule-breaking and male dominance in conversations. *Symbolic Interaction* 8(1), 15–32.

Owens, L., Shute, R. & Slee, P. (2000). 'Guess what I just heard!': Indirect aggression among teenage girls in Australia. *Aggressive Behavior* 26(1), 67–83.

Paquette, J.A. & Underwood, M.K. (1999). Young adolescents' experiences of peer victimization: Gender differences in accounts of Social and physical aggression. *Merrill-Palmer Quarterly* 45(2), 233–258.

Pell, M.D., Paulmann, S., Dara, C., Alasseri, A. & Kotz, S.A. (2009). Factors in the recognition of vocally expressed emotions: A comparison of four languages. *Journal of Phonetics* 37(4), 417–435.

Pell, M.D., & Skorup, V. (2008). Implicit processing of emotional prosody in a foreign versus native language. *Speech Communication* 50(6), 519–530.

Perrin, L., Deshaies, D. & Paradis, C. (2003). Pragmatic functions of local diaphonic repetitions in conversation. *Journal of Pragmatics* 35(12), 1843–1860.

Pesarin, A., Cristani, M., Murino, V. & Vinciarelli, A. (2012). Conversation analysis at work: Detection of conflict in competitive discussions through automatic turn-organization analysis. *Cognitive Process* 13(2), 533–540.

Piskorska, A. (2017). Editorial: Relevance theory and intercultural communication problems. *Research in Language* 15(1), 1–9.

Pittam, J. & Scherer, K.R. (1993). Vocal expression and communication of emotion. In M … Lewis & J.M. Haviland (eds.), *Handbook of Emotions* (pp. 185–198). New York: Guildford Press.

Poggi, I., D'Errico, F. & Vincze, L. (2012). Ridiculization in public debates: Making fun of the other as a discrediting move. In N. Calzolari*et al.* (eds.), *Proceedings of the 8th Conference on International Language Resources and Evaluation* (pp. 44–50). Istanbul: European Language Resources Association.

Popkova, E. (2015). The backyard of EFL teacing: Issues behind L1 prosodic interference in Russian English. *Journal of Language and Education* 1(4), 37–44.

Pronin, E., Ross, L. & Gilovich, T. (2004). Objectivity in the eye of the beholder: Divergent perceptions of bias in self versus others. *Psychological Review* 111(3), 781–799.

Pyszczynski, T.A. & Greenberg, J. (1981). Role of disconfirmed expectancies in the instigation of attributional processing. *Journal of Personality and Social Psychology* 40(1), 31–38.

Ratner, C. (2000). A cultural-psychological analysis of emotions. *Culture and Psychology* 6(1), 5–39.

Ray, G.B. (1986). Vocally cued personality prototypes: An implicit personality theory Approach. *Journal of Communication Monographs* 53(3), 266–276.

Ren, Z.P. (2014). Body language in different cultures. *US-China Foreign Language* 12 (12), 1029–1033.

Sabini, J., Siepmann, M. & Stein, J. (2001). The really fundamental attribution error in social psychological research. *Psychological Inquiry* 12(1), 1–15.

Sanchez-Cortes, D., Aran, O., Mast, M.S. & Gatica-Perez, D. (2010). Identifying emergent leadership in small groups using nonverbal communicative cues. *International Conference on Multimodal Interfaces (ICMI)*, 1–17. (Available from: https://infoscience.ep fl.ch/record/163173/files/Sanchez-Cortes_ICMI-MLMI2010_2010.pdf).

Scharrer, E. (2002). Third-person perception and television violence. *Communication Research* 29(6), 681–704.

Schein, E.H. (2004). *Organizational Culture and Leadership*. San Francisco, CA: Wiley & Sons.

Scherer, K.R., Banse, R., & Wallbott, H. (2001). Emotion inferences from vocal expression correlate across languages and cultures. *Journal of Cross-Cultural Psychology* 32(1), 76–92.

Sharma, N. (2011). Contribution of non verbal language in communication: A study of non-verbal communication. *ELT Voices October*, 81–87.

Sheldon, R.C. (1951). Some observations on theory in the social sciences. In T. Parsons & E.A. Shils (eds.), *Toward a General Theory of Action* (pp. 30–44). New York:Harper & Row Publishers.

Shouse, E. (2005). Feeling, emotion, affect. *M/C Journal* 8(6). (Available from: http://journal.media-culture.org.au/0512/03-shouse.php).

Simmons, R. (2002). *Odd Girl Out: The Hidden Culture of Aggression in Girls.* New York: Harcourt.

Spencer-Oatey, H. & Xing, J. (2000). A problematic Chinese business visit to Britain: Issues of face. In H. Spencer-Oatey (ed.), *Culturally Speaking* (pp. 272–288). London: Continuum.

Stadler, S. (2007). *Multimodal (Im)Politeness: The Verbal, Prosodic and Non-Verbal Realization of Disagreement in German and New Zealand English.* Hamburg: Verlag Dr. Kovač.

Street, R.L. (1991). Accommodation in medical consultations. In H. Giles, J. Coupland & N. Coupland (eds.), *Contexts of Accommodation* (pp. 131–156). Cambridge: Cambridge University Press.

Thompson, W. & Balkwill, L.-L. (2006). Decoding speech prosody in five languages. *Semiotica* 158(1/4), 407–424.

Ting-Toomey, S. (2012). *Communicating across Cultures.* New York:Guildford Press.

Uleman, J.S., Saribay, S.A. & Gonzalez, C.M. (2008). Spontaneous inferences, implicit impressions, and implicit theories. *Annual Review of Psychology* 59, 329–360.

Underwood, M.K. (2004). Glares of contempt, eye rolls of disgust and turning away to exclude: Non-verbal forms of social aggression among girls. *Feminism and Psychology* 14(3), 371–375.

van Heugten, K. (2010). Bullying of social workers: Outcomes of a grounded study into impacts and interventions. *British Journal of Social Work* 40(2), 638–655.

Vishnevskaya, G.M. (2012). English pronunciation norms and the case of Russian English. In T. Paunovic & B. Cubrovic (eds.), *Exploring English Phonetics* (pp. 225–240). Newcastle upon Tyne: Cambridge Scholars Publishing.

von Raffler-Engel, W. (1980). Developmental kinesis: The acquisition of conversational nonverbal behavior. In W. von Raffler-Engel (ed.), *Aspects of Nonverbal Behavior* (pp. 133–160). Lisse: Swets and Zeitlinger.

Weaver, G.R. (1986). Understanding and coping with cross-cultural adjustment stress. In R.M. Paige (ed.), *Cross-Cultural Orientation: New Conceptualizations and Applications* (pp. 111–145). Lanham, MD: University Press of America.

West, C. (1979). Against our will: Male interruptions of females in cross-sex conversations. InJ. Orasanu, M. Slater & L. Adler (eds.), *Language, Sex and Gender* (pp. 81–97). New York: New York Academy of Sciences.

Wichmann, A. (2004). The intonation of please-requests: A corpus-based study. *Journal of Pragmatics* 36(9), 1521–1549.

Wong, P.T.P. & Weiner, B. (1981). When people ask 'why' questions, and the heuristics of attributional search. *Journal of Personality and Social Psychology* 40(4), 650–663.

Yammiyavar, P., Clemmensen, T., & Kumar, J. (2008). Influence of cultural background on non-verbal communication in a usability testing situation. *International Journal of Design* 2(2), 31–40.

Zahn-Waxler, C. (2000). The development of empathy, guilt, and internalization of distress. In R. Davidson (ed.), *Anxiety, Depression, and Emotion: Wisconsin Symposium on Emotion*, Volume II (pp. 222–265). New York: Oxford University Press.

Zellner Keller, B. (2004). Prosodic styles and personality styles: Are the two interrelated? In B. Bel & I. Marlien (eds.), *Proceedings of Speech Prosody 2004* (pp. 383–386). Nara, Japan: SProSIG.

Zellner Keller, B. (2005). Speech prosody, voice quality and personality. *Logopedics-Phoniatrics Vocology* 30(2), 72–78.

Chapter 6

Interpersonal relationships and network structures

How we define relationships, what responsibilities and obligations we associate with them, and how our networks are structured and intertwined impacts fundamentally on how we approach conflict. This chapter is therefore dedicated to examining cultural differences in relationship formation, structure and maintenance.

Much of our interactional work is oriented towards the creation of new relationships or the maintenance of existing relationships. Situating inter-personal relationships in the belongingness hypothesis, Baumeister and Leary (1995) purport that 'human beings have a pervasive drive to form and maintain at least a minimum quantity of lasting, positive, and significant interpersonal relationships' (p. 497). Hence, no matter how task-oriented our interactions may be, we cannot de-couple relational purposes from communication. Our interactions thus always serve both a content function and a relationship function, which can be roughly separated into what is said (content) and how it is said (relational). I would argue that no interaction takes place that is completely void of concerns for the people we interact with. Not least because, if we neglect to foster relational aspects in meaningful ways, our content-oriented goals will not be met. So even if it is for purely self-serving reasons that we engage in communication, relational considerations are necessarily an inevitable constituent. This communicative orientation to relationship-building and maintenance is therefore invariably governed by concerns for politeness, face and solidarity.

The salience of relational considerations in communication is highlighted not only by the studies that describe its importance but also by a number of studies dedicated to researching the implications of the loss of relationship-oriented cues in more recent modes of communication, such as computer-mediated forms of communication (Walther & Burgoon, 1992; Kreijns, Kirschner & Jochems, 2003; Baumer & van Rensburg, 2011). What is important to establish then is how different cultures define relationships, how these concepts emerge, and what kind of relationship-maintenance work they require in order to enable successful communication across cultural boundaries.

6.1 Relationship formation

Like all other aspects of communication and human interaction in the wider sense, cultures differ in their approach, attitudes and expectations to how relationships are created, how fast they are established, what it takes to maintain them, their depth, as well as the commitments they entail. While Krappman (1996) discusses the notion of 'friendship' as a universal phenomenon, he asserts that the content and performance of friendships are determined by sociocultural factors and vary across cultural systems. Cultural diversity in the perception of friendships is further supported by Cargile (1998) and Krumrey-Fulks (2001). This applies to, for example, the pace at which friendships are formed. Hall (1959) said of Americans that, while they are quick to form relationships, in other countries friendships go deeper, last longer and are characterized by stronger obligations. Cultural differences can also be found in the type of support that is expected from friends. Ghanaian people apparently place more emphasis on friendships for practical assistance and advice, while Americans mention companionship and emotional support as defining features (Adams & Plaut, 2003). Differences regarding conceptualizations of friendships can even be found across ethnicities within the same culture. Samter et al. (1997, p. 425), for example, found that the 'capacity of same-sex friends to provide emotional support was given significantly more weight by Euro-American women than by African-American women'. Keller et al.'s (1998) study on Icelandic and Chinese adolescents reveals that while close friendships constitute an important social construct in both cultures, and while there is substantial overlap in perceptions of how close friends should be treated, they assert that the motivating factors for doing so differ substantially. While Icelandic youths are motivated by personal moral value judgements, Chinese youths are motivated by altruistic cultural values for harmony-preservation's sake. So even when they may look similar on a surface-level, our understandings of friendships may differ on fundamental cultural levels.

Attitude formation towards relationships starts from childhood socialization and early enculturation. Weisner (1989) and Cicirelli (1994) point to the fact that cultures differ with regard to perceptions of sibling roles, as well as actual practices of care-taking patterns, play interaction, friendship and support among siblings. Chen, Rubin and Sun (1992) found that different behaviours lead to social acceptance in different cultures. While shyness-sensitivity was negatively associated with peer acceptance in Canada, it was positively correlated with peer acceptance in Chinese children. They attribute this finding to general cultural values and socialization practices, seeing as children in China are encouraged to be dependent, cautious, behaviourally inhibited, and self-restrained (Ho, 1986; Tseng & Hsu, 1970; Rubin & Coplan, 1998), while the same behaviours in Western cultures are usually viewed as socially immature, deviant, fearful and lacking in self-confidence (Cheek & Buss, 1981). According to Rubin, Bukowski and Parker (1998), the meaning attributed to any given social behaviour is a function of the ecological niche within which it is produced, meaning we are all products of our cultural priming, which views behaviours (including relationships) uniquely and distinctly. These different attributions, in turn, lead to different relative weightage of concepts such as loyalty, interdependence, emotional intensity, affective salience, emotional closeness, and family support (Updegraff et al., 2005).

Cultures also systematically differ where family structures and functions are concerned (Georgas et al., 1997). Some of these differences in our orientations to relationships have been attributed to our situatedness in individualistic or collectivistic frameworks of operation. Fijneman, Willemsen and Poortinga (1996) have suggested that this dynamic can explain cross-cultural differences in behaviour over a wide range of situations. Georgeas et al. (1997) found that the strength of emotional closeness, the geographical proximity of living, and the frequency of meetings and telephone contacts with cousins, grandparents, and aunts/uncles was higher in the more collectivist European cultures than in the more individualist European cultures. Some researchers therefore draw a link between collectivism and the strength of social ties. Tjosvold et al. (2005) emphasize that Chinese culture values strong relationships, which are prevalent across many Asian, Latin American and Arab cultures.

Although arguments have been made that collectivistic outlooks are the root cause for this disposition, I am not sure such a one-sided view can accurately represent the complex nature of interpersonal connections. While collectivistic mindsets undoubtedly helped shape many a modern Asian society, in this day and age it is hard to argue for homogeneous practices of pure collectivism almost anywhere. China is heavily impacted by the aftermaths of the one-child policy and its generation of 'little emperors', a 'generation of pampered and entitled children who believe they sit at the center of the social universe because that's exactly how they've been treated' (Kluger, 2013). According to Chung et al. (2009), this is a generation of children who enjoyed undivided attention, and financial and emotional support, and can be equated to the generation Y of the Western world. Falbo (2018) speaks of increased levels of self-enhancement, Wang and Fong (2009) mention high levels of egocentrism, while Cai, Kwan and Sedikides (2012) and Brummelman et al. (2015) refer to the growth of narcissism of China's only children (see also Pascu, 2011). These Chinese children have often been described as 'uniquely spoiled', 'willful', 'egocentric', and 'disrespectful of elders' (Wang & Fong, 2009). Singapore is dominated by virtues of meritocracy, which validates first and foremost individual achievement (Tan, 2008; Ang, 2006), and *kiasuism*, which refers to the 'fear of losing out' and 'winning at all cost' (Ellis, 2014), and refers to individuals hogging or claiming things for themselves irrespective of whether they need or even want them. An end-unto-itself, as Kirby and Ross (2007) describe it (see Singapore's 2000 Hello Kitty craze that escalated into quarrels, vandalism and even fights; Ng, 2001). Leo (1995) has linked *kiasu* behaviour to the terms 'selfish', 'inconsiderate', 'greedy', and 'obnoxious' – hardly representative of the Confucian ideals associated with collectivism. Japanese society reaches record-highs of singletons (Hermann, 2011; Nippon, 2018; Aoki, 2016) and the entire country is geared out to cater predominantly to singles (e.g. housing, restaurant seating, serving size). Yamada (1999; 2000) refers to them as spoiled and even as parasites. Hence, in this climate of self-centred concerns, collectivism can hardly be viewed as the main, let alone the only driving force.

A further argument that speaks against the notion of collectivism as main consideration for relational ties is that cultures, which are characterized by strong relationships, such as Chinese or Japanese culture, are also defined by a lack of trust. Fukuyama (1995) asserts that intense family ties prevent trust from developing beyond the inner circle. Surprisingly, however, cultures with strong relationships have also been found to be less trusting in general (including the in-group) than cultures that are on the more individualistic end of the spectrum (Yamagishi, Cook & Watabe, 1998; Kiyonari & Yamagishi, 1996). Instead, Yamagishi, Cook and Watabe (1998) posit that social uncertainty is a far better predictor for commitment formation, as it has been found to promote commitment formation, especially in cultures low in trust.

I think it is safe to assert that it is rare in the intercultural domain that any predisposition is solely or even predominantly attributable to a single value, such as collectivism. Rather, a complex interplay of various values and preferences is at work at any one time. Beyond collectivism, trust and social uncertainty, other important elements include the nature and strength of the networks we are socialized into, considerations of obligations and reciprocity, and the perceived impact of conflict on relationships.

6.2 Social networks

Societies differ in type, number and permanence of the groups that people join, but people of all cultures naturally form groups (Coon, 1946; Baumeister & Leary, 1995). Though I have argued that the notions of individualism and collectivism do not necessarily constitute the most salient category in terms of what governs group behaviours, these concepts are interlinked with important network structures and patterns that do exert an enormous impact on our interactional behaviours. According to Pym (2007, p. 745), 'connections concern not just communication but also the potential to act through communication; and they concern not just agency but more specifically co-agency, the capacity to act in relation'. In other words, our orientations to networks and social relationship organization determine largely how we communicate because much (though by no means all) of our communication is a means to a (transactional) end. Pym (2007) further states that language and culture alone are not sufficient determinants when it comes to communication, as they create and act in their own space. And this space, I would argue, is co-dependent on other people. Through this notion of co-dependence, our interactional behaviours are predetermined by how strong and interconnected those networks are and, consequently, to what extent relationships will determine our linguistic actions. As such, networks are a crucial factor in explaining differences in relational and linguistic strategies.

Network structure is important in determining the outcome of many important social and economic relationships (Jackson & Watts, 1998). Social networks carry important social functions, including collective capital (intellectual and resource related), social influence, social control, companionship and support (Heaney & Israel, 2008). Two key structural concepts that determine the impact and influence of social networks on our interactional and behavioural patterns are the notions of network density and plexity.

6.2.1 Density

The concept of density refers to how strongly personal networks are interlinked, or as Sparrowe et al. (2001) describe it: 'density is analogous to the mean number of ties per group member' (p. 317). In other words, do the people one interacts with in one's social network also know the other people in one's social network or are these relationships relatively isolated? High network density is often closely tied to cultures with strong relationships, because strong relationships are almost invariably defined through interconnectedness of family, extended family and friendship ties. Adams and Plaut (2003) purport that friendships in these cultures are less based on voluntary participation and instead more on a reliance on existing relationships for practical ends, such as patronage networks and interfamilial alliances (Piot, 1999).

Case study: Patronage

Growing up in rural Bavaria (Germany), as a child of parents who owned a shop in a local village, my early childhood experience of local business models was one of mutually supportive patronage. Every single Sunday of my childhood was spent eating at restaurants (whether we enjoyed the food or not), whose owners bought goods at my parents shop in return. This extended to where we bought our groceries, stationery, clothes, petrol, cars, etc.

While the density of networks is linked to national culture to some extent, it is also linked to rural vs. urban cultures (Fischer, 1982; Höllinger & Haller, 1990), as this example of rural Bavaria demonstrates. While Bavaria is one of the most affluent states in Germany (*The Economist*, 2017), such practices represent the remnants of strong community ties associated with its farming past. Dense networks also generally tend to benefit poorer communities, communities that are geographically more isolated, or communities whose work relies on collective social action. Badstue et al. (2003) discuss the inter-reliance of farmers in rural communities in Mexico, who depend strongly on each other for support of resources and labour.

Case study: Almabtrieb

All of my childhood vacations were spent on a farm in a small village in Kärnten (Austria). One practice that left a lasting impression on me relates to the communal practice of the *Almabtrieb* (literally meaning: driving cattle downhill from a mountain hut). Because meadows in the valleys are limited, both for grazing and making hay for the winter, farmers drive their young stock up the mountain over the summer, so they can graze on the slopes there, which are inaccessible to machinery, instead of using up precious resources in the valley unnecessarily. One person (or couple) stays up on the mountain in a small hut over the summer, watching over the herd. During this time, a different person/family of the local community whose young stock is on the mountain, hikes up to the hut each week with provisions. At the end of the summer, the entire village joins in on a hike up the mountain in the early hours of the morning in order drive the cattle back down to the village.

Such practices are becoming increasingly rare. However, even in modern Western societies, collective social action has its place. Höllinger and Haller (1990), in their review on kinship and social network structures in North-western, Eastern and Southern Europe, assert that the expectation that industrialization and modernization lead to a disintegration of kin relations is not supported by research, as such relationship structures have deep sociocultural roots. Since dense networks have a distinct set of gains, they are favoured by certain cultures or communities to meet very specific needs, which depend strongly on an interconnection of multiple factors, including the social, demographic and geographic characteristics of a place.

Dense social networks are generally associated with positive attributes. Heaney and Israel (2008) discuss the beneficial impact of strong relationships on health and longevity. Lin (1999) regards dense networks as a means for maintaining collective capital. While Lin (1999) asserts that dense ties are not a necessity for social capital, dense networks do have a relative advantage in maintaining resources. According to Putnam (1993), East Asian societies emphasize the importance of dense social networks. He attributes China's economic growth and the success of American politics in earlier times to network density. Zhou et al. (2007) also discuss the strong economic benefits of *guanxi* relationships in Chinese culture and similar kinds of relationships in other cultures, such as post-Soviet Russia.

However, while dense social networks offer greater capacity for support overall, dense social networks do not necessarily reflect on the quality of support. Hirsch (1979), for example, purports that denser social networks offer substantially greater quantities of support, but less satisfying emotional support. Lin (1999) observed that different communities have a preference for dense or loose networks simply because of the specific benefits that they each have to offer. Putnam (1995) asserts that, while dense networks clearly have benefits, they should not be idealized. Closely knit social, economic and political organizations, he states, are also prone to inefficient cartelization and corruption. Zhou et al. (2007), for example, allude to the benefits that the speed and flexibility of loose networks offer. Leonhard and Onyx (2003) also clearly state that the two types of networks benefit communities in different ways. Specifically, they assert that denser networks are better for 'getting by', while looser networks are better for 'getting ahead'.

As literature on density exemplifies, network density offers different kinds of benefits for different communities. As a consequence, some communities invariably benefit more from denser networks, while other communities benefit more from looser network structures. Putnam (1995) speaks of the 'network capitalism' of East Asia. Eloundou-Enyegue and Shapiro (2004) highlight the density of social ties in Cameroon. Höllinger and Haller (1990) describe Italian and Hungarian adolescents as strongly family-bound, Germans as moderately family-bound, while Australians and Americans were least family-bound, with regard to a multitude of factors, such as spatial proximity and frequency of contact. Putnam (1995) even speaks of a decline of social capital in the US.

Social networks are only partially defined by network density. Another vital, and no less important, indicator for how relationships are established and maintained can be attributed to how singular or pluralistic each individual connection is.

6.2.2 Plexity

The concept of plexity is fairly closely connected to the concept of density, in the sense that communities with preferences for network density typically also score high in relationship plexity. Tie interdependence theory suggests that one type of tie often entails another (Lomi and Pattison, 2006). As such, it is hardly surprising that density and plexity are linked to some extent. Kapferer (1969) even argues that multiplexity should only be seen as relevant in reference to density.

Plexity refers to 'the extent to which two actors are linked together by more than one relationship in a network' (Ferriani, Fonti & Corrado, 2013, p. 7). That is to say, are workplace colleagues merely colleagues at work or do they socialize with one another or carry out other types of activities outside the workplace as well? The greater the amount and diversity of activities one engages in with any one person, the more multiplex a relationship is considered to be. Typically, relationships high in plexity are referred to as multiplex, while relationships low in plexity are referred to as simplex or uniplex relationships.

Tolsdorf (1976) describes multiplex relationships as more powerful, and, indeed, research supports that multiplex workplace relationships have been linked to higher levels of productivity and job satisfaction (Rath, 2006). Coleman (1988) also links dense and multiplex relations to greater social capital. Researchers have even suggested a linear additive effect within the next generation (cf. Nauck, 2001). However, Ingram and Zou (2008) acknowledge that multiplex relationships serve different functions and place different demands on those involved than do uniplex relationships. While Methot et al. (2016) also point out the benefits of multiplex relationships, they also highlight that there is a unique downside to such relationships, which they describe as 'energy sapping' (p. 314). Multiplex relationships, they assert, are characterized by 'complex individual roles and wide boundaries' (p. 314). Because there are stronger bonds, it means they also require greater care, consideration and investment of time and energy, which can be depleting (Cordes & Dougherty, 1993). Ingram and Zou (2008) also caution that affective relationships can compromise and undermine economic ones. As such, both uniplex and multiplex relationships have their advantages and disadvantages.

Whether cultures show a preference for multiplex or uniplex relationships, however, is not purely determined by choice, but is grounded in a complex interconnection of a variety of other cultural determinants. One significant factor includes geographical space, which McPherson, Smith-Lovin and Cook (2001) mention as a determining factor of the 'thickness' of relationships, influencing both multiplexity and frequency of contact. While urban spaces are characterized by greater diversity, rural spaces invariably encourage greater density and more multiplex networks. Workplace culture constitutes another factor in the development of social network formation, and may well dictate to what extent uniplex networks are even feasible in any given society, as is the case in Japan.

Case study: 'Overwork death' and 'drink meeting'

Japanese workplace culture is characterized by a multitude of factors that are unique to and characteristic of Japanese working life. Traditionally, Japanese employees were tied to the same workplace throughout their career. Though the economic climate and shift in culture have altered this to some extent, long-term (if not lifelong) workplace participation is still very common in Japanese culture. Because people work together for long periods of time, they tend to get to know each other fairly well, not least because Japanese employment is also characterized by long working hours and an expectation of complete commitment. Japanese culture is, sadly, known for a phenomenon called *karoshi*, which can be translated as 'overwork death'. It refers to people dying from exhaustion due to the long hours committed to work and the resultant lack of sleep. Part of this phenomenon can be attributed to another phenomenon called *nomikai*, which literally means 'drink meeting'. It refers to a practice of either taking clients out for a meal and drinks after work (though it can be considered less of a purely social event and part of the deal-making practices) or to socializing among staff. These events can run into the early hours of the morning, with the result that some people will go straight to the office afterwards, because there is not enough time, and/or no transportation, to make it home and back in time for the new work day.

Because work commitments take up most of a person's waking hours and regularly after-hours too, and because people stay in the same companies for long periods of time, work life and personal life inevitably become inseparable. It is not only difficult but impractical and nearly impossible to maintain relationships outside the workplace. As such, workplace culture necessarily enforces high plexity networks in Japanese culture.

Various factors are therefore responsible for determining network structures and need to be taken into consideration when discussing social links across societies and cultures. However, some more generic observations can be made that appear to hold true across cultures and influence behaviours in conflict situations: The notion is that the higher the density and plexity in one's network are, the more reliant people are on maintaining and enhancing existing relationships. Since multiplex networks have also been linked to greater emotional importance (Stanton-Salazar & Urso Spina, 2005), unsettling these relationships has a more profound impact on an individual. The more dense and multiplex a social network is, the greater the repercussions of any form of infringement, since density and plexity foster interconnectivity. The interlinkage of ties within multiplex networks also entails that bonds created in one network influence the formation or dissolution of ties in other networks (Lee & Monge, 2011). The looser the networks and the less joint activities a person has with another person, the more independent their actions will be, because they have less to loose.

6.3 Obligations and reciprocity

Cultures differ strongly, both in terms of how they define and perceive relationships, and with regard to the expectations they place on obligations that the various types of relationships entail. Obligations and expectations, in fact, have been mentioned as key factors in strong relationship ties (Burt, 1992; Coleman, 1990; Granovetter, 1985; Mauss, 1954). While we all have to rely on our social networks at times, who we rely on for what kind of support may vary considerably.

Case study: Financial problems

During my time as an undergraduate student in Germany, it never ceased to amaze me that whenever US American students ran into money issues, they would first approach their friends for help, refusing to ask their parents for assistance. In contrast, for the German students I knew, parents were always the first point of contact in a financial crisis.

Interestingly, while Hall (1959) claimed that Americans tend to have looser ties to friends than is the case in most other cultures, where financial assistance is concerned, they appear to rely more on friends than on family, indicating that support may well be a domain-specific phenomenon. Insights on Ghanaian friendships (Adams & Plaut, 2003) lead to a similar conclusion. They rely on friends less for emotional support and more for practical assistance, meaning that they are likely to seek emotional support predominantly from other social ties. While Santana González, Silot Moreno and Schneider (2004) found that different cultures showed some important commonalities in their expectations of friends (loyalty and acceptance), they also found that Canadian adolescents prioritize common interests and shared activities, while Cuban adolescents perceive the giving and receiving of help as the primary benefit of friendships. In other words, while we may share some of our expectations regarding the roles and obligations of friendships, all cultures have culture-specific priorities of what kind of obligations are tied to which form of relationship.

One of the most prominent and defining social networks is, without a doubt, the family unit, which is governed by vastly different individual and collective obligations relating to core and extended family. Latin American cultures, for example, are known for their loyalty and dedication to their families (Chilman, 1993). Asian cultures are known for family solidarity, respect and commitment (Uba, 1994). However, Fuligni, Tseng and Lam (1999) posit that younger generations may not subscribe to these same ideals to the same degree anymore. Apparently, familial duties constitute one of the most significant sources of conflict between parents and children within Asian and Latin American families (Zhou, 1997). Despite the propensity for change, however, Asian and Latin American youths (even among third-generation immigrants) still subscribe to future obligations to their families more strongly than their European American peers (Fuligni, Tseng & Lam, 1999), indicating that they still largely adhere to traditional cultural patterns. A similar pattern emerged in a comparative study between Canadian and Cuban adolescents, where Cuban children were found to emphasize giving and receiving of support (Santana González, Silot Moreno & Schneider, 2004) in a cultural system, which is defined by reciprocity of relationships. McGuire and Essock-Vitale (1987) refer to reciprocity as a safeguard in times of need. The Cameroon family system, for example, is one that is defined by solidarity, protection (Tiemoko, 2004), and shared long-term mutual benefits (Fleischer, 2007). The system is set up in such a way that it encourages support across extended family networks, including the common practice of fosterage, in a society where child rearing is seen as a collective and social duty (Eloundou-Enyegue & Shapiro, 2004; Fleischer, 2007). These cultures prioritize shared and mutual (practical) support and advice over the goals and obligations found in other cultures, such as shared activities and emotional support.

Entire financial systems, in fact, are built around a society's notion of, for example, family obligations. While German society has high tax rates, the tax schemes that German citizens contribute to during their working lives, sees the government support citizens in old age. This welfare system is set up in such a way that the state, rather than children, is responsible for financial care-taking in old age. While Dallinger (2001) and Pfau-Effinger (2005) argue that the family-oriented culture in Germany sees family members often caring for the elderly, care can be provided by professional care-givers and financial support is attributed in either scenario, though the proportion of elderly people who hire a professional carer is on the increase (Pabst, 1999). Singapore, which is strongly influenced by Confucian ideals and notions of filial piety, on the other hand, has filial responsi-bility statutes (Moskowitz, 2002; Rieger & Leibfried, 2003), meaning children are obliged to take care (physically and financially) of their parents in old age. The Singaporean government advocates self-reliance of the family and extended family (Lee, 1995). In Chinese culture, parental support is seen as continued loyalty to family bonds (Su & Littlefield, 2001). These obligations are more than mere moral commitments though. Parental support can be judicially enforced if necessary (Ting & Woo, 2009; Moskowitz, 2002). Though Ting and Woo (2009) claim that the traditional Chinese culture of filial propriety is diminishing, because of a change in values between younger and older generations, and that the elderly tend to rely less on financial support from children to maintain their living standards after retirement nowadays. Thus, while cultural attitudes and expectations may shift, financial systems largely reflect cultural expectations of what parents' and childrens' roles are throughout the course of their lives.

The concept of children 'paying back' parents for everything they have received during childhood is rooted in the notion of reciprocity. While Gouldner (1960) claims that reciprocity can be encountered in all cultures, in American culture, social responsibilities are regarded as more of a matter of choice than an obligation (Markus, Kitayama & Heiman, 1997). By contrast, in many Asian cultures, recipro-city is clearly construed as an obligation and constitutes a particularly salient concept to relationships. Reciprocity refers to what Laursen and Hartup (2002) describe as 'matched or mutually equivalent exchange or paying back of what one has received' (p. 30). This refers partly to tangible objects and partly to social and financial reci-procal exchanges. Reciprocity constitutes an important construct to social interac-tions and its importance should not be underestimated in cultures, such as the Chinese, where *guanxi* forms an inextricable element of relationships. Though the concept of *guanxi* applies not only to family but to most any kind of relationship (Yan, 1996), including expectations placed on friends. Pye (1992) describes *guanxi* as friendship or relationship-oriented towards continued exchange of favours.

Case study: Korean hospitality

Though I had been to Korea multiple times, including for salsa dancing, I had only visited salsa clubs in one particular area of Seoul before. One weekend, a friend, who was visiting from the US, took me to a salsa club in another part of town. I enjoyed this club immensely, especially the friendly family vibe. To my astonishment,

I was immediately welcomed and fully included in this club's customary practice of jointly going for breakfast (typically Korean BBQ) after the club closes (at 5 a.m.). A few months later I was invited to join the club on their annual vacation, where the core members of the club go on a joint vacation for 3–4 days (for most of the people involved, this was the only vacation for the entire year, as some Korean companies give no more than four days annual leave). Seeing as this treatment was reserved for only the most salient members, I was more than surprised to have been invited. The entire duration of this trip I felt fully included and felt like a part of this family of friends. However, half a year later, a new club opened and on Christmas Eve a friend and I decided to try it out. We went to the usual club afterwards, around 2 a.m., only to be met with a very frosty reception, and reprimanding looks and gestures. I was later told explicitly by the club owner that he expects me to arrive before midnight (even though there were hardly any people to dance with before midnight).

I was very much taken aback by the effect my late arrival had on the owners, something I was not at all prepared for. A friend later explained to me that Koreans are quick to offer friendship and include people into their in-group, but that this friendship comes with the expectation of full and complete loyalty and unquestioned patronage of the club, and that the group breakfasts are not just an offer of hospitality but also come with an obligation to join, if not always, then at least almost always.

As this incident shows, friendship expectations can be very strongly binding in societies that rely on close bonds, and any transgression can completely unhinge a friendship. While this friendship never fully recovered from this unintended mishap, the repercussions for fellow Koreans are even more grave, because they are expected to know these unwritten rules. A failure to meet such reciprocity obligations will therefore invariably cause serious damage to a relationship. Spencer-Oatey and Xing (2008) describe how a visiting delegation of Chinese managers had an established relationship with a British engineer, who put obligations to his family first, and did not oblige the Chinese delegation's requests to meet until Monday, which was construed as failing his friends and violating the norms of mutual friendship obligations. In a system where relationships are often based on interdependency, the ability to count on a friend, especially in times of need, are absolutely essential.

Reciprocity, however, has to be seen as more than just support of interdependency structures. Gouldner (1960, p. 175) describes it as serving 'important social functions by facilitating status placement, providing generational continuities, reducing conflict, and equalizing class differences'. The key to understanding this concept is to understand that, in cultures based on reciprocity, 'society is wholly networked and that all ... activities revolve around these networks' (Weir & Hutchings, 2005). Sawalha (2002) cautions though, not to confuse reciprocity concepts, such as the Arab *wasta* or the Chinese *guanxi*, with nepotism or corruption. Though I do not wish to portray Japanese culture as less benefit-driven than other cultures, Ohashi (2008) describes reciprocity obligations in Japanese culture as more strongly motivated by gratitude and thanking for gifts/benefits received. Other cultures practice reciprocity out of purely altruistic motivations (Jung et al., 2014). The concept of reciprocity simply expresses the value placed on interpersonal connections, social networks and social security for in-group members. It should therefore be viewed more in the sense of 'bounded solidarity' (Dominguez & Watkins, 2003; Lin, Ensel & Vaughn, 1981).

6.4 Summary

In this chapter, I have described the complex nature of the relationship and network structures we are all part of. While it is almost impossible to capture the complexity of these systems in their entirety, it is important to assess at least some of the most prevalent factors at play in order to determine the effect they have on our predispositions towards conflict. Szell et al. (2010) emphasize that the 'interaction and coexistence of multiple relations are crucial to describe the emergence of conflict in social systems' (p. 13640). The assessment of the multidimensionality of human relationships is therefore paramount to the understanding of our actions during conflicts and disputes.

References

Adams, G. & Plaut, V.C. (2003). The cultural grounding of personal relationship: Friendship in North American and West African worlds. *Personal Relationships* 10(3), 333–347.

Ang, L.Y.L. (2006). Steering debate and initiating dialogue: A review of the Singapore preschool curriculum. *Contemporary Issues in Early Childhood* 7(3), 203–212.

Aoki, M. (2016). In sexless Japan, almost half of the single young men and women are virgins: Survey. (Available from: https://www.japantimes.co.jp/news/2016/09/16/national/social-issues/sexless-japan-almost-half-young-men-women-virgins-survey/#.W-kRS9UzaUk).

Badstue, L.B., Bellon, M.R., Juarez, X., Manuel, I. & Solano, A.M. (2003). Social relations and seed transactions among smallscale maize farmers in the Central Valleys of Oaxaca, Mexico. Economics Working Paper 02–02. Mexico: CIMMYT.

Baumeister, R.F. & Leary, M.R. (1995). The need to belong: Desire for interpersonal attachments as a fundamental human motivation. *Psychological Bulletin* 117(3), 497–529.

Baumer, M. & van Rensburg, H. (2011). Cross-cultural pragmatic failure in computer-mediated communication. *Coolabah* 5, 34–53.

Brummelman, E., Thomaes, S., Nelemans, S.A., Orobio de Castro, B., Overbeek, G. & Bushman, B. (2015). Origins of narcissism in children. *PNAS* 112(12), 3659–3662.

Burt, R.S. (1992). *Structural Holes: The Social Structure of Competition*. Cambridge, MA: Harvard University Press.

Cai, H., Kwan, V.S.Y. & Sedikides, C. (2012). A sociocultural approach to narcissism: The case of modern China. *European Journal of Personality* 26(5), 529–535.

Cargile, A.C. (1998). Meanings and modes of friendship: Verbal descriptions by native Japanese. *Howard Journal of Communications* 9(4), 347–370.

Cheek, J.M. & Buss, A.H. (1981). Shyness and sociability. *Journal of Personality and Social Psychology* 41(2), 330–339.

Chen, X.Y., Rubin, K.H. & Sun, Y.R. (1992). Social reputation and peer relationships in Chinese and Canadian children: A cross-cultural study. *Child Development* 63(6), 1336–1343.

Chilman, C.S. (1993). Hispanic families in the United States: Research perspectives. In H.P. McAdoo (ed.), *Family Ethnicity: Strength in Diversity* (pp. 141–163). Newbury Park, CA: Sage.

Chung, K.C., Holdsworth, D.K., Li, Y.Q., & Fam, K.S. (2009). Chinese 'little emperor', cultural values and preferred communication sources for university choice. *Young Consumers: Insight and Ideas for Responsible Marketers* 10(2), 120–132.

Cicirelli, V.G. (1994). Sibling relationships in cross-cultural perspective. *Journal of Marriage and the Family* 56(1), 7–20

Coleman, J.S. (1988). Social capital in the creation of human capital. *American Journal of Sociology* 94(1), 95–120.

Coleman, J.S. (1990). *Foundations of Social Theory.* Cambridge, MA: Belknap Press.

Coon, C.S. (1946). The universality of natural groupings in human societies. *The Journal of Educational Sociology* 20(3), 163–168.

Cordes, C.L. & Dougherty, T.W. (1993). A review and an integration of research on job burnout. *Academy of Management Review* 18(4), 621–656.

Dallinger, U. (2001). Organisierte Solidarität und Wohlfahrtskultur. Das Beispiel des 'Generationenvertrages'. *Sociologica Internationalis* 39, 67–89.

Dominguez, S. & Watkins, C. (2003). Creating networks for survival and mobility: Social capital among African-American and Latin-American low-income mothers. *Social Problems* 50(1), 111–135.

Ellis, N.J. (2014). Afraid to lose out: The impact of kiasuism on practitioner research in Singapore schools. *Educational Action Research* 22(2), 235–250.

Eloundou-Enyegue, M.P. & Shapiro, D. (2004). Buffering inequalities: The safety net of extended families in Cameroon. SAGA Working Paper. Atlanta University: Cornell and Clark.

Falbo, T. (2018). Evaluations of the behavioral attributes of only children in Beijing, China: Moderating effects of gender and the one-child policy. *Heliyon* 4(4), 1–16.

Ferriani, S., Fonti, F. & Corrado, R. (2013). The social and economic bases of network multiplexity: Exploring the emergence of multiplex ties. *Journal of Early Childhood Research* 11(1), 7–34.

Fijneman, Y.A., Willemsen, M.E. & Poortinga, Y.H. (1996). Individualism-collectivism: A empirical study of a conceptual issue. *Journal of Cross-Cultural Psychology* 27(3), 281–402.

Fischer, C.S. (1982). *To Dwell among Friends.* Chicago, IL: Chicago University Press.

Fleischer, A. (2007). Family, obligations, and migration: The role of kinship in Cameroon. *Demographic Research* 16(13), 413–440.

Fukuyama, F. (1995). *Trust: The Social Virtues and the Creation of Prosperity.* New York: Free Press.

Fuligni, A.J., Tseng, V. & Lam, M. (1999). Attitudes toward family obligations among American adolescents with Asian, Latin American, and European backgrounds. *Child Development* 70(4), 1030–1044.

Georgas, J., Christakopoulou, S., Poortinga, Y.H., Angleitner, A., Goodwin, R., & Charalambous, N. (1997). The relationship of family bonds to family structure and function across cultures. *Journal of Cross-Cultural Psychology* 28(3), 302–320.

Gouldner, A.W. (1960). The norm of reciprocity: A preliminary statement. *American Sociological Review* 25(2), 161–178.

Granovetter, M.S. (1985). Economic action and social structure: The problem of embeddedness. *American Journal of Sociology* 91(3), 481–510.

Hall, E.T. (1959). *Silent Language*. New York:Doubleday.

Heaney, C.A. & Israel, B.A. (2008). Social networks and social support. In K. Glanz, B. K. Rimer & K. Viswanath (eds.), *Health Beahviour and Health Education* (pp. 189–210). San Francisco, CA: Jossey-Bass.

Hermann, L. (2011). Single people in Japan reaches record high. *World*. (Available from: www.digitaljournal.com/article/315234).

Hirsch, B.J. (1979). Psychological dimensions of social networks: A multimethod analysis. *American Journal of Community Psychology* 7(3), 263–277.

Ho, D.Y.F. (1986). Chinese pattern of socialization: A critical review. In M.H. Bond (ed.), *The Psychology of the Chinese People* (pp. 1–37). Oxford: Oxford University Press.

Höllinger, F. & Haller, M. (1990). Kinship and social networks in modern societies: A cross-cultural comparison among seven nations. *European Sociological Review* 6(2), 103–124.

Ingram, P. & Zou, X. (2008). Business friendships. *Research in Organizational Behaviour* 28, 167–184.

Jackson, M.O. & Watts, A. (1998). *The Evolution of Social and Economic Networks*. Social Science Working Paper 1044, Pasadena, CA.

Jung, Y.B., Hall, J., Hong, R.Y., Goh, T., Ong, N. & Tan, N. (2014). Payback: Effects of relationship and cultural norms on reciprocity. *Asian Journal of Social Psychology* 17 (3), 160–172.

Kapferer, B. (1969). Norms and manipulation of relationships in a work context. In J.C. Mitchell (ed.), *Social Networks in Urban Situations* (pp. 181–244). Manchester: Manchester University Press.

Keller, M., Edelstein, W., Schmid, C., Fang, F.X. & Fang, G. (1998). Reasoning about responsibilities and obligations in close relationships: A comparison across two cultures. *Developmental Psychology* 34(4), 731–741.

Kirby, E.G. & Ross, J.K. (2007). Kiasu tendency and tactics: A study of their impact on task performance. *Journal of Behavioral and Applied Management* 8(2), 108–121.

Kiyonari, T. & Yamagishi, T. (1996). Distrusting outsiders as a consequence of commitment formation. *Japanese Journal of Experimental Social Psychology* 36, 56–67.

Kluger, J. (2013). China's One-Child Policy: Curse of the 'Little Emperors'. (Available from: http://healthland.time.com/2013/01/10/little-emperors/).

Krappman, L. (1996). Amicitia, drujba, shin-yu, philia, freundschaft, friendship: On the cultural diversity of a human relationship. In W.M. Bukowski, A.F. Newcomb & W. W. Hartup (eds.), *The Company they Keep: Friendship in Childhood and Adolescence* (pp. 19–40). Cambridge: Cambridge University Press.

Kreijns, K., Kirschner, P.A., & Jochems, W. (2003). Identifying the pitfalls for social interaction I computer-supported collaborative learning environments: A review of the research. *Computers in Human Behaviour* 19(3), 335–353.

Krumrey-Fulks, K.S. (2001). At the margins of culture: Intercultural friendship between Americans and Chinese in an academic setting. Unpublished Doctoral Dissertation. University of Kentucky, Lexington.

Laursen, B. & Hartup, W.W. (2002). The origins of reciprocity and social exchange in friendships. *New Directions for Child and Adolescent Development* 95, 27–40.

Lee, A. (1995). Singapore's maintenance of parents act: A lesson to be learned from the United States. *Loyola of Los Angeles International and Comparative Law Review* 17(3), 671–699.

Lee, S. & Monge, P. (2011). The coevolution of multiplex communication networks in organizational communities. *Journal of Communication* 61(4), 758–779.

Leo, D. (1995). *Kiasu, Kiasi: You Think What?*Singapore: Times Books International.

Leonard, R. & Onyx, J. (2003). Networking through loose and strong ties: An Australian qualitative study. *International Journal of Voluntary and Nonprofit Organizations* 14 (2), 189–203.

Lin, N. (1999). Building a network theory of social capital. *Connections* 22(1), 28–51.

Lin, N., Ensel, W.M. & Vaughn, J.C. (1981). Social resources and strength of ties: Structural factors in occupational status attainments. *American Sociological Review* 46(4), 393–405.

Lomi, A. & Pattison, P.E. (2006). Manufacturing relations: An empirical study of the organization of production across multiple networks. *Organization Science* 17(3), 313–332.

McGuire, M.T. & Essock-Vitale, S. (1987). Altruistic and affiliative behaviour in the family and among friends: Possible interpretations. *Social Science Information* 26(2), 385–402.

McPherson, M., Smith-Lovin, L. & Cook, J.M. (2001). Birds of a feather: Homophily in social networks. *Annual Review of Sociology* 27, 415–444.

Markus, H.R., Kitayama, S. & Heiman, R.J. (1997). Culture and 'basic' psychological principles. In E.T. Higgins & A.W. Kruglanski (eds.), *Social Psychology: Handbook of Basic Principles* (pp. 857–913). New York:Guildford Press.

Mauss, M. (1954). *The Gift*. New York:Free Press.

Methot, J.R., Lepine, J.A., Podsakoff, N.P. & Christian, J.S. (2016). Are workplace friendships a mixed blessing? Exploring tradeoffs of multiplex relationships and their associations with job performance. *Personnel Psychology* 69(2), 311–355.

Moskowitz, S. (2002). Adult children and indigent parents: Intergenerational responsibilities in international perspective. *Marquette Law Review* 86(3), 401–455.

Nauck, B. (2001). Intercultural contact and intergenerational transmission in immigrant families. *Journal of Cross-Cultural Psychology* 32(2), 159–173.

Ng, W.M.B. (2001). The Hello Kitty craze in Singapore: A cultural and comparative analysis. *Asian Profile* 29(6), 481–491.

Nippon (2018). Single living trend continues to grow in Japan. (Available from: https://www.nippon.com/en/features/h00182/).

Ohashi, J. (2008). Linguistic rituals for thanking in Japanese: Balancing obligations. *Journal of Pragmatics* 40(12), 2150–2174.

Pabst, S. (1999). Mehr Arbeitsplätze für Geringqualifizierte nach Einführung der Pflegeversicherung? Beschäftigungswirkungen des SGB XI im ambulanten Bereich. *WSI Mitteilungen* 2, 234–240.

Pascu, M.L. (2011). China's 'one-child family' demographic policy – analyzing the consequences of the measures taken to confine the demographic growth of China. *Bulletin of Transilvania* 4(1), 103–110.

Pfau-Effinger, B. (2005). Culture and welfare state policies: Reflections on a complex interrelation. *Journal of Social Policy* 34(1), 3–20.

Piot, C. (1999). *Remotely Global: Village Modernity in West Africa*. Chicago, IL: Chicago University Press.

Putnam, R.D. (1993). The prosperous community: Social capital and public life. *American Prospect* 13, 35–42.

Putnam, R.D. (1995). Bowling alone: America's declining social capital. *Journal of Democracy* 6, 65–78.

Pye, L.W. (1992). *Chinese Negotiation Style*. New York:Quorum Books.

Pym, A. (2007). Cross-cultural networking: Translators in the French-German network of Petites Revues at the end of the Nineteenth century. *Meta* 52(4), 744–762.

Rath, T. (2006). *Vital Friends: The People You Can't Afford to Live Without*. New York: Gallup Press.

Rieger, E. & Leibfried, S. (2003). *Limits to Globalization: Welfare States and the World Economy*. Cambridge: Polity Press.

Rubin, K.H., Bukowski, W. & Parker, J.G. (1998). Peer interactions, relationships, and groups. In W. Damon & N. Eisenberg (eds.), *Handbook of Child Psychology*, Vol. 3: *Social, Emotional, and Personality Development* (pp. 619–700). New York:Wiley.

Rubin, K.H. & Coplan, R.J. (1998). Social and nonsocial play in childhood: An individual differences perspective. In O.N. Saracho & B. Spodek (eds.), *Multiple Perspectives on Play in Early Childhood Education* (pp. 144–170). Albany, NY: State University of New York Press.

Samter, W., Whaley, B.B., Mortenson, S.T. & BurlesonB.R. (1997). Ethnicity and emotional support in same-sex friendship: A comparison of Asian-Americans, African-Americans, and Euro-Americans. *Personal Relationships* 4(4), 413–430.

Santana González, Y., Silot Moreno, D. & Schneider, B.H. (2004). Friendship expectations of early adolescents in Cuba and Canada. *Journal of Cross-Cultural Psychology* 35 (4), 436–445.

SawalhaF. (2002). Study says 'wasta' difficult to stamp out when advocates remain in power. *Jordan Times*, 1 April.

Sparrowe, R.T., Liden, R.C., Wayne, S.J. & Kraimer, M.L. (2001). Social networks and the performance of individuals and groups. *Academy of Management Journal* 44(2), 316–325.

Spencer-Oatey, H. & Xing, J. (2008). A problematic Chinese business visit to Britain: Issues of face. In H. Spencer-Oatey (ed.), *Culturally Speaking* (pp. 272–288). London: Continuum.

Stanton-Salazar, R.D. & Urso Spina, S. (2005). Adolescent peer networks as a context for social and emotional support. *Youth Society* 36(4), 379–417.

Su, C.T. & Littlefield, J.E. (2001). Entering guanxi: A business ethical dilemma in mainland China. *Journal of Business Ethics* 33(3), 199–210.

Szell, M., Lambiotte, R. & Thurner, S. (2010). Multirelational organization of large-scale social networks in an online world. *Proceedings of the National Academy of Science* 107(31), 13636–13641.

Tan, K.P. (2008). Meritocracy and elitism in a global city: Ideological shifts in Singapore. *International Political Science Review* 29(1), 7–27.

The Economist. (2017). On almost every indicator, Germany's south is doing better than its north. (Available from: https://www.economist.com/kaffeeklatsch/2017/08/20/on-almost-every-indicator-germanys-south-is-doing-better-than-its-north).

Tiemoko, R. (2004). Migration, return and socio-economic change in West Africa: The role of family. *Population, Space and Place* 10, 155–174.

Ting, G.H.Y. & Woo, J. (2009). Elder care: Is legislation of family responsibility the solution? *Asian Journal of Gerontology and Geriatrics* 4(2), 72–75.

Tjosvold, D., Poon, M. & Yu, Z.Y. (2005). Team effectiveness in China: Cooperative conflict for relationship building. *Human Relations* 58(3), 341–367.

Tolsdorf, C.C. (1976). Social networks, support, and coping: An exploratory study. *Family Process* 15(4), 407–417.

Tseng, W.S. & Hsu, F.L.K. (1970). Chinese culture, personality formation and mental illness. *International Journal of Social Psychiatry* 16(1), 5–14.

Uba, L. (1994). *Asian Americans: Personality Patterns, Identity, and Mental Health.* New York: Guildford Press.

Updegraff, K.A., McHale, S.M., Whiteman, S.D., Thayer, S.M. & Delgado, M.Y. (2005). Adolescent sibling relationships in Mexican American families: Exploring the role of familism. *Journal of Family Psychology* 19(4), 512–522.

Walther, J.B. & Burgoon, J.K. (1992). Relational communication in computer-mediated interaction. *Human Communication Research* 19(1), 50–88.

Wang, Y. & Fong, V.L. (2009). Little emperors and the 4:2:1 generation: China's Singletons. *Journal of the American Academy of Child and Adolescent Psychiatry* 48(12), 1137–1139.

Weir, D. & Hutchings, K. (2005). Cultural embeddedness and contextual constraints: Knowledge sharing in Chinese and Arab cultures. *Knowledge and Process Management* 12(2), 89–98.

Weisner, T.S. (1989). Comparing sibling relationships across cultures. In P.G. Zukow (ed.), *Sibling Interaction Across Cultures: Theoretical and Methodological Issues* (pp. 11–25). New York:Springer.

Yamada, M. (1999). *Parasite Single No Jidai.* Tokyo: Chikuma Shobo.

Yamada, M. (2000). The growing crop of spoiled Singles. *Japan Echo* 27(3), 49–53.

Yamagishi, T., Cook, K.S. & Watabe, M. (1998). Uncertainty, trust, and commitment formation in the United States and Japan. *American Journal of Sociology* 104(1), 165–194.

Yan, Y.X. (1996). The culture of guanxi in a north China village. *The China Journal* 35, 1–25.

Zhou, L., Wu, W.P. & Luo, X. (2007). Internationalization and the performance of born-global SMEs: The mediating roles of social networks. *Journal of International Business Studies* 38(4), 673–690.

Zhou, M. (1997). Growing up American: The challenge confronting immigrant children and children of immigrants. *Annual Review of Sociology* 23, 63–95.

Chapter 7

Relational conflict

Harre et al. (1985) assert that individual action operates in a context. Communication should therefore be viewed as a dynamic relationship between actor and environment (Smith, 1999). Consequently, we cannot communicate without considering how our actions will impact others around us. This is all the more true where potentially sensitive topics, or so-called face-threatening acts, are concerned.

There is notable diversity across cultures in their perception, interpretation and orientation to the concept of face. Face can be understood as one's social and public self-image, and a fundamental human desire to be liked and accepted, or as Goffman (1955, p. 213) put it: 'face may be defined as the positive social value a person effectively claims for himself'. An extensive amount of research has been carried out into cultural differences regulating face-oriented behaviours and even fundamentally different understandings of the concept of 'face' (see Ting-Toomey, 2005). Notably, East–West comparisons in orientations to and importance of face (Hu & Grove, 1999; Hwang, 1987; Pan, 2000). These studies may differ in some of their views on specific aspects of face, but they all promote the notion that there are different cultural sensitivities, awareness and orientations at play. Nonetheless, one factor that is shared across all cultures is that, irrespective of the importance we attribute to face or how we define it, the fact remains that we all take it into consideration to some degree for relationship's sake. Ting-Toomey at al. (1991) suggest that people in all cultures try to maintain and negotiate face in all communication situations. Essentially we all define ourselves in relation to the groups we belong to, or as Durkheim (1933) put it, identification is eminently social. Hence, we cannot NOT take our social bonds into consideration when we interact, as the consequences of violations can be severe.

Studies have demonstrated that a violation of face sensitivities and perceived transgressions can easily cause offence and may well result in dissent or conflict (Ren & Gray, 2009; Cropanzano, Goldman & Folger, 2003). Laursen (1993) speaks of the inevitability of disagreements but also the need to recognize the role conflict plays in the formation, maintenance and termination of social relationships. Conflict, he purports, holds the potential for irreparably damaging a relationship, since 'conflict of any kind is an emotionally laden, face-threatening phenomenon' (Ting-Toomey, 2005, p. 72).

What has become unequivocally clear is that insensitive acts of communication can damage relationships beyond repair, and as a result, our communicative goals. Face-threatening speech acts, such as disagreement, argument and conflict, therefore make it difficult to balance our wish to voice our opinions and disagree with something we believe to be erroneous with our wish not to threaten social bonds while doing so. These speech acts therefore constitute relational minefields. Voicing one's dissent while retaining relational ties is a careful balancing act that requires a fair degree of interpersonal sensitivity and skilled relational work. This is probably the reason why some cultures try to avoid conflict, and even disagreement, altogether. Though socio-pragmatic and demographic concerns also influence a culture's propensity to conflict-(dis)engagement, to some extent, these preferences are also determined by how cultures view interpersonal relationships, specifically with regard to the perceived stability of relationships and the effect conflict would exert on them.

I deliberately employ the term 'perceived stability', since our behaviours regarding conflict have very little to do with the actual stability of a relationship and instead are based largely on our perceptions. Some researchers have in fact also defined conflict as a perceptual construct rather than as a behavioural construct (Pruitt & Rubin, 1986; Borisoff & Victor, 1989). Consequently, the connection between relationships and conflict rests largely on perception.

7.1 Relational stability

How we respond to others in conflict situations is tied to a substantial degree to how we perceive the roles, responsibilities and obligations adherent to our relationships, but even more so on how we view the stability of said relationships under duress. The concepts of conflict avoidance versus conflict-tolerance, I addressed in earlier chapters, are directly linked to our understanding to what extent dissent can cause harm to precious relationships. Croucher et al. (2010) and Martin and Anderson (1996) posit that argumentativeness is closely tied to expected relationship outcomes. Consequently, if we expect the outcome to be negatively impacting on relationships, we will be more prone to shy away from them. Grimshaw (1990) posits that 'interactants motivated to maintain a relationship and concerned that it was not a strong one would avoid conflict – while individuals confident about a relationship would more comfortably engage one another in dispute' (p. 300). Rusbult and Zembrodt (1983) also established that how interpersonal conflict is handled is tied to the stability of the relationship. The perceived strength of a relationship, therefore, serves as a strong indictor to whether, and how openly, people engage in conflict.

Ren and Gray (2009) purport that relationship conflicts produce severe negative consequences for individuals, including anxiety, psychological strain, decreased task performance, and a decline of satisfaction and commitment. In this light, it is understandable why people prefer to avoid conflict.

Japanese culture, for example, generally steers clear of rocking the relational boat, because conflict of any kind is seen as harmony destroying. The strong emphasis on interpersonal harmony in Japanese society has been widely documented (Uchida & Ogihara, 2012; Leung et al., 2002; Ohbuchi et al., 1999). This not only relates to the harmony among strong personal contacts but also to harmony in the wider societal sense. However, this dedication to peace and unity (Ciubancan, 2015), often comes at the expense of individual needs or even justice. Japanese people even go to the extent of repressing their emotions in order not to impede on others or disturb harmonious relations (Ruby et al., 2012; Tanaka et al., 2010; Oda, 2006). Cultures with a strong harmony orientation avoid conflict because they interpret is as a threat to relational ties (Koerner & Fitzpatrick, 2002). Prunty et al. (1990) posit that, because Japanese view arguments negatively, friendships – once disrupted by arguments – rarely recover. Conflict avoidance, therefore, constitutes a core principle of the non-confrontational communication style associated with Japan (Saito, 2011; Ohbuchi et al., 1999; Ohbuchi & Takahashi, 1994; Chen & Chung, 1994). This is taken to the extreme at times, where social harmony is given priority over justice. According to Ohbuchi (1998), Japanese people accept social harmony as a principle of justice, believing that this value is more important than fairness. Apparently, even the Japanese legal system discourages people from publicly pursuing conflicts in court (Ohbuchi, 1998).

Case study: Harmony over injustice

Johnson (1974) cites a case where the eldest brother was the sole inheritor of the parents' estate, but, as a result, also carried the obligation to care for his widowed mother. However, since the mother and daughter-in-law could not get along, the mother ended up living with, and being cared for, by the sister instead, even though the eldest son retained all of the inheritance. Despite this injustice, the sister neither fought with, nor criticized, her brother, stating that 'we were taught that all are human beings, and we must try to understand them' (p. 304).

This disposition makes it unequivocally clear that conflict is seen as something relationships cannot recover from. Rather than addressing the issues that caused the relationship problems, no one raised this issue with the brother. Grimshaw (1990) cautions that the absence of visible conflict does not imply that the apparent harmony between people is real. This critical incident vividly demonstrates this assertion. Though superficial-level harmony was prioritized, the relationship between brother and sister remained strained (Johnson, 1974).

However, this view is not necessarily shared across cultures, where certain types of disagreement or even conflict are seen as productive, interesting, constructive or sociable. While conflict holds potential for relational damage, it also holds promise for social relationships (Schantz & Hobart, 1989). Laursen and Haven (2010) established that conflict is not necessarily a direct threat to the stability of obligatory relationships, such as family relationships. Some scholars have even linked conflict to positive relationship outcomes (e.g. because conflict helps refine interpersonal collaboration skills, encourages greater affective perspective-taking and emotional sensitivity, and greater moral development), and to promoting overall well-being (Dunn, 2004; Smetana, Campione-Barr & Metzger, 2006; Dunn & Brown, 1994; Berkowitz & Gibbs, 1983). Moderate to high levels of argumentativeness were linked to positive relational outcomes across multiple social domains (Beatty et al., 1994; Avtgis & Rancer, 2007; Roach, 1995), though Avtgis et al. (2008) assert that a clear distinction has to be drawn between argumentativeness and aggression/hostility, the latter being described as destructive to human relationships. Research has clearly highlighted that in some cultures, disagreements, arguments and conflict can strengthen rather than disintegrate social bonds. Adams and Laursen (2007) discuss conflict in supportive relationships as constructive and beneficial. Schiffrin (1984), in her study titled 'Jewish argument as sociability' emphasizes this very point, as does Kuo (1992), who states that argument can be valued as a sign of involvement and intimacy. Stadler's (2002) German research participants indicated that they find heated debates (including disagreements) enjoyable. Kim et al. (2001), even argue that people with argumentative predispositions 'perceive refutation as an intellectual challenge [and] feel pleasantly excited before an argument and afterwards feel satisfied and refreshed' (p. 387). The idea behind this argumentative behaviour is not only that argumentative discussions are more interesting but also that the interlocutors demonstrate a willingness to engage in such an exchange with a particular person. This kind of involvement is not something we would necessarily share with any person, so it can be seen as interest to get to know the other person and their views better, and that their views are important enough to warrant our time and energy. Indeed, Sillars, Canary and Tafoya (2004) state that conflicts signal the significance of topics and relationships, and can serve as vehicle for relationship transformation. As such, argumentative discourse can be seen as an invitation to forming a new friendship. Among established friendships, the notion is that our social bonds are strong enough that a little dissent cannot rattle or harm them. In well-established relationships then, conflict can be construed as a sign of trust in the strength of the shared bond.

This view is further supported by Adams and Laursen's (2007) and Laursen and Haven's (2010) findings that the consequences of conflict depend on the quality of the relationship. Moderate conflict was associated with favourable outcomes among those who reported low levels of perceived negativity towards a relationship. In other words, where relationships are strong and positive, some conflict benefits rather than hampers a relationship. However, in negatively perceived relationships or in relationships defined by distrust, conflict has negative repercussions. Simons and Peterson (2000) construe trust as central to conflict behaviours, stating that when a person distrusts another, that person will interpret ambiguous conflict behaviours as sinister in intent. This insight then aligns fully with the earlier discussion that more collectivistic cultures have been shown to exhibit lower levels of trust, not only towards outsiders but also to members of their inner circles. If there is less trust in other people and in the strength of relational bonds, combined with greater levels of interdependency, it makes sense that conflict would be avoided.

In essence then, how we view the relationships we are engaged in, or which we create, has an enormous and inextricable impact on how we view conflict, how and to what extent we engage in it, and what strategies we employ to deal with disputes.

7.2 Conflict and social networks

Beyond the perceived stability of relationships, a critical factor to consider is how conflict relates to network structures, since social structures have implications for actors' behaviours and outcomes (Kilduff & Brass, 2010). Understanding conflict dynamics then calls for understanding the factors driving the 'formation, persistence, dissolution, and content of ties in the network', as Ahuja, Soda and Zaheer (2012, p. 437) put it. Earlier, I discussed how cultures approach and set up network structures in a variety of ways. These structures have a severe impact on how we approach conflict. While it is true, of course, that personality also plays a role in how prone we are to engage in conflict (Graziano, Jensen-Campbell & Hair, 1996), personality alone cannot account for conflict behaviours, seeing as no individual operates in a vacuum and we all rely to some extent on the social networks of which we are a part. O'Reilly and Chatman (1996) deem culture to be a powerful social control mechanism that limits and controls the range of acceptable behaviours. Cahn (1992) asserts that communication behaviours associated with conflict are crucial in shaping and guiding ongoing relationships. Baumgartner (1998) therefore regards loose and dense networks as systematically associated with particular approaches to grievance pursuit.

7.2.1 Conflict in dense multiplex networks

In dense and multiplex networks, due to their strong interconnectedness, a threat to one social link has the potential to collapse one's entire social network. While strong social networks may be beneficial in terms of support, the greater interconnectedness of relational links in dense and multiplex networks also means that conflict has wider-reaching repercussions. Friday and Hage (1976) argue that when multiple roles overlap in a relationship, integrative bonds are much stronger. Strong bonds, in turn affect our behaviours, since network structures have consequences not only for individual members but for the network as a whole (Klovdahl, 1985). In this light, it becomes self-evident why members of dense and multiplex networks have to be more cautious in how they approach conflict. For this reason, societies with strong network ties are more likely to make concessions for the benefit of group harmony. Hwang (1997) states that in conflict situations involving horizontal in-group relationships, Chinese tend to say 'we are all brothers, it is needless to argue' (p. 32) – an attitude highly representative of cultures that emphasis strong relationship ties. Koerner and Fitzpatrick (2002) speak of pressure to agree.

In general, strong ties have been found to encourage cooperativeness (Nahapiet & Goshal, 1998). This is of course not to say that conflict does not arise, but network structures have strong implications for conflict avoidance. A cultural preference for conflict avoidance thus does not in any way imply that individuals in such cultures do not experience conflict. Conflict avoidant cultures are not conflict-free cultures, though it may seem that way on the surface (Gelfand et al., 2008). Morrill (1991) states that disputes begin with real or imagined grievances against someone or something. Nader and Todd (1978) speak of a 'pre-conflict' or 'grievance' stage (p. 14). The difference is therefore not so much in whether or not an individual experiences conflict, but whether such issues subsequently become voiced and resolved, or suppressed and avoided.

Researchers have indicated that strong network ties are associated with lower levels of conflict (Nelson, 1989). Kim et al.'s (2001) findings indicate that interdependence negatively and significantly affects argumentativeness. The lower propensity for conflict is twofold. On the one hand strong ties constitute conflict reduction mechanisms in their own right (Krackhardt & Stern, 1988; Curşeu, Janssen & Raab, 2012). Sytch and Tatarynowicz (2014) consider conflicts, especially severe conflict with little chance for reconciliation, less likely in collaborative and multiplex relationships, since density enhances uniformity (Wellman & Berkowitz, 1988). Presumably, this can be attributed in part to the fact that such groups have more shared goals and a more communal outlook to start with. Krohn (1986), at least, mentions that individuals are bonded to groups not only through institutions but also through goals and beliefs. Wellman and Berkowitz (1988) also allude to a connection between multiplex networks and attitude similarity. Koerner and Fitzpatrick (2002) further mention conformity orientation. Though they refer more to family culture rather than communities of practices at large, they assert that families with high conformity orientation create a climate that stresses homogeneity of attitudes, values and beliefs (see also Fitzpatrick & Ritchie, 1994). Family culture may well be a central aspect in shaping relationship practices, since Kadushin (2012) mentions that the concept of mutuality begins early in life, which he regards as a key factor in human development. Koerner and Fitzpatrick (1997) found that conformity orientation in families is positively correlated with conflict avoidance, while Wrench and Socha-McGee (as cited in Koerner & Fitzpatrick, 2006, p. 168) discovered a negative correlation between conformity orientation and conflict strategies. As such, from early childhood socialization, cultures seem to be geared towards conflict avoidance where strong in-group bonds prevail, because open debate of conflict is perceived as undesirable, as having little utility, or even as dangerous (Gelfand et al., 2008).

On the other hand, strong relationship networks also prevent conflict because people will refrain more readily from disintegrating strong network ties. Krohn (1986) and Haynie (2001) assert that participation in a social network constrains individual behaviours and that behaviour 'consistent with the continuance of their network relationships will increase' (Krohn, 1986, p. 83). In other words, strong relational ties are associated with the suppression of destructive behaviours and an increase in face-oriented behaviours. Sytch and Tatarynowicz (2014) and Rosenkopf, Metiu and George (2001) speak of a protective function that social relationships provide. Hwang (1997) says of Chinese culture that victims in such networks lean towards endurance over confrontation. Brown (1995) claims that in Tenejapan society, conflict, overt anger and scolding are 'normatively disapproved of' (p. 162), and consequently tend to be suppressed. Kagan, Knight and Martinez-Romero (1982) also assert that Mexicans tend to use more passive, avoidant conflict strategies. Indeed, Oetzel (1998) found a correlation between interdependence and conflict avoidance. Maintaining harmony, preserving face, and cooperation (Triandis et al., 1990) are second nature to members of what Landrine (1995) refers to as 'socio-centric' cultures (p. 755). Within such cultural systems, conflict is viewed as disruptive, and consequently either avoided altogether or kept covert (Lebra, 1984; Gelfand et al., 2001). Rohlen (1974) discusses how the strong social ties in Japanese companies, both to co-workers and the company, see Japanese people adopt avoidant, non-confrontational strategies. Where disagreement, criticism and unhappiness occur, they are likely to be expressed only through 'acts of subtle nonconformity' (p. 111), or suppressed altogether. Barnlund (1989) assesses direct verbal confrontation in Japan as serious blunder. Rohlen (1974) positions the high levels of solidarity among Japanese workers as well as their devotion to an organization as conflict-deterrents.

The concept of mutuality, as Kadushin (2012) and Wellman and Wortley (1990) call it, or of reciprocity, as it is typically referred to, is particularly relevant when considering behavioural conduct in conflict situations. Due to reciprocal arrangements, strong inter-unit ties constrain action more than week ties (Hansen, 1999). In relationships dominated by reciprocity considerations, conflict can be especially harmful. Socio-centric communities therefore tend to emphasize reconciliation over escalation. Davidheiser (2006) states that Gambians emphasize forgiveness over principled negotiation, along the lines of 'if you forgive now, then when you (or your kinsperson, associate, or animal) make a similar mistake, people will be willing to forgive you' (p. 843). Reciprocity should therefore not only be regarded as 'paying back' favours but also as 'paying forward', in order to cash in favours in the future. If peoples' livelihood depends on mutual assistance, as with Mexican maize farming or Austrian cattle farming (as described in Chapter 6), then it becomes evident why the suppression of minor grievances is in an individual's best (self-) interest. Therefore, even Gambian mediation practices are more geared towards persuading disputants to reconcile rather than towards negotiation and problem-solving (Davidheiser, 2006).

Conflict avoidance or minimization, however, are not solely employed for the benefit of the greater good of the community. Diamond (1996) argues that there are 'very necessary and important reasons to minimize, deny or refute the existence of conflict' (p. 118). She lists 'fear of reprisals' as chief reason. Network structures lie at the centre of such considerations. Though repercussions also pertain to power, status and hierarchical differences, the interdependence inherent in close-knit groups also prevents conflict from being escalated. Sytch and Tatarynowicz (2014) assert that conflict diminishes the likelihood of future collaborative relationships, consequently, it can impinge on the economic goals of a group. Diamond (1996) further alludes to the difficulty of raising dissent or disagreement in a large group. Though voicing conflict in close-knit networks does not necessarily imply raising issues in front of a large group of people, it is akin to such an action, as conflict in dense and multiplex networks rarely remains contained to the individuals who are directly affected by it. Rather, it tends to set off a reaction of social sanctions applied to those violating expectations of harmony, respect and reciprocity. Szell, Lambiotte and Turner (2010) purport that networks representing hostile actions may serve as catalyst for the network of punishments. While they refer to social networks in virtual realities, they argue that these carry implications for social network structures at large. This seems to be indeed the case, as enforcement of alignment through punishment seems to be a standard practice for ensuring cooperation with a society's expectations for normative behaviour. According to Gómez (2008), in dense, multiplex societies, compliance regarding these norms is also achieved by way of coercion via shaming, gossiping or threat of social isolation. This can take many forms, such as spreading rumours, social exclusion, manipulation or backbiting (Richardson & Green, 1997; Archer, 2010). Ellwardt, Steglich and Wittek (2012) mention the strategic use of gossip about norm violators as a sanction to maintain a society's norms. Wilson et al. (2000) also found that gossip was perceived as appropriate when it served the interests of the group. Though it does not seem to be pleasant for those on the receiving end, such indirectly aggressive strategies appear to be essentially targeting group affiliation rather than ostracization. Walgrave and Aertsen (1996) portray shaming as a re-integrative strategy that is essentially oriented towards providing an opportunity for restoration of the situation and reintegration into the community. Researchers, in general, have established a clear link between strong network ties and more indirect forms of aggression (Lagerspetz et al., 1988; Green, Richardson & Lago, 1996; Archer, 2010). Though it is somewhat questionable whether indirect aggression constitutes a less harmful outlet for conflict as far as interpersonal relationships are concerned, it does unequivocally serve as an effective tool of social enforcement. Richardson and Green (1997) in fact state that one could argue that such non-direct aggression, or what they refer to as circuitous harm, might even be more aversive than direct confrontation.

In some communities, however, transgressions can incur even stronger sanctions. Brown (1990) says of Tenejapan society that women are expected to be self-annihilating kinesically and 'operate under very stringent interactional constraints including strong inhibitions against public displays of emotion or public confrontation'. Failure to comply, she states, may result not only in indirect forms of aggression such as ridicule by one's peers but also potential physical punishment. Fear of repercussions is therefore clearly warranted in tight-knit societies, and can potentially explain the lower levels of trust even within the in-group, if in-group members may turn against someone for social sanctions' sake.

Conflict avoidance can thus be regarded as a natural response to greater shared perspectives and viewpoints, to greater responsibility to society, to greater reciprocal obligations, and to greater repercussions, both for the network and the individual involved.

7.2.2 Conflict in loose uniplex networks

Preferred conflict strategies are inextricably linked to relationship and network ties, and this does not merely apply to dense and multiplex networks, where people rely on their network connections more strongly. Croucher et al. (2010) purport that an independent self-construal, which views the individual as autonomous entity, is most often associated with high levels of argumentativeness. Gelfand et al. (2012) link direct, confrontational verbal behaviours and the open expression of emotions and interests to loose social structures and low-density social networks. A preference for active, confrontational strategies in loose, uniplex societies is further supported by Kagan, Knight and Martinez-Romero (1982). Folger, Poole and Stutman (1993) view this propensity for argumentativeness as an important predisposition that impacts on processes and outcomes of interpersonal conflicts.

Lazega and Mounier (2002) claim that, since the contacts of an autonomous actor are not connected to each other, they cannot put together a strong constraint on his/her behaviour. Individuals involved in loose social networks, therefore, enjoy more behavioural freedom. German conflict style has been described as confrontational and argumentative (Oetzel, Garcia & Ting-Toomey, 2008), and is associated with asserting one's own wishes (Clackworthy, 1996). This freedom is provided, in part, because individuals may feel more comfortable sharing with individuals, with whom they do not share overlapping relationships (Wright, Rains & Banas, 2010). In part, this freedom also stems from the fact that weak-tie networks, as Wright, Rains and Banas (2010) state, 'do not typically share an intimate relational history', making them 'less likely to judge or feel judged by one another' (p. 610). Members of loose networks therefore benefit from more liberty to openly address dissident issues and, in addition, the consequences of their open argumentativeness are subject to a substantially lower risk-factor.

In loose and uniplex social networks, ties are generally formed more quickly, there are fewer links between individual contacts, and participants of such networks rely less on one specific person to meet several of their needs and goals. Should conflict threaten one such relationship, it might cause disastrous consequences to this one particular connection, but it is not very likely to spill over to many other connections within a person's network structure. Since loose, uniplex networks are defined by a multitude of different relationships that operate in relative isolation, the repercussions of conflict have very different consequences for individuals. Holt and DeVore (2005) purport that people who are less concerned with preserving the goodwill of others have more freedom to pursue their own interactional goals and can therefore engage in more confrontational conflict styles. Pruitt and Carnevale's (1993) findings also suggest that lower expectations of long-term dependency on the other party are tied to lower concern for others.

While strong arguments have been made in favour of the strong social support networks prevalent in dense and multiplex societies, loose ties also have some advantages when it comes to social support. Dense social networks might have more social support available, but looser networks offer a wider pool of knowledge and support, which offers its own specific set of benefits (Hansen, 1999). Granovetter (1983) regards weak ties as a means to providing access to information and resources that are not available in one's own social circle. Maintaining strong relations, Hansen (1999) asserts, also requires more energy than weak ones, and people can therefore afford to maintain relations with only few units, making them all the more interdependent and susceptible to negative conflict outcomes.

The lack of interdependent needs and goals also allows for more objective, disimpassioned support (Adelman et al., 1987). Nannestad et al. (2008) associate bridging contacts (i.e. loose uniplex contacts) with positive social capital, integration and social mobility. Ryan (2011) therefore cautions not to overestimate the social benefits of dense multiplex networks, because they are also characterized by ethnic enclaves and ghettoization, which are viewed by Crowley and Hickman (2008) as threat to social cohesion in certain social contexts. LaGaipa (1990) even suggests that 'social obligations may override the positive effect of companionship and social support' (p. 126) of strong ties. Strong reciprocal obligations cause more stress to the individual, while weak ties have been associated with lower levels of stress (Wright, Rains & Banas, 2010), presumably because always having to consider the repercussions of one's actions on the self and on others constitutes a substantial burden. Weak ties, consequently, offer some great advantages in conflict situations. Wellman and Wortley (1990) speak of more sparsely knit relations as simply offering more specialized, compartmentalized forms of support. Lepore (1992) suggests that individuals with diverse social support resources are more resilient in the face of negative social interactions. The ability to draw on support from multiple domains aids an individual in coping with social negativity, he purports. Prell, Hubacek and Reed (2009) also speak of weak ties making a network more resilient and adaptive, while Crowell (2004) mentions the mediating social effect that weak ties can have. The independence of weak ties can therefore provide strong advantages to individuals in conflict situations.

However, members of loose networks do not only benefit from lower levels of negative aftermaths of conflict, but often also value the benefits of conflict resolution. While conflict can be harmful to relationships, not resolving conflict can have the same effect. Gelfand et al. (2008) describe conflict in conflict avoidant cultures as 'the elephant in the room that no one talks about' (p. 145). Suppressing conflict is akin to sweeping dissident issues under the rug. In other words, conflicts may not be immediately visible, but tend to linger under the surface. Conflict avoidance is therefore not categorically preferable.

Though members of loose, uniplex social networks enjoy more freedom for self-expression and have fewer consequences to fear, it would be unfair to argue that they have categorically lower concerns for others and others' face-needs. Their higher propensity for argumentativeness should be viewed in the light of argumentativeness being a necessary bi-product of conflict resolution. Greco Morasso (2011) positions argumentative discussion as a necessary and constructive element of conflict resolution. It might even be plausible that the resolution of a conflict, without the lingering resentments and hostility that can accompany conflict suppression, are in and of themselves other-oriented strategies. Greco Morasso (2011), in fact, alludes to conflict resolution offering disputants the possibility to 'restore jeopardized relationships' (p. 2). While certainly more confrontational, the very willingness to engage in conflict, for the sake of burying the hatchet, can also be seen as socially directed communication strategy.

7.3 Summary

The different approaches of avoidance/suppression and engagement/confrontation are both socially motivated, even if these motivations stem from divergent underlying premises. The different social network structures naturally predispose individuals to judge, assess and evaluate their interpersonal relationships differently. Consequently, they are also prone to assess conflict outcomes and their repercussions in starkly different ways. While perceptions of relational ties influence conflict attitudes, they also assert a strong effect on preferred conflict negotiation and conflict management strategies.

References

Adams, R.E. & Laursen, B. (2007). The correlates of conflict: Disagreement is not necessarily detrimental. *Journal of Family Psychology* 21(3), 445–458.

Adelman, M.B., Parks, M.R. & Albrecht, T.L. (1987). Beyond close relationships: Support in weak ties. In T.L. Albrecht, M.B. Adelman et al. (eds.), *Communicating Social Support* (pp. 126–147). Newbury Park, CA: Sage.

Ahuja, G., Soda, G. & Zaheer, A. (2012). The genesis and dynamics of organizational networks. *Organization Science* 23(2), 434–448.

Archer, J. (2010). What is Indirect Aggression in Adults? In K. Osterman (ed.), *Indirect and Direct Aggression* (pp. 3–16). Frankfurt am Main: Peter Lang.

Avtgis, T.A. & Rancer, A.S. (2007). The theory of independent mindedness: An organizational theory for individualistic cultures. In M. Hinner (ed.), *The Role of Communication in Business Transactions and Relationships: Freiberger Beitrage zur Interkulturellen und Wirtschaftskommunikation* (pp. 183–201). Frankfurt: Peter Lang.

Avtgis, T.A., Rancer, A.S., Kanjeva, P.A. & Chory, R.M. (2008). Argumentative and aggressive communication in Bulgaria: Testing for conceptual and methodological equivalence. *Journal of Intercultural Communication Research* 37(1), 17–24.

Barnlund, D. (1989). *Communication Styles of Japanese and Americans*. Belmont, CA: Wadsworth.

Baumgartner, M.P. (1988). *The Moral Order of a Suburb*. New York: Oxford University Press.

Beatty, M.J., Zelley, J.R., Dobos, J.A. & Rudd, J.A. (1994). Fathers' trait verbal aggressiveness and argumentativeness as predictors of adult son's perceptions of fathers' sarcasm, criticism, and verbal aggressiveness. *Communication Quarterly* 42(4), 407–415.

Berkowitz, M.W. & Gibbs, J.C. (1983). Measuring the developmental features of moral discussion. *Merrill-Palmer Quarterly* 29(4), 341–357.

Borisoff, D. & Victor, D. (1989). *Conflict Management: A Communication Skills Approach*. Englewood Cliffs, NJ: Prentice-Hall.

Brown, P. (1990). Gender, politeness, and confrontation in Tenejapa. *Discourse Processes* 13(1), 123–141.

Brown, P. (1995). Politeness strategies and the attribution of intentions: The case of Tzeltal irony. In E. Goody (ed.), *Implications of a Social Origin for Human Intelligence* (pp. 153–174). Cambridge: Cambridge University Press.

Cahn, D.D. (1992). *Conflict in Intimate Relationships*. New York: Guildford Press.

Chen, G.M. & Chung, J. (1994). The impact of Confucianism on organizational communication. *Communication Quarterly* 42(2), 93–105.

Ciubancan, M. (2015). Principles of communication in Japanese indirectness and hedging. *Romanian Economic and Business Review* 10(4), 246–253.

Clackworthy, D. (1996). Training Germans and Americans in conflict management. In M. Berger (ed.), *Cross-Cultural Team Building: Guidelines for more Effective Communication and Negotiation* (pp. 91–100). London: McGraw-Hill.

Cropanzano, R., Goldman, B. & Folger, R. (2003). Deontic justice: The role of moral principles in workplace fairness. *Journal of Organizational Behavior* 24(8), 1019–1024.

Croucher, S.M., Oommen, D., Hicks, M.V., Holody, K.J., Anarbaeva, S., Yoon, K., Spencer, A.T., Marsh, C. & Aljahli, A.I. (2010). The effects of self-construal and religiousness on argumentativeness: A cross-cultural analysis. *Communication Studies* 61 (2), 135–155.

Crowell, L.F. (2004). Weak ties: A mechanism for helping women expand their social networks and increase their capital. *The Social Science Journal* 41(1), 15–28.

Crowley, H. & Hickman, M.J. (2008). Migration, postindustrialism and the globalized nation state: Social capital and social cohesion re-examined. *Ethnic and Racial Studies* 31(7), 122–124.

Curşeu, P.L., Janssen, S.E.A. & Raab, J. (2012). Connecting the dots: Social network structure, conflict, and group cognitive complexity. *Higher Education* 63(5), 621–629.

Davidheiser, M. (2006). Joking for peace. Social organization, tradition, and change in Gambian conflict management. *Cahiers d'Études Africaines* 184(4), 835–859.

Diamond, J. (1996). *Status and Power in Verbal Interaction: A Study of Discourse in a Close-Knit Social Network.* Philadelphia, PA: John Benjamins.

Dunn, J. (2004). *Understanding Children's Worlds.* Malden, MA: Blackwell.

Dunn, J. & Brown, J. (1994). Affect expression in the family, children's understanding of emotions, and their interactions with others. *Merrill-Palmer Quarterly* 40(1), 120–137.

Durkheim, E. (1933). *The Division of Labour in Society.* New York: Macmillan.

Ellwardt, L., Steglich, C. & Wittek, R. (2012). The co-evolution of gossip and friendship in workplace social networks. *Social Networks* 34(4), 623–633.

Fitzpatrick, M.A. & Ritchie, L.D. (1994). Communication schemata within the family: Multiple perspectives on family interaction. *Human Communication Research* 20(3), 275–301.

Folger, J.P., Poole, M.S. & Stutman, R.K. (1993). *Working through Conflict.* New York: HarperCollins.

Friday, P.C. & Hage, J. (1976). Youth crime and post industrial societies: An integrated perspective. *Criminology* 14, 331–346.

Gelfand, M.J., Leslie, L.M. & Ketter, K.M. (2008). On the etiology of conflict cultures. *Research in Organizational Behavior* 28, 137–166.

Gelfand, M.J., Nishii, L.H., Holcombe, K.M., Dyer, N., Ohbuchi, K-I. & Fukuno, M. (2001). Cultural influences on cognitive representations of conflict: Interpretations of conflict episodes in the United States and Japan. Cornell University ILR School. (Available from: https://digitalcommons.ilr.cornell.edu/cgi/viewcontent.cgi?article=2268&context=articles).

Gelfand, M.J., Severance, L., Fulmer, C.A. & Al Dabbagh, M. (2012). Explaining and predicting cultural differences in negotiation. In G.E. Bolton & R.T.A. Croson (eds.), *The Oxford Handbook of Economic Conflict Resolution.* Oxford: Oxford University Press.

Goffman, E. (1955). On face work: An analysis of ritual elements in social interaction. *Psychiatry* 18, 213–231.

Gómez, M.A. (2008). All in the family: The influence of social networks on dispute processing. *Georgia Journal of International and Comparative Law* 36(2), 291–354.

Granovetter, M. (1983). The strength of weak ties: A network theory revisited. *Sociological Theory* 1, 201–233.

Graziano, W., Jensen-Campbell, L. & Hair, E. (1996). Perceiving interpersonal conflict and reacting to it: The case for agreeableness. *Journal of Personality and Social Psychology* 70(4), 820–835.

Greco Morasso, S. (2011). *Argumentation in Dispute Mediation: A Reasonable Way to Handle Conflict.* Amsterdam: John Benjamins.

Green, L.R., Richardson, D.R. & Lago, T. (1996). How do friendship, indirect, and direct aggression relate? *Aggressive Behavior* 22(2), 81–86.

Grimshaw, A.D. (1990). *Conflict Talk: Sociolinguistic Investigations of Arguments in Conversations.* Cambridge: Cambridge University Press.

Hansen, J.T. (1999). The search-transfer problem: The role of weak ties in sharing knowledge across organization subunits. *Administrative Science Quarterly* 44(1), 82–111.

Harre, R., Clarke, D. & DeCarlo, N. (1985). *Motives and Mechanisms: An Introduction to the Psychology of Action.* New York: Methuen.

Haynie, D.L. (2001). Delinquent peers revisited: Does network structure matter. *American Journal of Sociology* 106(4), 1013–1057.

Holt, J.L. & DeVore, C.J. (2005). Culture, gender, organizational role, and styles of conflict resolution: A meta-analysis. *International Journal of Intercultural Relations* 29(2), 165–196.

Hu, W. & Grove, C. (1999). *Encountering the Chinese: A Guide for Americans.* Boston, MA: Intercultural Press.

Hwang, K.K. (1987). Face and favor: The Chinese power game. *The American Journal of Sociology* 92(4), 944–974.

Hwang, K.K. (1997). Guanxi and mientze: Conflict resolution in Chinese society. *Intercultural Communication Studies* 7(1), 17–38.

Johnson, C.L. (1974). Gift giving and reciprocity among the Japanese Americans in Honolulu. *American Ethnologist* 1(2), 295–308.

Kadushin, C. (2012). *Understanding Social Networks: Theories, Concepts, and Findings.* Oxford: Oxford University Press.

Kagan, S., Knight, G. & Martinez-Romero, S. (1982). Culture and the development of conflict resolution style. *Journal of Cross-Cultural Psychology* 13(1), 43–59.

Kilduff, M. & Brass, D.J. (2010). Organizational social network research: Core ideas and key debates. *Academy of Management Annals* 4(1), 317–357.

Kim, M.S., Aune, K.S., Hunter, J.E., Kim, H.J. & Kim, J.S. (2001). The effect of culture and self-construals on predispositions toward verbal communication. *Human Communication Research* 27(3), 382–408.

Klovdahl, S. (1985). Social Networks and the Spread of Infectious Diseases: The AIDS Example. *SocialScience and Medicine* 21(11), 1203–1216.

Koerner, A.F. & Fitzpatrick, M.A. (1997). Family type and conflict: The impact of conversation orientation and conformity orientation on conflict in the family. *Communication Studies* 48(1), 59–75.

Koerner, A.F. & Fitzpatrick, M.A. (2002). You never leave your family in a fight: The impact of family of origin on conflict-behaviour in romantic relationships. *Communication Studies* 53(3), 234–251.

Koerner, A.F. & Fitzpatrick, M.A. (2006). Family conflict communication. In J.G. Oetzel & S. Ting-Toomey (Eds.), *The Sage Handbook of Conflict Communication: Integrating Theory, Research, and Practice* (pp. 159-183). Thousand Oaks, CA: Sage Publications.

Krackhardt, D. & Stern, R.N. (1988). Structuring of information organizations and the management of crises. *Social Psychology Quarterly* 51(2), 123–140.

Krohn, M.D. (1986). The web of conformity: A network approach to the explanation of delinquent behaviour. *Social Problems* 33(6), 81–93.

Kuo, S.H. (1992). Formulaic opposition markers in Chinese conflict talk. In J.E. Alatis (ed.), *Georgetown University Roundtable on Languages and Linguistics 1992* (pp. 388–402). Washington, D.C.: Georgetown University Press.

LaGaipa, J.L. (1990). The negative effects of informal support systems. In S. Duck & R. C. Silver (eds.), *Personal Relationships and Social Support* (pp. 122–139). Newbury Park, CA: Sage.

Lagerspetz, K., Björkqvist, K. & Peltonen, T. (1988). Is indirect aggression typical of females? Gender differences in aggressiveness in 11- to 12-year-old chidren. *Aggressive Behavior* 14(5), 403–414.

Landrine, H. (1995). Clinical implications of cultural differences: The referential versus the indexical self. In N.R. Goldberger & J.B. Veroff (eds.), *The Culture and Psychology Reader* (pp. 744–766). New York: New York University Press.

Laursen, B. (1993). The perceived impact of conflict on adolescent relationships. *Merrill-Palmer Quarterly* 39(4), 535–550.

Laursen, B. & Haven, C. (2010). Future directions in the study of close relationships: Conflict is bad (except when it's not). *Societal Development* 19(4), 858–872.

Lazega, E. & Mounier, L. (2002). Interdependent entrepreneurs and the social discipline of their cooperation: The research program of structural economic sociology for a society of organizations. InO. Favereau & E. Lazega (eds.), *Conventions and Structures in Economic Organization: Markets, Networks, and Hierarchies* (pp. 147–199). Cheltenham: Edward Elgar Publishing.

Lebra, T.S. (1984). Nonconfrontational strategies for the management of interpersonal conflicts. In E.S. Krauss, T.P. Rohlen & P.G. Steinhoff (eds.), *Conflict in Japan* (pp. 41–60). Honolulu, HI: University of Hawai'i Press.

Lepore, S.J. (1992). Social conflict, social support, and psychological distress: Evidence of cross-domain buffering effects. *Journal of Personality and Social Psychology* 63(5), 857–867.

Leung, K., Tremain Koch, P. & Lu, L. (2002). A dualistic model of harmony and its implications for conflict management. *Asia Pacific Journal of Management* 19(2/3), 201–220.

Martin, M.M. & Anderson, C.M. (1996). Argumentativeness and verbal aggressiveness. *Journal of Social Behavior and Personality* 11(3), 547–554.

Morrill, C. (1991). The customs of conflict management among corporate executives. *American Anthropologist* 93(4), 871–893.

Nader, L. & Todd, H.F. (1978). *The Disputing Process: Law in Ten Societies*. New York: Columbia University Press.

Nahapiet, J. & Goshal, S. (1998). Social capital intellectual capital, and the organizational advantage. *TheAcademy of Management Review* 23(2), 242–266.

Nannestad, P., Svendsen, G.L. & Svendsen, G.T. (2008). Bridge over troubled water? Migration and social capital. *Journal of Ethnic and Migration Studies* 34(4), 607–631.

Nelson, R.E. (1989). The strength of strong ties: Social networks and intergroup conflict in organizations. *Academy of Management Journal* 32(2), 377–481.

Oda, S. (2006). Laughter and the traditional Japanese smile. In J. Milner Davis (ed.), *Understanding Humour in Japan* (pp. 15–26). Detroit, MI: Wayne State University Press.

Oetzel, J.G. (1998). The effects of ethnicity and self-construals on self-reported conflict styles. *Communication Reports* 11(2), 133–144.

Oetzel, J., Garcia, A.J. & Ting-Toomey, S. (2008). An analysis of the relationships among face concerns and facework behaviours in perceived conflict situations. *International Journal of Conflict Management* 19(4), 382–403.

Ohbuchi, K. (1998). Conflict management in Japan: Cultural values and efficacy. In K. Leung & D. Tjosvold (eds.), *Conflict management in the Asia Pacific: Assumptions and Approaches in Diverse Cultures* (pp. 49–72). Singapore: Wiley & Sons.

Ohbuchi, K., Fukushima, O., & Tedeschi, J.T. (1999). Cultural values in conflict management. *Journal of Cross-Cultural Psychology* 30(1), 51–71.

Ohbuchi, K. & Takahashi, Y. (1994). Cultural styles of conflict management in Japanese and Americans. *Journal of Applied Social Psychology* 24(15), 1345–1366.

O'Reilly, C. & Chatman, J. (1996). Culture as social control: Corporations, cults and commitment. In B. Shaw & L. Cummings (eds), *Research in Organizational Behavior* (pp. 157–200). Stamford, CT: JAI Press.

Pan, Y. (2000). *Politeness in Chinese Face-to-Face Interaction*. Stamford, CT: Ablex.

Prell, C., Hubacek, K. & Reed, M. (2009). Stakeholder analysis and social network analysis in natural resource management. *Society and Natural Resources* 22(6), 501–518.

Pruitt, D.G. & Carnevale, P.J. (1993). *Negotiation in Social Conflict*. Pacific Grove, CA: Brooks/Cole.

Pruitt, D.G. & Rubin, J.Z. (1986). *Social Conflict: Escalation, Impasse, and Resolution*. Reading, MA: Addison-Wesley.

Prunty, A., Klopf, D. & Ishii, S. (1990). Argumentativeness: Japanese and American tendencies to approach and avoid conflict. *Communication Research Reports* 7(1), 75–79.

Ren, H. & Gray, B. (2009). Repairing relationship conflict: How violation types and culture influence the effectiveness of restoration rituals. *Academy of Management Review* 34(1), 105–128.

Richardson, D.R. & Green, L.R. (1997). Circuitous harm. In R.M. Kowalski (ed.), *Aversive Interpersonal Behaviors* (pp. 171–188). New York: Plenum Press.

Roach, K.D. (1995). Teaching assistant argumentativeness: Effects on affective learning and students perceptions of power use. *Communication Education* 44(1), 15–29.

Rohlen, T.P. (1974). *For Harmony and Strength: Japanese White-Collar Organization in Anthropological Perspective*. Berkeley, CA: University of California Press.

Rosenkopf, L., Metiu, A. & George, V.P. (2001). From the bottom up? Technical committee activity and alliance formation. *Administrative Science Quarterly* 46(4), 748–772.

Ruby, M.B., Falk, C.F., Heine, S.J., Villa, C., & Silberstein, O. (2012). Not all collectivisms are equal: Opposing preferences for ideal affect between East Asians and Mexicans. *Emotion* 12(6), 1206–1209.

Rusbult, C.E. & Zembrodt, I.M. (1983). Responses to dissatisfaction in romantic involvements: A multidimensional scaling analysis. *Journal of Experimental Social Psychology* 19(3), 274–293.

Ryan, L. (2011). Migrants' social networks and weak ties: Accessing resources and constructing relationships post-migration. *The Sociological Review* 59(4), 707–724.

Saito, J. (2011). Managing confrontational situations: Japanese male superiors' interactional styles in directive discourse in the workplace. *Journal of Pragmatics* 43(6), 1689–1706.

Schantz, C.U. & Hobart, C.J. (1989). Social conflict and development: Peers and siblings. In T.J. Berndt & G.W. Ladd (eds.), *Peer Relationships in Child Development* (pp. 71–94). New York: Wiley.

Schiffrin, D. (1984). Jewish argument as sociability. *Language in Society* 13(3), 311–335.

Sillars, A., Canary, D.J. & Tafoya, M. (2004). Communication, conflict, and the quality of family relationships. In A.L. Vangelisti (ed.), *Handbook of Family Communication* (pp. 413–446). Mahwah, NJ: Erlbaum.

Simons, T.L. & Peterson, R.S. (2000). Task conflict and relationship conflict in top management teams: The pivotal role of intragroup trust. *Journal of Applied Psychology* 85(1), 102–111.

Smetana, J.G., Campione-Barr, N. & Metzger, A. (2006). Adolescent development in interpersonal and societal contexts. *Annual Review of Psychology* 57, 255–284.

Smith, L.R. (1999). Intercultural network theory: A cross-paradigmatic approach to acculturation. *International Journal of Intercultural Relations* 23(4), 629–658.

Stadler, S. (2002). *Learning to Disagree in German: The Case of New Zealand University Students*. Unpublished MA Thesis, Victoria University of Wellington.

Sytch, M. & Tatarynowicz, A. (2014). Friends and foes: The dynamics of dual social structures. *Academy of Management Journal* 57(2), 585–613.

Szell, M., Lambiotte, R. & Thurner, S. (2010). Multirelational organization of large-scale social networks in an online world. *Proceedings of the National Academy of Science* 107(31), 13636–13641.

Tanaka, A., Koizumi, A., Imai, H., Hiramatsu, S., Hiramoto, E. & de Gelder, B. (2010). I feel your voice: cultural differences in the multisensory perception of emotion. *Psychological Science* 21(9), 1259–1262.

Ting-Toomey, S. (2005). The matrix of face: An updated face-negotiation theory. In W.B. Gudykunst (ed.), *Theorizing about Intercultural Communication* (pp. 71–92). Thousand Oaks, CA: Sage.

Ting-Toomey, S., Gao, G., Trubisky, P., Yang, Z., Kim, H.S., Lin, S.L. & Nishida, T. (1991). Culture, face maintenance, and styles of handling interpersonal conflict: A study in five cultures. *The International Journal of Conflict Management* 2(4), 275–296.

Triandis, H.C., McCusker, C. & Hui, C.H. (1990). Multimethod probes of individualism and collectivism. *Journal of Personality and Social Psychology* 59(5), 1006–1020.

Uchida, Y. & Ogihara, Y. (2012). Personal or interpersonal construal of happiness: A cultural psychological perspective. *International Journal of Wellbeing* 2(4), 354–369.

Walgrave, L. & Aertsen, I. (1996). Reintegrative shaming and restorative justice. *European Journal of Criminal Policy and Research* 4(4), 67–85.

Wellman, B. & Berkowitz, S.D. (1988). *Social Structures: A Network Approach*. Cambridge: Cambridge University Press.

Wellman, B. & Wortley, S. (1990). Different strokes from different folks: Community ties and social support. *American Journal of Sociology* 96(3), 558–588.

Wilson, D.S., Wilcynski, C., Wells, A. & Weiser, L. (2000). Gossib and other aspects of language as group-level adaptations. In C. Heyes (ed.), *Cognition and Evolution* (pp. 347–366.). Cambridge, MA: MIT Press.

Wrench, J.S. & Socha-McGee, D. (1999). The influence of saliency and family communication patterns on adolescent perceptions of adolescent and parent conflict management strategies. Paper presented at the annual meeting of the International Communication Association.

Wright, K.B., Rains, S. & Banas, J. (2010). Weak-tie support network preference and perceived life stress among participants in health-related, computer-mediated support groups. *Journal of Computer-Mediated Communication* 15(4), 606–624.

Chapter 8

Conflict negotiation

Conflict is part and parcel of our lives. Where there are two or more people, the occurrence of at least some level of conflict is natural, normal and inevitable. Diamond (1996) speaks of conflict as being inherent in all interpersonal relationships. Lederach (1995) describes conflict as 'natural, common experience present in all relationships and cultures' (p. 9). Lee and Rogan (1991) refer to conflict as an omnipresent and ubiquitous phenomenon. Brahman et al. (2005) denote conflict as an unavoidable component of human activity, Pološki Vokić and Sonton (2010) call it a natural, everyday phenomenon in all private and working spheres, and Kaushal and Kwantes (2006) speak of conflict as 'a common facet of our everyday lives', which derives from a 'misalignment of goals, motivations, or actions' (p. 580). Hence, even the most conflict-avoidant cultures will engage in conflict situations at some point.

While I have discussed at great length what drives certain cultures or communities to engage in or disengage from conflict, in this chapter, I will assess how cultures approach conflict once it has manifested to such an extent that it becomes unavoidable. In other words, this chapter addresses less how and if people engage in conflict, and more, as Alagozlu and Makihara (2015) put it, 'how they find a way out' (p. 177).

8.1 Cultural conflict approaches

De Dreu and Gelfand (2008) deem social conflict to be universal, occurring across all human cultures, ranging from small-scale societies to modern nations. The solutions to conflict, on the other hand, are highly culturally variable as Gelfand et al. (2012) and Brett and Gelfand (2006) purport. Lee et al. (2013) also assert that culture shapes how we negotiate conflict and operates on multiple levels.

Conflict can therefore be construed as a culturally defined and regulated event, according to Hocker and Wilmot (1991). Consequently, conflict management also differs across cultures. All conflict involves culture, as Pedersen and Jandt (1996) assert. They therefore implore that we recognize the importance of the relationship between conflict and cultural context, as do a multitude of other researchers (Cingöz-Ulu & Lalonde, 2007; Holt & DeVore, 2005; Xie, Song & Stringfellow, 1998; Nadler, Nadler & Broome, 1985; Tafoya, 1983). Marsella (2005, p. 653) calls culture a 'critical determinant of conflict'. He asserts that culture constitutes 'both a source of the conflict and the means for its resolution'.

According to Tyler et al. (1997), cultural values influence people's reactions to conflict and to conflict resolution. Leung et al. (1992) refer to culture-specific procedural preferences. Leung and Wu (1990) and Marsella (2005) further assert that cultural differences in values, beliefs, communication styles and history, determine how individuals prefer to deal with conflicts. Kaushal and Kwantes' (2006) findings also demonstrate clearly that cultural values and social beliefs are determining factors in predicting a person's choice of conflict resolution strategies. In particular, they draw links between high concern for the self, combined with low concern for others as an indicator for conflict engagement.

For conflict negotiation and resolution practices to work, questions of transferability and appropriateness of conflict management strategies need to be considered. Yarn (2002) speaks of a cultural imperialism in conflict management approaches across cultures, which involves the imposition of culturally inappropriate models of conflict resolution. Cultural sensitivity, as he asserts, is key.

8.2 Negotiation strategies

According to van de Vliert's (1997) overview, early literature classified intercultural conflict resolution styles as fight–fight (Cannon, 1929), as cooperation–competition (Deutsch, 1973a), as moving away, moving towards, and moving against (Horney, 1945), and as withdrawing, yielding, problem-solving, and inaction (Rubin et al., 1994).

Hammer (2005), based on Blake and Mouton's (1964) publication, alludes to the fact that modern approaches to conflict resolution still predominantly take a dichotomous approach, defined by greater concern for either self-interests or other-interests. Van de Vliert and Kabanoff (1990) also assert that Blake and Mouton's (1964) early work has made a comeback and still largely defines current conflict resolution approaches. Today, conflict management styles are typically described as falling within one of five prevalent stylistic patterns. While terminology varies somewhat, the commonly employed terms include accommodating/obliging, collaborating/integrating, dominating/competing, avoiding, and compromising (Rahim, 1983; Thomas, 1992). Though Pološki Vokić and Sonton (2010) claim that only a compromising style takes into consideration the interests of both parties and focuses on mutual rather than individual gains, they also assert that no one conflict handling style is appropriate under all given circumstances, but is strongly dependent on the context in which it occurs. Cingöz-Ulu and Lalonde (2007) also point to the importance of contextual factors in conflict management. Despite this idealistic notion that conflict management styles should be adapted to the situation and context at hand, there are clearly cultural trends for favoured conflict management styles, more or less irrespective of their appropriateness in a given situation or whether they work with interactional partners from different cultural backgrounds. Conflict, as Lederach (1995) asserts, does not automatically end in negotiation. Essentially, negotiation only becomes possible when 'the needs and interests of all those involved and affected by the conflict are ... articulated' (Lederach, 1995, p. 14). Before conflict can be managed, it must first be acknowledged (Pinkley & Northcraft, 1994).

Not all cultures, however, want to acknowledge, let alone resolve, conflict. The tendency not to even acknowledge the existence of conflict is widespread among other-oriented and relationship-oriented cultures. Being prone to avoidance versus engagement therefore does not only apply to whether conflict arises in the first place, but also with regard to how conflict is dealt with retrospectively. The notions of avoidance therefore also extend to the negotiation strategies prevalent in a cultural setting.

8.2.1 Withdrawal versus engagement

Leung, Koch and Lu (2002) assert that the single-most important concept in conflict management in East Asian cultures is the Confucian concept of harmony. Haar and Krahé (1999) refer to the creation and maintenance of harmony as a core ethical principle in Javanese society, and Indonesian society in more general terms (Mulder, 1996). Kelley (2008) lists harmony, empathy, loyalty and patience as the foundation of the Japanese social system. McLaughlin and Braun (1998) say of harmony-oriented cultures, such as Asian and Pacific Island cultures, that they are generally less likely to share bad news, while Saldov, Kakai and McLaughlin (1997) assert that harmony-oriented cultures are more inclined to keep their true desires to themselves if they believe it would inconvenience or disturb the group, even if it implies personal hardship and pain. In such cultures, endurance is typically chosen over confrontation (Hwang, 1997–1998, p. 29). Cultures that place greater emphasis on the group than on the self therefore often have very negative attitudes to conflict on the whole.

Traditionally, conflict has been viewed as aversive and, thusly, as something to be avoided, especially in cultures such as China (Botvinick, 2007; Tjosvold et al., 2003). Wang et al. (2005) purport that Asian cultures, East Asian cultures in particular, hold the believe that conflict has a negative effect on the balance of feelings within a unit. Jia (2002) even asserts that Chinese culture sees conflict as bad and evil. As such, it is unsurprising that they are not only predisposed to try to avoid conflict from arising, but also exhibit a preference for withdrawal or non-confrontational strategies when it comes to conflict resolution practices. Tjosvold et al. (2003, p. 70) describe the risks of approaching conflict as 'particularly high in societies where relationships are highly valued'. Dealing with conflict directly is therefore something they label 'unlikely'. In conflict management, the harmony model tries to maintain group harmony by relying on non-confrontational means, including avoiding and compromising (Kozan, 1997). Kozan (1997) views this approach to conflict as typical of Middle Eastern, Asian and Latin American cultures. Withdrawal or even flight, temporarily or permanently, have been reported for Finnish culture (Fry, 1999), Fijian culture (Hickson, 1986), Mexican Zapotec culture (O'Nell, 1989), Indonesian culture (Hollan, 1997), and the Buid of the Philippines (Gibson, 1989). Lee et al. (2013), therefore, speak of 'culturally sanctioned conflict avoidance' (p. 516) in particular cultural contexts.

According to Gabrielidis et al. (1997), withdrawal is a strategy whereby 'individuals allow conflicts to go unresolved or permit others to take responsibility for solving the problem' (p. 662). Though preventing conflict from arising is the preferred approach, when conflict does manifest, East Asian managers fail to acknowledge them (Bond & Wang, 1983). Conflicts are repressed rather than made public and resolved (Moran et al., 1994). Song, Dyer and Thieme (2006) list ignoring, withdrawal and inaction as common evasive strategies. Friedman et al. (2000) explain that the desire to downplay or ignore disputes is stronger in such cultures than the desire to resolve them. Ohbuchi and Takahashi (1994) speak of a downright refusal to overtly recognize the existence of conflict. The parties engaged in a conflict thereby hope that the conflict will somehow go away on its own accord, if left alone (Pruitt & Rubin, 1986).

Even if two conflicting parties do not withdraw from conflict entirely, Sillars and Vangelisti (2006) speak of a deliberately employed, strategic ambiguity in conflict communication in order to alleviate immediate pressure to respond to an interlocutor, ultimately directed at relationship-preservation. This form of avoidance is reflective of a high concern for others (Gabrielidis et al., 1997), which is associated with the positive value of maintaining harmony and preserving face, both for the self and the other (Redding, Norman & Schlander, 1994: Ting-Toomey et al., 1991). Wang et al. (2005) therefore implore that conflict orientation should always be approached by taking cultural value systems into account.

Though Gabrielidis et al. (1997) reject a correlation between collectivism and conflict withdrawal, partly based on Gire and Carment's (1992) findings that some individualistic cultures show preference for harmony-orientation in conflict resolution (e.g. Canada), while some collectivistic cultures do not show a preference for harmony-orientation (e.g. Nigeria), they see a link between interdependence, other-orientation and accommodation strategies. Tjosvold et al. (2003) also point to interdependence as a central factor in conflict withdrawal. Cultures high in concern for others, typically with multiplex and dense social network structures are more prone to opt for withdrawal strategies in conflict negotiation also. Swierczek (1994) asserts that in cultures with strong other-orientation, conflict tends to be subdued. For example, in handling interpersonal conflict, Arab Middles Eastern executives have been found to resort more to conflict avoidance (Elsayed-EkJiouly & Buda, 1996). Gabrielidis et al. (1997) found that Mexicans displayed a strong tendency to avoid conflicts. Krauss, Rohlen and Steinhoff (1984) assert that the Japanese cultural ideal of harmony prohibits engagement in conflict. Ohbuchi et al. (1999) indicate that Japanese people prefer avoidance tactics in conflict management. Lee et al. (2013) found that Japanese and Koreans withdraw from conflict. Hwang (1997–1998) states that Chinese people will not disagree openly. Friedman, Chi and Liu (2006) and Kirkbride, Tang and Westwood (1991) speak of a Chinese tendency to avoid conflict. Ma's (2007) findings on Chinese culture also indicate a preference for non-confrontational conflict resolution styles. Though researchers have raised questions regarding the effectiveness of conflict avoidance and withdrawal mechanisms, Roloff and Ifert (2000) assert that they can function successfully, but that they require an ideology of tolerance.

In most Western cultures, on the other hand, avoidance and withdrawal are viewed negatively, because sidestepping an issue is not perceived as constructive (Wang et al., 2005). Instead, the preference is to openly acknowledge conflicts and take steps towards resolving it. According to Haar and Krahé (1999), Western societies expect a direct approach, whereby conflict is confronted in an explicit manner. In their study on conflict resolution styles in German and Indonesian adolescents, they uncovered that German adolescents endorsed confrontational approaches in dealing with interpersonal conflict more frequently than their Indonesian counterparts, though they concede that responses differed somewhat depending on status, gender and addressee-relations. Swierczek (1994) describes the European conflict management style in general as confrontational, with a propensity for arguments if no agreement can be reached.

American conflict negotiation style has been described as competitive, confrontational, focused on differences and legalities by LePoole (1989), and as independent, persistent and authoritative by Harris and Moran (1991). Wolfson and Norden (1984) report generally more active strategies in handling conflicts in US subjects and Lee and Rogen (1991) assert that, in the US, conflict is managed through competitive strategies. Friedman, Chi and Liu (2006) speak of a nearly universal preference for being direct among Americans, though they admit that, within this group, there were different preferences in how to go about it.

Though the general trajectory may be more towards approaching conflict openly and directly, cultures with a preference for engaging in conflict tend to differ in how to approach conflict negotiation and resolution. Though Weinberger et al. (2013) describe German and Finnish culture as very similar and compatible in many ways, they found that German students were more conflict-oriented than Finnish groups, and that both groups had different preferences for conflict resolution. While Finnish students preferred an integrating and consensus-building approach, German students preferred an approach that highlighted understanding, but continuation of discourse rather than resolution.

When two contrasting approaches to conflict collide, they can exert serious consequences on interpersonal and organizational relationships.

Case study: Clashes in conflict engagement

A Swiss man told me that his relationship to an Indonesian woman suffered because they had starkly different ways of dealing with relationship problems. Whenever they experienced conflicting views, his preference was to address the issue openly, discuss it, resolve it and thereby clear the issue and the air between them. However, her preferred approach was to ignore the issue, sweep it under the rug and pretend it never happened.

The effect of parties from a conflict-avoidant and a conflict-engaging style trying to deal with conflict situations can be challenging and demanding. Friedman, Chi and Liu (2006) call it an impediment to Western–Chinese business relationships.

8.2.2 Deflection versus resolution

Though conflict may be useful in solving problems, it may come at the expense of the relationship (Amason, 1996). This is a risk that many cultures are wont to take. While resolution is often considered the goal of conflict negotiation, this does not invariably apply to how conflict is approached. Swierczek (1994) states of other-oriented cultures that 'if conflict does emerge, conflict management includes appropriate behaviours to smooth the conflicts and return the relationship to balance' (p. 42). Optimal conflict outcomes are therefore situated more in relationship-preservation than in fair and just settlement. Uwazie (2000) says of the African Igbo culture that reconciliation is the paramount goal. Deflection and circumvention of a conflict are practised for the greater good of the group. Johnson's (1974) example of Japanese cultural deflection practices (refer to Chapter 7 for details) serves as a good example. Her case study clearly indicates that in Japanese culture, for the sake of harmony and the preservation of family ties, people are disinclined to engage in conflict, and instead distance themselves from the people they are in conflict with. This means that while relationships may grow distant, conflict does not need to arise. This constitutes a very other-oriented approach, where individual self-interest is put aside. Lebra (1984) speaks of Japanese conflict management style as 'egoless' (p. 55). Instead, the preservation of a relationship – at least on the surface level – is foregrounded, irrespective of the personal costs this may entail.

The idea behind deflection is not that conflicts are settled, nor is the restoration of sincere and holistic harmonious relationships a primary concern. Instead the focus is on the restoration of equilibrium and of surface-level harmony. Social harmony in such cultures is practised chiefly at the surface level, with turbulence concealed beneath superficial politeness (Chang, 2001). Huang (1999) distinguishes between 'genuine' and 'surface' harmony. Surface harmony refers to seemingly smooth relationships with latent conflict. The emphasis of this type of harmony is not true, genuine harmony, but what Leung, Wang and Deng (2016) call disintegration avoidance. In this way, as Anedo (2012) explains, the status quo of the relationship is maintained, though the problems remain unresolved.

According to Leung, Koch and Lu (2002), Leung and Wu (1998) acknowledge that, though surface-level harmony is not considered optimal, Chinese culture generally prefers it over direct confrontation. Lee (2006) speaks of conflict as a taboo topic in some interpersonal relationships. In cultures where the preservation of relationships is foregrounded, conflict therefore often simply gets ignored (Rahim, Antonioni & Psenicka, 2001; Lim & Yazdanifard, 2012) rather than resolved. Western theory regards withdrawal from conflict as problematic, because it blocks opportunities for compromise, conflict resolution, and change (Nichols, 2012; Lee et al., 2013). Dyer and Song (1998) purport that surface harmony simply glosses over and suppresses disagreement, which merely achieves to forestall actual conflict resolution.

8.3 Unresolved lingering conflict

While deflection may well avoid dealing with the conflict at hand, the consequences are not invariably positive. Tjosvold et al. (2003) assert that trying to avoid conflict does not mean that conflict disappears. As Ajayi and Buhari (2014) put it: 'The repercussions of conflicts between person to person, group to group, community to community, state to state or nation to nation rarely cease with the termination of overt hostilities' (p. 141). Roloff and Ifert (2000, p. 152) caution that to leave conflict unresolved constitutes a 'risky course of action', while Xie, Song and Stringfellow (1998) deem ignoring conflict to be 'very harmful'. Cloke and Goldsmith (2000) and Capazzoli (1999) outline a multitude of negative repercussions stemming from poor conflict management, including loss of trust and reduced motivation. Baumeister, Stillwell and Wotman (1990) contend that unresolved conflict can fester to the point of causing an explosion. Barker, Tjosvold and Andrews (1988) therefore speak of conflict avoidance as ineffectual.

Although Johnson (1974) makes it clear that Japanese culture will go to some length to avoid conflict, she also articulates clearly that the consequence of doing so may result in lingering resentment and strained relationships. This is no isolated occurrence. Research has generally demonstrated that unresolved conflict can exert rather negative consequences, especially on interpersonal relationships. According to Leung (1997, p. 644), avoiding actions 'will strain a relationship and lead to its weakening and dissolving'. In her study on intercultural friendships, Lee (2006) found that where conflict was not managed in an effective manner, friendships 'backwarded' (p. 17) to earlier stages of their friendship. Progression of a friendship can therefore become impeded and friendships can grow more distant. Wallenfelsz and Hample (2010) also allude to the damage unvoiced conflict can do to relationships, while Peterson and

Schwind (1977) speak of ineffective communication, difficulty in information exchange, and a lack of open discussion as major problems in international collaboration. In other words, irrespective of the type and nature of the relationship, conflict avoidance or withdrawal appear to incur counter-productive consequences. Indeed, Bowman (1990) and McGonagle, Kessler and Gotlib (1993) report a negative correlation between conflict avoidance and relationship satisfaction and stability. DeChurch and Marks (2001) assert that passive conflict management (i.e. avoidance) harmed group performance. In her study on Israeli nurses and physicians, Desivilya and Yagil (2005) uncovered that cooperative patterns of conflict management were associated with positive intragroup emotional states, that contentious (dominating) patterns were partly associated with positive emotions, but that avoidance patterns were only associated with negative emotions, indicating that avoidance had the most aversive effect on intragroup cohesion out of all possible conflict management styles. Conflict avoidance thus appears to be not only counter-productive but even downright detrimental under just about any circumstances or contexts.

Case study: Roomies and loomies

In Singaporean university dormitories, it is customary for two students to share a room (typically referred to as 'roomies'). In some of the older dormitories, in addition to sharing a room, two rooms (i.e. four students) also share the same bathroom/toilet facilities (which the students commonly refer to as 'loomies'). One of my students reported to me that, for some time, she shared a room and bathroom facilities with a Mainland Chinese student, but was unhappy with her roomie's cleaning, which did not meet her personal expectations of cleanliness. She articulated that she was especially upset about the fact that the Chinese student never contributed to cleaning the toilet. When I inquired whether she ever raised this issue and discussed it with her roomie, she said she would never openly address this issue with her. She admitted that she felt very resentful about it, resulting clearly in lingering resentment, negative stereotyping and a self-admitted refusal to ever share facilities with a Mainland Chinese student again. The Mainland Chinese student was probably entirely unaware that her behaviour caused problems, and since this issue was not brought to her attention, she was not given the chance to rectify her behaviours. Despite this lack of awareness of the conflict, their relationship was damaged irreparably because of this un-surfaced conflict.

Though conflict avoidance serves the purpose of harmony, ergo the drive to experience less conflict, Friedman et al. (2000) assert that, ironically, conflict-avoidant styles are likely to experience more conflict, not less. Contrary to the intentions behind conflict avoidance, Tjosvold et al. (2003) purport that conflict avoidance has actually been found to predict competition, because when conflict does surface despite attempts to avoid it, it is typically handled in a more uncompromising manner and with a competitive win-lose approach. Baumeister, Stillwell and Wotman (1990) explain that initially stifled anger in conflict victims may be expressed stronger in response to continued provocations. The conflict perpetrator, on the other hand, only sees what they perceive as an overreaction to a single incident. Lingering conflict can therefore escalate with much more solidified positions between the two parties, with far more negative affective stances than when conflict is addressed immediately. Active conflict avoidance has therefore been construed as a failure to resolve the conflict situation (Johnson et al., 2001).

8.4 Benefits of resolving conflict

While there is a clear line of argument that assumes that conflict is detrimental to interpersonal relationships and should therefore be avoided, there is also evidence to the contrary. Whether conflict affects relationships depends both on the nature of conflict, the persistence of conflict and the way conflict is managed. Roskos et al. (2010) identified that both the continued presence of either conflict or conflict avoidance exert equally detrimental effects on mental health. The only form of conflict that is not reported to have negative consequences is the constructive management of conflict that leads to conflict resolution.

Ubinger, Handal and Massura (2013), for example, report positive outcomes for conflict resolution. When managed successfully, conflict can even yield important benefits (Baron, 1991). Fitzpatrick and Badzinski (1985) also found that even serious conflict had no impact on a couple's satisfaction with the relationship. Lee (2006) seconds this opinion, stating that 'conflict should not always be associated with negative connotations' (p. 18), as her research uncovered that conflict can bring people closer together, because it helped dyadic pairs learn more about each other in the process of conflict negotiation, so long as this was handled in an open and respectful manner. Constructive conflict management, as Lee (2006) discovered, can therefore facilitate the development of intercultural friendships.

This applies not only in the private domain, since open approaches to discussing opposing views have been associated with stronger, more cooperative relationships in general (Tjosvold, Dann & Wong, 1992; Tjosvold & McNeely, 1988). Todor and Owen (1991) assert that one of the positive effects of conflict is the potential for improvement in employee attitudes, as well as in the organizational climate overall. Baron (1991) reports that when encountering conflict, members of a group often experience increased loyalty and cohesiveness, which are not only beneficial to interpersonal relationships, but also positively affect performance and productivity. Deutsch (1973b) proposes that through managing conflict, people reaffirm that they have a strong, mutually beneficial relationship and are more inclined to strengthen than weaken a relationship. Though DeChurch and Marks (2001) found that it depends on the type and nature of conflict management strategies, active conflict management was found to be beneficial to group performance and that conflict, when managed appropriately, actually promoted group satisfaction.

Instead of viewing a predisposition for argumentativeness as harmful, Infante (1987) regards it as a constructive communication trait. Confrontational approaches can be constructive or destructive, according to Harrison and Wendorf Muhamad (2018). They therefore speak of engagement in conflict as both a problem and an opportunity, as it can represent a meaningful action towards resolution. Gottman (1993) views a confrontational problem-solving style as preferable over an avoidant one. Koerner and Fitzpatrick (1997) thus emphasize the importance of conflict resolution. Ideally, normative pragmatics proposes, argumentation should lead to consensus and resolution, rather than acquiescence, settlement or forced decision-making (van Eemeren et al., 1993; Harrison & Wendorf Muhamad, 2018).

In the US and Germany, for example, confrontation and conflict resolution are the norm (Clackworthy, 1996). In cultures that value conflict resolution, priority is given to truth and justice, and so long as these are achieved, the end justifies the means. Gelfand, Leslie and Keller (2008) speak of 'dominating conflict cultures', which are characterized by active and open conflict resolution, where 'truth through conflict wins' (p. 143). They state that, within the framework of such cultures, saying what one thinks, open and heated debates, and other forms of controlled aggression are acceptable, are considered effective tools, and are even perceived as honourable and admirable. Onyekwere, Rubin and Infante (1991) also argue that people high in argumentativeness were perceived as more appropriate and effective. Clearly then, within loose and uniplex networks, argumentativeness is positively valenced rather than discouraged, and associated with positive and desirable traits. Indeed, argumentativeness has been linked positively to learning, intellectual development, problem-solving benefits and job satisfaction (Infante, 1982; Infante & Gordon, 1987). Collaborative behaviours in such cultures are not valued, Gelfand, Leslie and Keller (2008) assert, but are instead viewed as a weakness.

However, conflict resolution has not only been proven to benefit cultures that are naturally inclined to surface rather than avoid conflict, but also to benefit harmony-oriented cultures. Tjosvold et al.'s (2003) results indicate a positive role for conflict in China. Ajayi and Buhari (2014) assert that in African societies, conflict resolution performs a healing function, since conflict resolution 'promotes consensus-building, social bridge reconstructions, and the re-enactment of order in society' (p. 152).

8.5 Summary

Understanding differences, situated in cultural preferences for certain conflict resolution practices, can aid tremendously in revising and refining current approaches to conflict management. The attitudes cultures hold towards avoidance and withdrawal versus engagement and resolution carry fundamentally important implications not only for a person's behaviour during conflict situations but also for the most effective and appropriate mediation practices. As Ma (2007) put it: 'Incorporating ideas and practices of other cultures can help develop more enduring, elegant, and universal theories' (p. 4).

Nevertheless, while each culturally preferred approach has its benefits, research across cultures has clearly established that conflict resolution is preferable over avoidance and deflection practices. The question then, lies more in which conflict resolution practices constitute the most effective and meaningful approaches rather than whether to opt for avoidance or engagement.

References

Ajayi, A.T. & Buhari, L.O. (2014). Methods of conflict resolution in African traditional society. *African Research Review* 8(2), 138–157.

Alagozlu, N. & Makihara, M. (2015). Conflict resolution strategies in Turkish and American speech communities. *International Online Journal of Education and Teaching* 2(3), 177–197.

Amason, A.C. (1996). Distinguishing the effects of functional and dysfunctional conflict on strategic decision making: Resolving a paradox for top management teams. *Academy of Management Journal* 39(1), 123–148.

Anedo, O. (2012). A cultural analysis of harmony and conflict: Towards an integrated model of conflict styles. *Unizik Journal of Arts and Humanities* 13(2), 16–52.

Barker, J., Tjosvold, D. & Andrews, I.R. (1988). Conflict approaches of effective and ineffective managers: A field study in a matrix organization. *Journal of Management Studies* 25(2), 167–178.

Baron, R.A. (1991). Positive effects of conflict: A cognitive perspective. *Employee Responsibilities and Rights Journal* 4(1), 25–36.

Baumeister, R.F., Stillwell, A. & Wotman, S.R. (1990). Victim and perpetrator accounts of interpersonal conflict: Autobiographical narratives about anger. *Journal of Personality and Social Psychology* 59(5), 994–1005.

Blake, R.R. & Mouton, J.S. (1964). *The Managerial Grid*. Houston, TX: Gulf.

Bond, M.H. & Wang, S.H. (1983). Aggressive behaviour in Chinese society: The problem of maintaining order and harmony. In A.P. Goldstein & M. Segall (eds.), *Global Perspectives on Aggression*. Elmsford, NY: Pergamon.

Botvinick, M.M. (2007). Conflict monitoring and decision making: Reconciling two perspectives on anterior cingulate function. *Cognitive, Affective & Behavioral Neuroscience* 7(4), 356–366.

Bowman, M.L. (1990). Coping efforts and marital satisfaction: Measuring marital coping and its correlates. *Journal of Marriage and Family* 52(2), 463–474.

Brahman, S.D., Margavio, T.M., Hignite, M.A., Barrier, T.B. & Chin, J.M. (2005). A bender-based categorization for conflict resolution. *Journal of Management Development* 24(3), 197–208.

Brett, J.M. & Gelfand, M.J. (2006). A cultural analysis of the underlying assumptions of negotiation theory. In L. Thompson (ed.), *Negotiation Theory and Research* (pp. 173–201). New York: Psychology Press.

Cannon, W.B. (1929). *Bodily Changes in Pain, Hunger, Fear and Rage*. New York: Appleton-Century.

Capazzoli, T.K. (1999). Conflict resolution: A key ingredient in successful teams. *Journal for Quality and Supervision* 56(12), 3–5.

Chang, H.C. (2001). Harmony as performance: The turbulence under Chinese interpersonal communication. *Discourse Studies* 3(2), 155–179.

Cingöz-Ulu, B. & Lalonde, R.N. (2007). The role of culture and relational context in interpersonal conflict: Do Turks and Canadians use different conflict management strategies? *International Journal of Intercultural Relations* 31(4), 443–458.

Clackworthy, D. (1996). Training Germans and Americans in conflict management. In M. Berger (ed.), *Cross-Cultural Team Building: Guidelines for more Effective Communication and Negotiation* (pp. 91–100). London: McGraw-Hill.

Cloke, K. & Goldsmith, J. (2000). Conflict resolution that reaps great rewards. *The Journal for Quality and Participation* 23(3), 27–30.

DeChurch, L.A. & Marks, M.A. (2001). Maximizing the benefits of task conflict: The role of conflict management. *International Journal of Conflict Management* 12(1), 4–22.

De Dreu, C.K.W. & Gelfand, M.J. (2008). Conflict in the workplace. Sources, functions, and dynamics across multiple levels of analysis. In C.K.W. De Dreu & M.J. Gelfand (eds.) *The Psychology of Conflict and Conflict Management in Organizations* (pp. 3–54). New York: Erlbaum.

Desivilya, H.S. & Yagil, D. (2005). The role of emotions in conflict management: The case of work teams. *International Journal of Conflict Management* 16(1), 55–69.

Deutsch, M. (1973a). Conflicts: Productive and destructive. In F.E. Jandt (ed.), *Conflict Resolution through Communication* (pp. 155–197). New York: Harper & Row.

Deutsch, M. (1973b). *The Resolution of Conflict*. New Haven, CT: Yale University Press.

Diamond, J. (1996). *Status and Power in Verbal Interaction: A Study of Discourse in a Close-Knit Social Network*. Philadelphia, PA: John Benjamins.

Dyer, B. & Song, M. (1998). Innovation strategy and sanctioned conflict: A new edge in innovation? *The Journal of Product Innovation Management* 15(6), 505–519.

Elsayed-EkJiouly, S.M. & Buda, R. (1996). Organizational conflict: A comparative analysis of conflict styles across cultures. *International Journal of Conflict Management* 7(1), 71–81.

Fitzpatrick, M.A. & Badzinski, D.M. (1985). All in the family: Interpersonal communication in kin relationships. In M.L. Knapp & G.R. Miller (eds.), *Handbook of Interpersonal Communication* (pp. 687–737). London: Sage.

Friedman, R.A., Tidd, S.T., Currall, S.C. & Tsai, J.C. (2000). What goes around comes around: The impact of personal conflict style on work conflict and stress. *International Journal of Conflict Management* 11(1), 32–55.

Friedman, R., Chi, S.C. & Liu, L.A. (2006). An expectancy model of Chinese-American differences in conflict-avoiding. *Journal of International Business Studies* 37(4), 76–91.

Fry, D.P. (1999). Altruism and aggression. In L.R. Kurtz (ed.), *Encyclopedia of Violence, Peace, and Conflict* (pp. 17–33). San Diego, CA: Academic Press.

Gabrielidis, C., Stephan, S.W., Ybarra, O., Pearson, D.S. & Villareal, L. (1997). Preferred styles of conflict resolution. *Journal of Cross-Cultural Psychology* 28(6), 661–677.

Gelfand, M.J., Leslie, L.M. & Keller, K.M. (2008). On the etiology of conflict cultures. *Research in Organizational Behavior* 28, 137–166.

Gelfand, M.J., Severance, L., Fulmer, C.A. & Al Dabbagh, M. (2012). Explaining and predicting cultural differences in negotiation. In G.E. Bolton & R.T.A. Croson (eds.),

The Oxford Handbook of Economic Conflict Resolution (pp. 332–358). Oxford: Oxford University Press.

Gibson, T. (1989). Symbolic representations of tranquility and aggression among the Buid. In S. Howell & R. Willis (eds.), *Societies at Peace: Anthropological Perspectives* (pp. 60–78). London: Routledge.

Gire, J.T. & Carment, D.W. (1992). Dealing with disputes: The influence of individuals-collectivism. *Journal of Social Psychology* 133(1), 81–95.

Gottman, J.M. (1993). The roles of conflict engagement, escalation, and avoidance in marital interaction. *Journal of Consulting and Clinical Psychology* 61(1), 6–15.

Haar, B.F. & Krahé, B. (1999). Strategies for resolving interpersonal conflicts in adolescence: A German-Indonesian comparison. *Journal of Cross-Cultural Psychology* 30(6), 667–683.

Hammer, M.R. (2005). The intercultural conflict style inventory: A conceptual framework and measure of intercultural conflict resolution approaches. *International Journal of Intercultural Relations* 29(6), 675–695.

Harris, P.R. & Moran, R.T. (1991). *Managing Cultural Differences: High-Performance Strategies for a New World of Business*. Houston, TX: Gulf Publishing.

Harrison, T.R. & Wendorf Muhamad, J. (2018). Engagement in conflict. In K.A. Johnston & M. Taylor (eds.), *The Handbook of Communication Engagement* (pp. 187–204). Hoboken, NJ: Wiley Blackwell.

Hickson, L. (1986). The social contexts of apology in dispute settlement: A cross-cultural study. *Ethnology* 25(4), 283–294.

Hocker, H.L. & Wilmot, W.W. (1991). *Interpersonal Conflict*. Dubuque, IA: W.C. Brown.

Hollan, D. (1997). Conflict avoidance and resolution among the Toraja of South Sulawesi, Indonesia. In D.P. Fry & K. Björkvist (eds.), *Cultural Variation in Conflict Resolution: Alternatives to Violence* (pp. 59–68). Mahwah, NJ: Erlbaum.

Holt, J.L. & DeVore, C.J. (2005). Culture-gender, organizational role, and styles of conflict resolution: A meta-analysis. *International Journal of Intercultural Relations* 29(2), 165–196.

Horney, K. (1945). *Our Inner Conflicts*. New York: W.W. Norton.

Huang, L.L. (1999). *Interpersonal Harmony and Conflict: Indigenous Theories and Research*. Taipei: Gui Guan.

Hwang, K.K. (1997–1998). Guanxi and mientze: Conflict resolution in Chinese Society. *Intercultural Communication Studies* 7(1), 17–42.

Infante, D.A. (1982). The argumentative student in the speech communication classroom: An investigation and implications. *Communication Education* 31(2), 141–148.

Infante, D.A. (1987). Aggressiveness. In J. McCroskey & J. Daly (eds.), *Personality and Interpersonal Communication* (pp. 157–192). Newbury Park, CA: Sage.

Infante, D.A. & Gordon, W.I. (1987). Superior and subordinate communication profiles: Implications for independent-mindedness and upward effectiveness. *Central States Speech Journal* 38(2), 73–80.

Jia, W.S. (2002). Chinese mediation and its cultural formation. In G.M. Chen & R. Ma (eds.), *Chinese Conflict Management and Resolution* (pp. 289–296). London: Ablex.

Johnson, C.L. (1974). Gift giving and reciprocity among the Japanese Americans in Honolulu. *American Ethnologist* 1(2), 295–308.

Johnson, H.D., LaVoie, J.C., Spenceri, M.C. & Mahoney-Wernli, M.A. (2001). Peer conflict avoidance: Associations with loneliness, social anxiety, and social avoidance. *Psychological Reports* 88(1), 227–235.

Kaushal, R. & Kwantes, C.T. (2006). The role of culture and personality in choice of conflict management strategy. *International Journal of Intercultural Relations* 30(5), 579–603.

Kelley, J.E. (2008). Harmony, empathy, loyalty, and patience in Japanese children's literature. *The Social Studies* 99(2), 61–70.

Kirkbride, P.S., Tang, S.F.Y. & Westwood, R.I. (1991). Chinese conflict preferences and negotiating behaviour: Cultural and psychological influences. *Organization Studies* 12(3), 365–386.

Koerner, A.F. & Fitzpatrick, M.A. (1997). Family type and conflict: The impact of conversation orientation and conformity orientation on conflict in the family. *Communication Studies* 48(1), 59–75.

Kozan, M.K. (1997). Culture and conflict management: A theoretical framework. *The International Journal of Conflict Management* 8(4), 338–360.

Krauss, E.S., Rohlen, T.P. & Steinhoff, P.G. (1984). *Conflict in Japan*. Honolulu, HI: University of Hawai'i Press.

Lebra, T.S. (1984). Nonconfrontational strategies for management of interpersonal conflict. In E.S. Krauss, T.P. Rohlen & P.G. Steinhoff (eds.), *Conflict in Japan* (pp. 41–60). Honolulu, HI: University of Hawai'i Press.

Lederach, J.P. (1995). *Preparing for Peace: Conflict Transformation across Cultures*. New York: Syracuse University Press.

Lee, P.W. (2006). Bridging cultures: Understanding the construction of relational identity in intercultural friendships. *Journal of Intercultural Communication Research* 35(1), 3–22.

Lee, H.O. & Rogan, R.G. (1991). A cross-cultural comparison of organizational conflict management behaviours. *International Journal of Conflict Management* 2(3), 181–199.

Lee, W.Y., Nakamura, S.I., Chung, M.J., Young, J.C., Fu, M., Liang, S.C. & Liu, C.L. (2013). Asian couples in negotiation: A mixed-method observational study of cultural variations across five Asian regions. *Family Process* 52(3), 499–518.

LePoole, S. (1989). John Wayne goes to Brussels. In R.J. Lewicki, J.A. Litterer, D.M. Saunders & J.W. Minton (eds.), *Negotiation* (pp. 553–557). Burr Ridge, IL: Irwin.

Leung, K. (1997). Negotiation and reward allocations across cultures. In P.E. Early & M. Erez (eds.), *New Perspective on International Industrial Organizational Psychology* (pp. 640–675). San Francisco, CA: New Lexington.

Leung, K., Au, Y.F., Fernández-Sol, J.M. & Iwawaki, S. (1992). Preferences for methods of conflict processing in two collectivist cultures. *International Journal of Psychology* 27(2), 195–209.

Leung, K., Koch, P.T. & Lu, L. (2002). A dualistic model of harmony and its implications for conflict management in Asia. *Asia Pacific Journal of Management* 19(2/3), 201–220.

Leung, K., Wang, J. & Deng, H. (2016). How can indigenous research contribute to universal knowledge? An illustration with research on interpersonal harmony. *Japanese Psychological Research* 58(1), 110–124.

Leung, K. & Wu, P.G. (1990). Dispute processing: A cross-cultural analysis. In R.W. Brislin (ed.), *Applied Cross-Cultural Psychology* (pp. 209–231). Newbury Park, CA: Sage.

Leung, K. & Wu, P.G. (1998). Harmony as a double-edged sword in management. In B.S. Cheng, K.L. Huang & C.C. Kuo (eds.), *Human Resources Management in Taiwan and China*. Taiwan: Yuan Liou Publishing.

Lim, J.H. & Yazdanifard, R. (2012). The difference of conflict management styles and conflict resolution in workplace. *Business and Entrepreneurship Journal* 1(1), 141–155.

Ma, Z.Z. (2007). Competing or accommodating? An empirical test of Chinese conflict management styles. *Contemporary Management Research* 3(1), 3–22.

McGonagle, K.A., Kessler, R.C. & Gotlib, I.H. (1993). The effects of marital disagreement style, frequency and outcome on marital disruption. *Journal of Social and Personal Relationships* 10(3), 385–404.

McLaughlin, L.A. & Braun, K.L. (1998). Asian and Pacific Islander cultural values. *Health and Social Work* 23(2), 116–126.

Marsella, A.J. (2005). Culture and conflict: Understanding, negotiating, and reconciling conflicting constructions of reality. *International Journal of Intercultural Relations* 29(6), 651–673.

Moran, R.T., Allen, J., Wichman, R., Ando, T. & Sasano, M. (1994). Japan. In M.A. Rahim & A.A. Blum (eds.), *Global Perspectives on Organizational Conflict* (pp. 33–52). Westport, CT: Praeger.

Mulder, N. (1996). *Inside Indonesian Society*. Amsterdam: Pepin Press.

Nadler, L.B., Nadler, M.K. & Broome, B.J. (1985). Culture and the management of conflict situations. In W.B. Gudykunst, L.P. Stewart & S. Ting-Toomey (eds.), *Communication, Culture, and Organizational Processes* (pp. 71–86). Beverly Hills, CA: Sage.

Nichols, M.P. (2012). *Family Therapy: Concepts and Methods*. Upper Saddle River, NJ: Pearson.

Ohbuchi, K., Fukushima, O. & Tedeschi, J.T. (1999). Cultural values in conflict management. *Journal of Cross-Cultural Psychology* 30(1), 51–71.

Ohbuchi, K.Y. & Takahashi, Y. (1994). Cultural styles of conflict management in Japanese and Americans: Passivity, covertness, and effectiveness of strategies. *Journal of Applied Social Psychology* 24(15), 1345–1366.

O'Nell, C.W. (1989). The non-violent Zapotec. In S. Howell &R. Willis (eds.), *Societies at Peace: Anthropological Perspectives* (pp. 117–132). London: Routledge.

Onyekwere, E.O., Rubin, R.B. & Infante, D.A. (1991). Interpersonal perception and communication satisfaction as a function of argumentativeness and ego-involvement. *Communication Quarterly* 39(1), 35–47.

Pedersen, P.G. & Jandt, F.E. (1996). Culturally contextual models for creative conflict management. In F.E. Jandt & P.G. Pedersen (eds.), *Constructive Conflict Management* (pp. 3–28). Thousand Oaks, CA: Sage.

Peterson, R.B. & Schwind, H.F. (1977). A Comparative Study of Personnel Problems in International Companiew and Joint Ventures in Japan. *Journal of International Business Studies* 8(1), 45–55.

Pinkley, R.L. & Northcraft, G.B. (1994). Conflict frames of reference: Implications for dispute processes and outcomes. *Academy of Management Journal* 37(1), 193–205.

Pološki Vokić, N. & Sonton, S. (2010). The relationship between individual characteristics and conflict handling styles – The case of Croatia. *Problems and Perspective in Management* 8(3), 56–67.

Pruitt, D.G. & Rubin, J.Z. (1986). *Social Conflict Escalation, Stalemate, and Settlement*. New York: Random House.

Rahim, M.A. (1983). A measure of styles of handling interpersonal conflict. *Academy of Management Journal* 26(2), 368–376.

Rahim, M.A., Antonioni, D. & Psenicka, C. (2001). A structural equations model of leader power, subordinates' styles of handling conflict, and job performance. *International Journal of Conflict Management* 12(3), 191–211.

Redding, S.G., Norman, A. & Schlander, A. (1994). The nature of individual attachment to the organization: A review of East Asian variations. In H.C. Triandis, M.D. Dunnette & L.M. Hough (eds.), *Handbook of Industrial and Organizational Psychology* (pp. 647–688). Palo Alto, CA: Consulting Psychologists Press.

Roloff, M.E. & Ifert, D.E. (2000). Conflict management through avoidance: Withholding complaints, suppressing arguments, and declaring topics taboo. In S. Petronio (ed.), *Balancing the Secrets of Private Disclosures* (pp. 151–163). Mahwah, NJ: Erlbaum.

Roskos, P.T., Handal, P.J. & Ubinger, M. (2010). Family conflict resolution: Its measurement and relationship with family conflict and psychological adjustment. *Psychology* 1, 370–376.

Rubin, J.Z., Pruitt, D.G. & Kim, S.H. (1994). *Social Conflict*. New York: McGraw-Hill.

Saldov, M., Kakari, H. & McLaughlin, L. (1997). *Obtaining Informed Consent from Traditional Japanese Elders for Treatment in Oncology*. Honolulu, HI: University of Hawai'i.

Sillars, A.L. & Vangelisti, A.L. (2006). Communication: Basic properties and their relevance to relationship research. In A.L. Vangelisti & D. Perlman (eds.), *The Cambridge Handbook of Personal Relationships* (pp. 331–351). New York: Cambridge University Press.

Song, M., Dyer, B. & Thieme, R.J. (2006). Conflict management and innovation performance: An integrated contingency perspective. *Journal of the Academy of Marketing Science* 34(3), 341–356.

Swierczek, F.W. (1994). Culture and conflict in joint ventures in Asia. *International Journal of Project Management* 12(1), 39–47.

Tafoya, D. (1983). The roots of conflict: A theory and a typology. In W. Gudykunst (ed.), *Intercultural Communication Theory* (pp. 205–238). Beverly Hills, CA: Sage.

Thomas, K.W. (1992). Conflict and conflict management: Reflections and update. *Journal of Organizational Behavior* 13(3), 265–274.

Ting-Toomey, S., Gao, G., Trubisky, P., Yang, Z., Kim, H.S., Lin, S.L. & Nishida, T. (1991). Culture, face maintenance, and styles of handling interpersonal conflict: A study of five cultures. *International Journal of Conflict Management* 2(4), 275–296.

Tjosvold, D. & McNeely, L.T. (1988). Innovation through communication in an educational bureaucracy. *Communication Research* 15(5), 568–581.

Tjosvold, D., Dann, V. & Wong, C.L. (1992). Managing conflict between departments to serve customers. *Human Relations* 45(10), 1035–1054.

Tjosvold, D., Hui, C., Ding, D.Z. & Hu, J.C. (2003). Conflict values and team relationships: Conflict's contribution t team effectiveness and citizenship in China. *Journal of Organizational Behavior* 24(1), 69–88.

Todor, W.D. & Owen, C.L. (1991). Deriving benefits from conflict resolution: A macro justice assessment. *Employee Responsibilities and Rights Journal* 4(1), 37–49.

Tyler, T.R., Boeckmann, R.J., Smith, H.J. & Guo, Y.J. (1997). *Social Justice in a Diverse Society*. Boulder, CO: Westview.

Ubinger, M.E., Handal, P.J. & Massura, C.E. (2013). Adolescent adjustment: The hazards of conflict avoidance and the benefits of conflict resolution. *Psychology* 4(1), 50–58.

Uwazie, E.E. (2000). Social relations and peacekeeping among the Igbo. In I.W. Zartman (ed.), *Traditional Cures for Modern Conflicts: African Conflict 'Medicine'* (pp. 15–30). Boulder, CO: Lynne Rienner Publishers.

van de Vliert, E. (1997). *Complex Interpersonal Conflict Behavior: Theoretical Frontiers*. Hove: Psychology Press.

van de Vliert, E. & Kabanoff, B. (1990). Toward theory-based measures of conflict management. *Academy of Management Journal* 33(1), 199–209.

van Eemeren, F.H., Grootendorst, R., Jackson, S. & Jacobs, S. (1993). *Reconstructing Argumentative Discourse*. Tuscaloosa, AL: University of Alabama Press.

Wallenfelsz, K.P. & Hample, D. (2010). The role of taking conflict personally in imagined interactions about conflict. *Southern Communication Journal* 75(5), 471–487.

Wang, C.L., Lin, X.H., Chan, A.K.K. & Shi, Y.Z. (2005). Conflict handling styles in international joint ventures: A cross-cultural and cross-national comparison. *Management International Review* 45(1), 3–21.

Weinberger, A., Marttunen, M., Laurinen, L. & Stegmann, K. (2013). Inducing socio-cognitive conflict in Finnish and German groups of online learners by CSCL script. *International Journal of Computer-Supported Collaborative Learning* 8(3), 333–349.

Wolfson, K. & Norden, M. (1984). Measuring responses to filmed interpersonal conflict: A rules approach. In W.B. Gudykunst & Y.Y. Kim (eds.), *Methods for Intercultural Communication Research* (pp. 155–166). Beverly Hills, CA: Sage.

Xie, J.H., Song, X.M. & Stringfellow, A. (1998). Interfunctional conflict, conflict resolution styles and new product success: A four-culture comparison. *Management Science* 44(12), 192–206.

Yarn, D.H. (2002). Transnational conflict resolution practice: A brief introduction to the context, issues, and search for best practice in exporting conflict resolution. *Conflict Resolution Quarterly* 19(3), 303–319.

Chapter 9

Conflict mediation

As with all aspects related to conflict, the approach to how conflict is resolved, if avoidance and withdrawal are no longer an option, is highly culture-dependent. It is therefore no surprise that Lind, Huo and Tyler (1994) and Wheeler, Updegraff and Thayer (2010) found that culture serves as an important indicator for preferred conflict resolution approaches. Since managing conflict has been deemed crucial to most any kind of relationship, the most prevalent and effective conflict resolution styles are intricately tied to a culture's conceptualization of interpersonal, social and working relationships.

Pološki, Vokić and Sonton (2010) purport that in response to growing demands for workplace harmony and the resultant increased workplace productivity, effective conflict management has become essential. While they list a vast array of factors paramount to conflict handling styles, including gender, age, education, hierarchical orientation, experience, personality, power, etc., the prominence of cultural factors is not only highlighted in their research findings but also in numerous other studies. Tinsley (1998) found that conflict resolution preferences could be accounted for predominantly by cultural group membership. Augsburger (1992) refers to resolution processes as culturally prescribed. Lee Agee and Kabasakal (1993) emphasize that cultural differences can play a critical role in negotiations and conflict resolution, which they perceive as important to strengthening the coming world economy. Gelfand, Leslie and Keller (2008) refer to organizational dispute resolution systems, which can be resolved through informal resolution practices or formal channels, such as through collective bargaining, grievance systems, mediation, ombudsmen and arbitration (cf. Friedman, Hunter & Chen, 2008; Goldman et al., 2008; Ury et al., 1988). Which form of conflict resolution is deemed appropriate is therefore apparently a cultural construct. Morris et al. (1998) highlight the challenging nature of intercultural conflict resolution processes with their observation that, although cultural differences present a challenge in any form of negotiation across cultures, 'the problem of cultural differences is even more endemic ... where managers need to resolve everyday conflicts with co-workers from other cultures' (p. 730).

9.1 Contract-based versus relationship-based working practices

Beyond the myriad of factors already discussed, one major criterion in the assessment of people's attitudes towards conflict is based on how reliant relationships (especially relating to workplace structures and financial outcomes) are on interpersonal connections and social ties. How people approach mediation practices is strongly tied to relationship and social network practices. Kramer and Messick (1995) posit that conflict processes are commonly embedded in ongoing interpersonal and intergroup relationships. In Chapter 6, I discussed in some detail that different cultures evaluate and emphasize interpersonal relationships in different ways, with the concepts of independence and interdependence playing a central role. Lin and Wang (2002) assert that 'conflict resolution strategies not only affect the immediate resolution of a specific disagreement, but also have critical relational consequences' (p. 24). The nature of the relationship, as Lin and Wang (2002) observe, has important implications to the conflict resolution process. Boyle et al. (1992) and Mohr and Nevin (1990) also assert that relationship structure is likely to affect the nature of conflict resolution approaches. It is therefore pertinent to address contract-based, as opposed to relationship-based working practices across cultures.

Cultures with oral traditions and some cultures that emphasize relationships place far greater importance on spoken words, verbal agreements, agreement by handshake, and the centrality of an established relationship than on contracts. Uzzi (1997) says of the Japanese auto and the Italian knitwear industries that they are characterized by trust and personal ties, rather than explicit contracts. Calantone and Zhao (2001) assert that in Asian countries, the social context and personal relations that surround a formal contract are far more important than the written legal document. This stands in stark contrast to most North American and Northern European cultures, where the written word and contract is the sole binding form of agreement. Trust is placed in the words printed on paper instead of in the people one establishes the contract with. These differences can cause a substantial amount of grieve and conflict, but also impact on how conflict is handled subsequently.

The Treaty of Waitangi serves as a prime example that highlights not only cultural differences in the understanding and interpretation of cultural concepts behind lexical items such as 'government' but also the inevitable consequences when people, who place more trust in the relationships they have with people rather than in the written contracts that they sign, establish contracts with people who rely predominantly on contracts.

Case study: Treaty of Waitangi

The Treaty of Waitangi refers to an agreement made between the British Crown and 540 Māori chiefs in 1840 in Waitangi, New Zealand. From the beginning until the present day, this treaty has been surrounded by confusion. Orange (1987) states that the treaty contained the seeds of continuing conflict, particularly over land, power and authority. These are partly due to error-riddled translations (Mulholland & Tawhai, 2010), poor understanding of the content (Waikawa Marae, 2005), the choice of lexical items that inaccurately reflect Māori cultural concepts (Wikipedia; Moon & Fenton, 2002; Jackson, 2016), a discrepancy between verbal assurances and written accounts, and the fact that Māori culture, with its oral traditions (Wehi, Whaanga & Roa, 2009), relied more heavily on what was promised to them verbally than what they signed on paper (Belich, 1996). Orange (1987) refers to the oral nature of the Waitangi deliberations to have been of paramount importance.

These issues were never fully settled and this fight for a degree of autonomy, for a fairer share in the nation's decision-making, for land, fishery and other rights continues to the present day.

The fact that this conflict has continued for nearly two centuries shows how grave the consequences of a clash in cultural norms can be. While relationship-based versus contract-based agreement practices only form one part of this enduring conflict, it demonstrates the aggravating nature of this discrepant view of working relations.

The centrality of relationships over contracts in these cultures leads to much confusion between different parties. Contract-based cultures prefer to meet and immediately get down to business, drawing up contracts without much prior interpersonal contact, which are then regarded as safeguards for the relationship and are considered binding and fixed. Relationship-based cultures, on the other hand, are not inclined to start engaging in business interactions until they set aside time for relationship-building first. Once a certain level of trust is reached and parties feel like they get a sense of the other person, then business can start. Time for relationship-building and socializing in these cultures is not seen as wasted time, but as an investment in long-lasting, mutually beneficial working relations. Weir and Hutchings (2005) describe this process as 'very time con-suming, yet once a relationship has been established, verbal contracts are absolute and an individual's word is his/her bond' (p. 92). Bourdieu (1986) speaks of a durable network as a possession. Lin (2001) describes this focus on relationships as investment in social relations with expected returns in the marketplace. While agreements are binding, the relationship-based conceptions of contracts are seen as retrospectively modifiable, because the reliance on the relationship rather than on the printed contract forms the core of the agreement. Alston (1989) states that the Japanese view contracts as personal agreements that should be changed when conditions change. In a similar vein, Chinese contract law is described as more flexible than that in the West (Zhao, 2000).

Though both approaches make sense in their own right, Rousseau (1989) asserts that subjectivity can occur in written and oral agreements. Conse-quently, it makes sense that some cultures (especially those lower in trust and more reliant on strong social networks) invest time to size up potential partners prior to any agreements – written or otherwise.

Hutchings and Weir (2006) speak of a need to 'have acquired knowledge of ... business counterparts and built a trust relationship prior to engaging in business' (pp. 145–146) across Arab cultures. Khakhar and Rammal (2013) say of the Arab world that there is a focus on building relationships and accommodating others for the sake of harmony and avoidance of confrontation (Nelson, Al Batal & El Bakary, 2002), similar to the conceptualizations of working relations in Chinese and Japanese culture. Zirin (1997) also states that by avoiding a legalistic approach to conflict resolution and instead relying more on impersonal negotiation strategies, East Asian cultures avoid either side losing face and thereby preserve working relationships. Exchange partners in these cultural systems believe that an ongoing relationship is so important as to warrant maximum efforts at maintaining it (Morgan & Hunt, 1994).

In cultures that place such great emphasis on relationships, the concept of reciprocity plays a central role. Rousseau (1989) posits that the belief that reciprocity will occur is akin to developing a psychological contract. While such psychological contracts are not written, they are regarded as morally binding. Dominguez and Watkins (2003) speak of 'enforceable trust' (p. 113). This is all the more true if an oral promise is made. Expectations that psychological contracts based on verbalized assurances are binding are even higher, seeing as public commitments exert stronger influence on cognitions and behaviours than implied ones (Salancik & Pfeffer, 1978). Weir and Hutchings (2005) explain that 'failure to meet verbally agreed obligations will certainly lead to a termination of a business relationship' (p. 92). However, verbalized or not, the trust lies in the relationship ties and in abiding by reciprocally beneficial moral obligations.

Conflict is of course particularly undesirable where working practices are relationship-based, especially because investment in relationships typically means an investment in long-term business and trading relations as well as long-term expectations for profit. As a consequence, conflict avoidance and relationship-based working practices seem to go more or less hand-in-hand. Zirin (1997) explains that the Chinese abhor litigation. When conflict cannot be avoided, relationship-based cultures proceed extremely carefully, and it appears that these cultures favour the involvement of third-party go-betweens in order help resolve the conflict with minimal damage to the relationships. While Jia (2002) asserts that mediation practices in Chinese culture are first and foremost directed towards conflict prevention, when conflict does arise, third-party involvement is the favoured option for conflict resolution too.

9.2 Conflict facilitation, intermediaries and mediation

While European and even more so North American cultures typically rely on litigation processes to settle conflicts, many cultures, especially those in Asia and the South Pacific, shy away from this form of pursuing justice. Barnes (1994) asserts that members of Asian cultures tend not to turn to official institutions, such as the police, government or justice officials in conflict situations. In Indonesian society, for example, pursuing a grievance in court is an option that is rarely used (Just, 1991). In Japan, even the Japanese legal system itself discourages people from publicly pursuing conflicts in court (Ohbuchi, 1998). Barnes (1994) asserts that in the Asia-Pacific region, conflict management emphasizes diverting disputes from the court system in order to preserve social solidarity. This preference for mediation over litigation has nothing to do with sophisticated legal systems not existing in these cultures, and everything to do with people's attitudes and priorities. The pursuit of justice is what lies at the core of many European or North American attitudes to conflict resolution, while the restoration of harmony and maintenance of relationships forms the prime concern for a multitude of other cultures.

In harmony-oriented cultures, third parties are more frequently involved in conflicts (Kozan, 1997). Bingham (1985), in fact, defines mediation as 'the assistance of a "neutral" third party to a negotiation' (p. 5). Seeing as conflict is not perceived to be only a problem for the disputant parties, but for the collective (Wall et al., 1995), it justifies the involvement of a mediatorial conflict resolution style. Augsburger (1992) also asserts that, in what he refers to as 'traditional cultures', conflict is seen as a communal concern, whose preferred style of conflict engagement is by way of mediation through third parties, so that conflict resolution is achieved in 'indirect, lateral and systemic ways' (p. 8). The implication is that bringing in an intermediary as a neutral person prevents people from becoming emotional and for dissent to escalate into open conflict, whereas an intermediary can negotiate between parties in an uninvolved, neutral manner and thus prevent conflict from becoming heated and aggravated. The communication of negative feelings towards an intermediary instead of directly to the party is not only easier on the disputants but also helps save face, because more indirect communication means that the parties involved can avoid embarrassing public results. This relational outlook is reported for Chinese (Cohen, 1991) and Japanese (Moran et al., 1994) culture. Cushman and King (1985) report that Japanese culture values maintaining public face in the conflict process. 'The traditional Chinese approach to conflict resolution is based on saving face for all parties through secret negotiations to bypass direct confrontation' (Pedersen & Jandt, 1996, p. 9). Seeing as in Chinese culture, resolving conflict is driven by the desire to avoid open conflict (Tang & Ward, 2003), Gao (1998) and Walker et al. (1996) speak of compromise, intervention, mediation and the use of intermediaries as an integral part of Chinese conflict management. Barnes (1994) asserts that in cultures of the Pacific Basin, mediation practices have a historical and cultural tradition, including China, Taiwan, the Philippines and Japan. Barnes (1991) found that approximately 7 million disputes are mediated per year in China alone. He calls it the 'method of choice' for almost all civil disputes (1994, p. 119).

This preference, however, is by no means restricted to Chinese and Japanese culture, but constitutes the preferred approach for a much wider range of cultures. Kozan and Ergin (1998), for example, uncovered that Turkish subjects preferred to negotiate through an intermediary, whereas US subjects preferred direct negotiation. Kozan and Ilter (1994) further highlighted the preference of mediation in a Turkish cultural context with their finding that mediation facilitated conflict management in Turkish organizations. Faure (2000) refers to similarities between African and Chinese traditional approaches to conflict management. African societies have been found to lean towards mediation practices for dispute settlement and justice dispensation (Ajayi & Buhari, 2014; Nwolise, 2005). Davidheiser (2006, p. 836) calls the way Gambians conceptualize conflict and conflict management 'markedly different' from those typically encountered in the North-Atlantic region. The focus across many African societies, as Choudree (1999) asserts, is rooted in the desire to contain conflict and the potential for disruption.

Korean-Americans have also been found to rely on mediation (Pedersen & Jandt, 1996). This is very much in line with conflict management approaches in traditional Korean culture.

Case study: Korean vacation

A group of friends of 14 people (12 of them Korean) went for a short vacation trip. It is typical for Korean culture to do all activities together as a group. However, due to the relatively large group size we had to take multiple taxis. After one dinner, four of us went back to the apartment we all stayed in, while the rest went out for drinks, which they had forgotten to tell us about. Despite the fact that we tried to contact them, we could not reach them. Although none of the four of us were upset about this, when the rest of the group arrived back at the apartment, a huge heated discussion broke out involving both many accusations and many apologies. After this had been going on for quite some time, one of the 'forgotten' four, a Korean male, made a remark along the lines of 'it's enough now' to a slightly older female. This was deemed so inappropriate that the female addressee was livid with rage and resulted in her storming out of the apartment.

What ensued was that several group members ran after the offended female to console her and calm her down and convince her to come back. While the rest of the group talked to the offending male, reprimanding him and advising him how he should have behaved and what he should do when she comes back.

Third-party involvement of this kind is extremely common in Korean culture and I observed this on multiple occasions during my various extended stays in Korea. Though, overall, Korean culture is defined by harmony-orientation (Zhang et al., 2005), Koreans are often perceived by outsiders as a passionate culture (Kim and Morrison 2005), and refer to themselves as the Italians of Asia, i.e. as passionate high-involvement culture, where tempers flare relatively easily. Kim et al.'s (2007) findings also indicate that Koreans are less likely than

Chinese or Japanese to use avoiding styles. In fact, Lee and Rogan (1991) found no differences in the amount of avoidance strategies used by Korean as compared to US American subjects.

The types of altercations described in the case study above are not rare, and I have even witnessed several very public shouting matches, and a fist fight. While Koreans are not as categorically prone to conflict avoidance as the Japanese, for example, they emphasize harmony restoration and intervening. Since Koreans are extremely group-oriented in their activities, in-group members are quick to step in to facilitate between the offending and offended parties and to act as go-between if and when necessary. Though the parties in conflict eventually exchange a few words of reconciliation, the main conflict resolution is handled by in-group members, while the two parties are given time to cool their heels. Lee and Rogan (1991) assert that Koreans are most likely to solve conflict by integrating differences between parties. However, they also found that, among Koreans, the approach to conflict changes with age. As discussed in Chapter 1, age plays an important role in Korean culture and the reliance on non-confrontational conflict resolution strategies decreases with age, as reported by Lee and Rogan (1991).

Bowling and Hoffman (2000) describe mediation as a 'safe forum for airing grievances and venting emotion' (p. 6). They even claim that the sheer presence of a mediator who listens and reframes can be sufficient, even when a mediator is not trained or especially skilled. As such, mediation does not have to come in the form of specialists, but is often settled through the involvement of colleagues or family members. The neutrality of third parties serves as guarantor for avoiding unreasonableness and unnecessary aggression. This neutrality or impartiality is regarded as a crucial factor in successful mediation practices (Pruitt, 1981; Smith, 1985). However, neutrality or impartiality may neither be feasible nor necessarily desirable (see 9.5 for details). Goodenough (2000) and McGuigan (2009), in fact, emphasize that there is no such thing as an objective conflict and that it is impossible for a mediator to remain entirely neutral. Wehr and Lederach (1991) even argue that outsider-neutrals are not always the most desirable mediation option. In their exploration of conflict management practices in Nicaragua, they uncovered the important implications that the local trust-based (confianza) mediation style of insider-partial mediators can have for our understanding and approach to conflict management on a wider scale. According to Fry (2000), the Dou Donggo of Indonesia also rely on elders (i.e. insider-partials) to mediate a dispute. Stewart (1990) reports a similar process for Bedouin tribes, who also rely on respected men within their own social structure to negotiate and make decisions regarding conflicts. Instead, maybe Boulie's (1996, pp. 84–84) terms 'empathetic' and 'non-judgmental', which he lists among the key characteristics of a successful mediator, are more useful in the conceptualization of effective conflict management. Indeed, results indicate high levels of settlement and participant satisfaction (Bowling & Hoffman, 2000), because a conflict mediator introduces a certain amount of 'good sense' into the process, as Kozan (1997, p. 347) put it.

The preferred outcome in harmony-oriented cultures is not necessarily to do with the bottom line. Rather, the foremost goal is to restore harmony between disputant parties (Jia, 2002). Mediators are therefore mostly concerned with the preservation of relationships, protecting the parties' sense of pride, status and honour, and as such are in a way more abstract than concrete. This not only applies to Asian cultures but is also reported to be of pivotal importance to, for example, Bedouin tribes, where reputation, face and honour constitute primary considerations in conflict mediation (Stewart, 1990). Davidheiser (2006) explains that for the Mandinka in Gambia, mediation is more of a matter of 'persuading disputants to end their conflict and reconcile than as a structured process of facilitated problem solving' (p. 836). Bennett (1993) describes reconciliation of the conflictant parties as the essence of the African conflict resolution process.

However, Kozan (1997) also describes third-party involvement as quite intrusive. It is, therefore, understandable that some cultures prefer to resolve conflicts in a less public manner. Diamond (1996) speaks of social and situational constraints on conflict, in the sense that North American and Western European cultures prefer to deal with conflict situations privately, instead of airing their dirty laundry publicly. In this sense, then, the differences in attitudes towards conflict as a private/personal matter versus conflict as a relational/group matter affect whether a culture is open to resorting to other-involvement in the conflict resolution process. However, the main difference, as some researchers see it, lies in the perception of fairness and justice.

Successful conflict resolution centres on perceived fairness of procedures and outcomes (Folger & Greenberg, 1985). The perceptual difference, as Todor and Owen (1991) see it, lies in micro versus macro justice. They assert that treating groups fairly may produce unfair treatment for individuals, because, in some cases, some individuals must be treated unfairly to create a fair distribution of outcomes at the macro level. Micro justice, on the other hand assesses fairness at an individual level of analysis (Brickman et al., 1981). Whether mediation or legislation constitute preferred conflict management techniques then depends largely on whether collective or individual outcomes are the overarching goal of conflict intervention.

9.3 Regulation and legislation

Cultures that prioritize individual justice over interpersonal harmony tend to use more adversarial approaches to dispute resolution, based on precise legal documentation. The Western world, for the most part, therefore generally places emphasis on a judicial system presided over by lawyers and judges (Nwolise, 2005). Gómez (2008) speaks of private and public official institutions of industrialized, developed nations that deal with dispute management processes, with lawyers as intermediaries.

Contract-based cultures typically value overt codes and formal descriptions (Tinsley, 1998), and what counts is what is written in legal documents (Hall, 1976). These cultures therefore appear to favour the regulative model. Regulative conflict management means can either come in the form of bureaucratic procedures that safeguard working processes or in the form of litigation practices. Kozan (1997) purports that countries, such as Germany and France, prefer to rely on workflow bureaucracy, which serves to aid problem solving and tension reduction. Other countries prefer to rely more on the legal system to facilitate in conflict situations. Seeing as written contracts prevail in less relationship-oriented cultures, with detailed written procedures outlining due process in case of a dispute (Kozan, 1997), legalistic strategies are the standard in conflict resolution (Wang et al., 2005). According to Frazier and Summers (1984), parties then either resort to promising rewards and sanctions for adhering to contractual obligations or threaten with legal actions to gain compliance. Legally enforceable contracts and legally binding documents therefore provide an institutional framework to carry out conflict resolution. Yazzie (2004) speaks of coercive power to address conflicts. This applies to interpersonal conflicts as much as to workplace disputes, where the ability to set up and operate effective mechanisms for dealing with organizational conflict is viewed as an important organizational function (Pondy, 1967), and therefore perceived as an integral part of operations.

However, the functionality of such a system has been questioned and criticized, not least because litigation has been referred to as a 'rich man's game' where power and financial resources influence outcomes (Wang, 2010, p. 203). This is supported by Krahane (2004, p. 33), who says of supposedly neutral facilitation that they 'systematically favour more powerful parties'. Where international disputes are concerned, the issue is even more skewed, because, lacking a truly international court (at least for the resolution of transnational commercial disputes), litigation has to take place before a domestic court. It is little surprising that disputants are reluctant to litigate in their opponent's country, since the court is perceived to be biased in favour of local interests (Wang, 2010).

Considerations of fairness, however, are not the only pressing concern with litigation approaches to conflict resolution. Western capitalism rejects the values placed on reputation prevalent in the face-to-face community (Abel, 1982), and this has not been regarded as a forte. Bennett (1993) describes the Western model of conflict resolution as one 'designed to alienate and confuse the litigant' (p. 32) – hardly conducive to continued long-term relationship maintenance. The way Wang (2010, pp. 190f.) sees it,

> dispute resolution by way of litigation has been developed in the West to advance the interests of the 'rightful' parties against the interests of others, even though, in doing so, they damage the interest of all parties in the process. An example for this may be that interest of all may be imperiled

because the parties are unable and are extremely reluctant to continue with their otherwise pleasant business relationship after their extensive 'legal battle' against each other in court.

Cappelletti (1992) therefore criticizes the Western orientation to a rights culture, which focuses on contentious justice as an ideal. He regards other forms of justice preferential that focus on mending rather than terminating relationships. Lauchli (2000) encourages a reorientation to alterocentric instead of egocentric thinking.

Wang et al. (2005) also question the effectiveness of legal enforcement, given that even contract-based cultures are not void of relational considerations, especially where strategic alliances are concerned, and that no written document is comprehensive enough to provide unambiguous solutions for all possible contingencies (Koot, 1988; Lin & Miller, 2003). Needless to say, legal actions may also incur costly consequences, seeing as they breed mistrust and are not conducive to future cooperation prospects. Due to their win-lose orientation, forcing strategies are oriented towards short-term solutions not ongoing partnerships (Lin & Wang, 2002). Perlmutter and Heenan (1986) therefore call alliances that resort to forcing strategies inherently weak.

Lin and Wang (2002) position legalistic mechanisms relative to trust, whereby an increase in trust is positively correlated with a decrease in legal actions (cf. Dwyer, Schurr & Oh, 1987), while a lack of trust is positively correlated with an increase in legalism in conflict resolution (cf. Sitkin & Roth, 1993). De Waal (1996) therefore deem focusing attention on relationships in conflict negotiation and reconciliation appropriate. Bennett (1993) even argues that the African judicial process, in several respects, contains a better guarantee of procedural fairness than the Western system. Fry (2000) therefore rightly asserts that written legal codes and court systems 'are not the only paths to justice and social order' (p. 348).

9.4 New light on old ways

Ancient Greek philosophy speaks of a golden middle way as a desirable solution situated half-way between two extremes. The question that arises then is: is there a middle way between litigation and mediation, between cultures with a focus on individual outcomes and those focused on group cohesion? While there might not be an ideal solution that consolidates these preferences in conflict resolution practices across all cultures, there are several approaches that have been proven successful across cultures and times.

The ancient Hawaiian conflict mediation practice *ho'oponopono* serves as a prime example. By viewing the self as relational rather than as autonomous and by emphasizing peaceful resolution through the involvement of facilitation through trusted insider-partial mediators, it manages to resolve conflicts while still managing to preserve relationships. This method is so successful in fact that

it has seen a revitalization in a modern socio-cultural context and has been successfully integrated into current counselling practices (Lee, Oh & Mountcastle,
1992; Brinson & Fisher, 1999). Apparently it has not only proven to be effective
within Hawaiian culture but has also been successfully adopted by practitioners
outside Hawaii (Kamhis, 1992; Hurdle, 2002). The focus of peaceful conflict
resolution can also be found in the Samoan *ifoga* practice. According to Betham
(2008), with regard to the *ifoga* practice, settlement of a conflict is not achieved
until forgiveness has been granted by the injured party. This practice has been
used in circumstances involving serious acts of violence (e.g. murder or injuring
another) or acts against a person's honour (e.g. adultery or slander), and have
proven to successfully prevent the escalation of socially and economically disruptive inter-group conflicts (Macpherson & Macpherson, 2005).

The effectiveness of these approaches to resolving conflict lies in the fact that
they do not merely emphasize the restoration of surface-level harmony, as is
the case in other cultures, which merely patches up the conflict, but does not
in any way address the underlying problems. Instead, these ancient approaches
prioritize healing, peace and true harmony. Ropeti (2016) speaks of restorative
justice, seeing as the goals are repentance, atonement and forgiveness. Conflict
resolution is referred to as peacemaking, and is more conciliation than mediation. Peacemaking focuses on 'deep listening, not defending, arguing, forcing'
(LeResche, 1993, p. 321), and has connectedness, unity, harmony, and balance
at its core. Researchers, in fact, emphasize the spiritual focus of these practices
(Betham, 2008; Brinson & Fisher, 1999; Lavatai, 2016; Ropeti, 2016). LeR-
esche (1993) even refers to Native American peacemaking as 'inherently spiritual' (p. 321). The Navajo conflict resolution system, as Yazzie (2004) explains,
is focused on healing and relies on many of the same principles as healing ill-
nesses. In that sense, Yazzie (2004) sees the Navajo process as not only focused
on restoring good relations among people but 'most importantly it restores
good relations with self' (p. 181). Their mediation processes, Bluehouse and
Zion (1993) caution, cannot be likened to mediation practices as we commonly conceptualize them. The Navajo mediation system is characterized by
k'e and *k'ei*, which translate to the English concepts of compassion, cooperation, friendliness, unselfishness and peacefulness. Peacemakers are intent on
identifying the sources of disharmony and conflict, and explore concrete and
constructive means for repairing disharmony. Bluehouse and Zion (1993)
describe it as intervention without coercion. Barnes (1994) asserts that such a
form of participative dispute resolution allows disputants to reach an agreement
with help, rather than submit to an outside arbitrator or judge. It seeks synergistic solutions, which can be seen as more of a win–win situation, rather than
the win–lose outcome inherent in the litigation process. Witherspoon (1975)
speaks of an orientation to creating intense, diffuse and enduring solidarity.

Maybe there are lessons to be learned from such ancient approaches and
practices. The fact that Hawaiian *ho'oponopono* practices have proven successful
in conflict mediation across fields and cultures certainly indicates that they hold

potential, not only for the past but also for our future. In First Nations' mediation practices in the US and Canada, traditional approaches to mediation are also seeing a revival. According to Bluehouse and Zion (1993), there is a return to old justice ways among the Navajo communities in Arizona, New Mexico and Utah. Despite the struggles outlined by various researchers that traditional communities face in consolidating traditional cultural means of resolving conflict with pressures of modern litigation systems, there is a move towards alternative approaches to conflict resolution even in litigation-based societies (cf. Macpherson & Macpherson, 2005; Bluehouse & Zion, 1993). Osi (2008) speaks of a revival of sorts of indigenous dispute resolution processes in Canada. Duryea and Potts (1993) say of Canadian initiatives towards an integration of traditional indigenous with traditional Western approaches that 'Canadian steps toward the incorporation of Native values in dispute-processing systems are significant' (pp. 387f.).

It appears that the European-American community is becoming increasingly receptive to principled negotiation, which Lauchli (2000) describes as rooted in the Greco-Roman tradition. Osi (2008) even asserts that alternative dispute resolution has been touted as one of the greatest developments of the modern legal system. At the very least, he himself sees it as a 'more expedient, cheaper, more creative, less complicated, less cumbersome, more participative, and more effective' alternative to protracted and fraught-laden litigation (Osi, 2008, p. 164). He, however, emphasizes that this co-existential form of justice has always been part of the traditions of other cultures, especially indigenous cultures. Yazzie (2004) therefore stresses that Navajo justice systems should not be viewed as modern ADR (alternative dispute resolution) solutions, but as traditional justice methods that have been in use since time immemorial. Though Osi (2008) states that indigenous cultures have often been perceived as 'backward' and have been overlooked or neglected, their traditional approaches to conflict resolution form the most useful platform for modern ADR practices. As the Chief Justice Robert Yazzie (2005) said about Navajo conflict resolution practices: 'We are ahead of the curve when it comes to restorative or reparative justice.' A step back to tradition may well prove to be a step forward for mediation outcomes across cultures.

9.5 Summary

While it is difficult to insinuate that there is any such thing as one ideal approach to conflict resolution across all cultures, it appears that avoidance, withdrawal and surface-harmony are equally as counter-productive as aggression, litigation and the resultant alienation. Neither approach seems to be particularly successful or conducive for long-term relationship preservation or constructive working practices. What does emerge from the various findings and insights researchers have contributed on these topics is that relational considerations can and should not be taken out of the equation, but that fruitful and beneficial outcomes can only be achieved when conflict is truly settled.

Mediation appears to lead to more desirable long-term outcomes than litigation, but only if the focus is on peaceful yet complete settlement that is embraced by both parties.

The presumption that simply adopting ancient practices could eradicate the difficulties inherent in the process somewhat undermines the complexities of conflict resolution across cultural domains. However, given that litigation practices are criticized even within the cultures by which they are embraced, a move towards more alterocentric practices, as Lauchli (2000) put it, may well prove to be in the best interest of all parties, irrespective of their cultural affiliation. Despite their need for adaptation to modern contexts, turning to and learning from conflict resolution processes that have stood the test of time and have proven to be transferrable and effective across cultures could be a useful starting point for creating an interculturally valid mediation system that strives for synergetic solutions and mediation outcomes.

References

Abel, R.L. (1982). *The Politics of Informal Justice*. New York: Academic Press.
Ajayi, A.T. & Buhari, L.O. (2014). Methods of conflict resolution in African traditional society. *African Research Review* 8(2), 138–157.
Alston, J.P. (1989). Wa, guanxi, and inwha: Managerial principles in Japan, China, and Korea. *Business Horizons* 32(2), 26–31.
Augsburger, D.W. (1992). *Conflict Mediation across Cultures*. London: Westminster John Knox Press.
Barnes, B.E. (1991). *Mediation in the Pacific Pentangle*. Working Paper No. 3. Honolulu, HI, Program on Conflict Resolution.
Barnes, B.E. (1994). Conflict resolution across cultures: A Hawaii perceptive and pacific mediation model. *Mediation Quarterly* 12(2), 117–133.
Belich, J. (1996). *Making Peoples: A History of the New Zealanders from Polynesian Settlement to the End of the Nineteenth Century*. Auckland: Penguin.
Bennett, T.W. (1993). Human rights and the African cultural tradition. *Transformation* 22, 30–40.
Betham, S.E. (2008). Aspects of Samoan indigenous spirituality and Christian spirituality and spiritual Direction. *Spiritual Growth Ministries* (pp. 2–15).
Bingham, G. (1985). *Resolving Environmental Disputes*. Washington, DC: Conservation Foundation. (Available from: www.sgm.org.nz/uploads/2/0/1/6/20165561/aspects_of_samoan_indigenous_spirituality_-_emanuela_bet.pdf).
Bluehouse, P. & Zion, J.W. (1993). Hozhooji naat'aanii: The Navajo justice and harmony ceremony. *Mediation Quarterly* 10(4), 327–337.
Boulie, B. (1996). *Mediation: Principle, Process, Practice*. London: Butterworth.
Bourdieu, P. (1986). The forms of capital. In J. Richardson (ed.), *Handbook of Theory and Research in the Sociology of Education* (pp. 241–258). Westport, CT: Greenwood Press.
Bowling, D. & Hoffman, D. (2000). Bringing peace into the room. *Negotiation Journal* 16(1), 5–28.
Boyle, B.F., Dwyer, R., Robicheaux, R.A. & Simpson, J.T. (1992). Influence strategies in marketing channels: Measures and use in different relationship structures. *Journal of Marketing Research* 29(4), 462–473.

Brickman, P., Folger, R., Goode, E. & Schul, Y. (1981). Microjustice and macrojustice. In M.J. Lerner & S.C. Lerner (eds.), *The Justice Motive in Social Behavior* (pp. 173–204). New York: Plenum Press.

Brinson, J. & Fisher, T.A. (1999). The ho'oponopono group: A conflict resolution model for school couselors. *Journal for Specialists in Group Work* 24(4), 369–382.

Calantone, R.J. & Zhao, Y.S. (2001). Joint ventures in China: A comparative study of Japanese, Korean and U.S. partners. *Journal of International Marketing* 9(1), 1–23.

Cappelletti, M. (1992). Access to justice as a theoretical approach to law and a practical programme for reform. *South African Law Journal* 109, 22–39.

Choudree, R.B.G. (1999). Traditions of conflict resolution in South Africa. *African Journal on Conflict Resolution* 1(1). (Available from: www.accord.org.za/publications/j1/choudree.htm).

Cohen, R. (1991). *Negotiation across Cultures: Communication Obstacles in International Diplomacy.* Washington, DC: U.S. Institute of Peace Press.

Cushman, D.P. & King, S.S. (1985). National and organizational cultures in conflict resolution: Japan, the United States and Yugoslavia. In W.B. Gudykkunst, L. Stewart & S. Ting-Toomey (eds.), *Culture and Organizational Processes: Conflict, Negotiation and Decision-Making* (pp. 114–133). Beverly Hills, CA: Sage.

Davidheiser, M. (2006). Joking for peace. Social organization, tradition, and change in Gambian conflict management. *Cahiers d'Études Africaines* 184, 835–859.

de Waal, F. (1996). *Good Natured: The origins of Right and Wrong in Humans and Other Animals.* Cambridge, MA: Harvard University Press.

Diamond, J. (1996). *Status and Power in Verbal Interaction: A Study of Discourse in a Close-Knit Social Network.* Philadelphia, PA: John Benjamins.

Dominguez, S. & Watkins, C. (2003). Creating networks for survival and mobility: Social capital among African-American and Latin-American low-income mothers. *Social Problems* 50(1), 111–135.

Duryea, M.L. & Potts, J. (1993). Story and legend: Powerful tools for conflict resolution. *Mediation Quarterly* 10(4), 387–395.

Dwyer, F.R., Schurr, P.H. & Oh, S. (1987). Developing Buyer-Seller Relationships. *Journal of Marketing* 51(2), 11–27.

Faure, G.O. (2000). Traditional conflict management in Africa and China. In I.W. Zartman (ed.), *Traditional Cures for Modern Conflicts: African Conflict 'Medicine'* (pp. 153–168). Boulder, CO: Lynne Rienner Publishers.

Folger, R. & Greenberg, J. (1985). Procedural justice: An interpretive analysis of personnel systems. In K. Rowland & G. Ferris (eds.), *Research in Personnel and Human Resources Management* (pp. 141–183). Greenwich, CT: JAI Press.

Frazier, G. & Summers, J.O. (1984). Inter-firm influence strategies and their application within distribution channels. *Journal of Marketing* 48(3), 43–55.

Friedman, R., Hunter, L. & Chen, Y. (2008). Union–management conflict: Historical trends and new directions. In C. De Dreu & M. Gelfand (eds.), *The Psychology of Conflict and Conflict Management in Organizations* (pp. 353–384). New York: Lawrence Erlbaum.

Fry, D.P. (2000). Conflict management in cross-cultural perspective. In F. Aureli & F.B. M. de Waal (eds.), *Natural Conflict Resolution* (pp. 334–351). Berkeley, CA: University of California Press.

Gao, G. (1998). Don't take my word for it – Understanding Chinese speaking practices. *International Journal of Intercultural Relations* 22(2), 163–186.

Gelfand, M.J., Leslie, L.M. & Keller, K.M. (2008). On the etiology of conflict cultures. *Research in Organizational Behavior* 28, 137–166.

Goldman, B., Cropanzano, R., Stein, J. & Benson, L. (2008). The role of third parties/mediation in managing conflict in organizations. In C. De Dreu & M. Gelfand (eds.), *The Psychology of Conflict and Conflict Management in Organizations* (pp. 291–320). New York: Lawrence Erlbaum.

Gómez, M.A. (2008). All in the family: The influence of social networks on dispute processing. *Georgia Journal of International and Comparative Law* 36(2), 291–354.

Goodenough, W.R. (2000). Object relations perspectives of masculine initiation. In E. R. Barton (ed.), *Mythopoetic Perspectives of Men's Healing Work: An Anthology for Therapists and Others*. Westport, CT: Bergin & Garvey.

Hall, E.T. (1976). *Beyond Culture*. Garden City, NY: Anchor Books.

Hurdle, D.E. (2002). Native Hawaiian traditional healing: Culturally cased interventions for social work practice. *Social Work* 47(2), 183–192.

Hutchings, K. & Weir, D. (2006). Guanxi and wasta: A comparison. *Thunderbird International Business Review* 48(1), 141–156.

Jackson, M. (2016). Facing the truth about the wars. (Available from: https://e-tangata. co.nz/history/moana-jackson-facing-the-truth-about-the-wars/).

Jia, W.S. (2002). Chinese mediation and its cultural formation. In G.M. Chen & R. Ma (eds.), *Chinese Conflict Management and Resolution* (pp. 289–296). London: Ablex.

Just, P. (1991). Going through the emotions: Passion, violence, and 'other-control' among the Dou Donggo. *Journal of the Society for Psychological Anthropology* 19(3), 288–312.

Kamhis, J. (1992). Healing with ho'oponopono. *Aloha* 6, 44–49.

Khakhar, P. & Rammal, H.G. (2013). Culture and business networks: International business negotiations with Arab managers. *International Business Review* 22(3), 578–590.

Kim, S.S. & Morrison, A.M. (2005). Change of images of South Korea among foreign tourists after the 2002 FIFA World Cup. *Tourism Management* 26(2), 233–247.

Kim, T.Y., Wang, C.W., Kondo, M. & Kim, T.H. (2007). Conflict management styles: The differences among the Chinese, Japanese, and Koreans. *International Journal of Conflict Management* 18(1), 23–41.

Koot, W. (1988). Underlying dilemmas in the management of international joint ventures. In F. Contractor & P. Lorange (eds.), *Cooperative Strategies in International Business* (pp. 347–367). Lexington: Lexington Books.

Kozan, M.K. (1997). Culture and conflict management: A theoretical framework. *The International Journal of Conflict Management* 8(4), 338–360.

Kozan, M.K. & Ergin, C. (1998). Preference for third party help in conflict management in the United States and Turkey: An experimental study. *Journal of Cross-Cultural Psychology* 29(4), 525–539.

Kozan, M.K. & Ilter, S.S. (1994). Third-party roles played by Turkish managers in subordinates' conflicts. *Journal of Organizational Behavior* 15(5), 453–466.

Krahane, D. (2004). What is culture? In C. Bell & D. Krahane (eds.), *Intercultural Dispute Resolution in Aboriginal Contexts* (pp. 28–56). Vancouver: UBC Press.

Kramer, R.M. & Messick, D.M. (1995). *Negotiation as a Social Process*. Thousand Oaks, CA: Sage Publications.

Lauchli, U.M. (2000). Cross-cultural negotiations, with a special focus on ADR with the Chinese. *William Mitchell Law Review* 26(4), 1045–1073.

Lavatai, S.F. (2016). *The Ifoga Ritual in Samoa in Anthropological and in Biblical Perspectives*. Hamburg: Missionshilfe Verlag.

Lee Agee, M. & Kabasakal, H.E. (1993). Exploring conflict resolution styles: A study of Turkish and American University Business Students. *International Journal of Social Economics* 20(9), 3–14.

Lee, C.C., Oh, M.Y. & Mountcastle, A.R. (1992). Indigenous models of helping in non-Western countries: Implications for multicultural counseling. *Journal of Multicultural Counseling and Development* 20(1), 3–10.

Lee, H.O. & Rogan, R.G. (1991). A cross-cultural comparison of organizational conflict management behaviours. *International Journal of Conflict Management* 2(3), 181–199.

LeResche, D. (1993). Editor's note. *Mediation Quarterly* 10(4), 321–325.

Lin, N. (2001). *Social Capital*. Cambridge: Cambridge University Press.

Lin, X. & Miller, S.J. (2003). Negotiation approaches: Direct and indirect effect of national cultures. *International Marketing Review* 20(3), 286–303.

Lin, X. & Wang, C.C.L. (2002). Relational contexts of conflict resolution strategies in international joint ventures. *Journal of Relationships Marketing* 1(3–4), 23–38.

Lind, E.A., Huo, Y.J. & Tyler, T.R. (1994). And justice for all: Ethnicity, gender, and preferences for dispute resolution procedures. *Law and Human Behavior* 18(3), 269–290.

Macpherson, C. & Macpherson, L.A. (2005). The Ifoga: The exchange value of social honour in Samoa. *The Journal of the Polynesian Society* 114(2), 109–133.

McGuigan, R. (2009). Shadows, conflict, and the mediator. *Conflict Resolution Quarterly* 26(3), 349–364.

Mohr, J. & Nevin, J. (1990). Communication Strategies in Marketing Channels: A Theoretical Perspective. *Journal of Marketing* 54(4), 36–51.

Moon, P. & Fenton, S. (2002). Bound into a fateful union: Henry Williams' translation of The Treaty of Waitangi into Maori in February 1840. *The Journal of the Polynesian Society* 111(1), 51–63.

Moran, R.T., Allen, J., Wichman, R., Ando, T. & Sasano, M. (1994). Japan. In M.A. Rahim & A.A. Blum (eds.), *Global Perspectives on Organizational Conflict* (pp. 33–52). Westport, CT: Praeger.

Morgan, R.M. & Hunt, S.D. (1994). The Commitment-Trust Theory of Relationship Marketing. *Journal of Marketing* 58(3), 20–38.

Morris, M.W., Williams, K.Y., Leung, K., Larrick, R., Mendoza, M.T., Bhatnagar, D., Li, J.F., Kondo, M., Luo, J.L. & Hu, J.C. (1998). Conflict management style: Accounting for cross-national differences. *Journal of International Business Studies* 29(4), 729–748.

Mulholland, M. and Tawhai, V. (2010). *Weeping Waters*. Wellington: Huia Publishers.

Nelson, G.L., Al Batal, M. & El Bakary, W. (2002). Directness vs. indirectness: Egyptian Arabic and US English communication style. *International Journal of Intercultural Relations* 26(1), 39–57.

Nwolise, O.B. (2005). *Traditional Models of Bargaining and Conflict Resolution in Africa: Perspective on Peace and Conflict in Africa*. Ibadan: John Archers.

Ohbuchi, K. (1998). Conflict management in Japan: Cultural values and efficacy. In K. Leung & D. Tjosvold (eds.), *Conflict management in the Asia Pacific: Assumptions and Approaches in Diverse Cultures* (pp. 49–72). Singapore: Wiley & Sons.

Orange, C. (1987). *The Treaty of Waitangi*. Wellington: Bridget Williams Books.

Osi, C. (2008). Understanding indigenous dispute resolution processes and western alternative dispute resolution. *Cardozo Journal of Conflict Resolution* 10(1), 163–231.

Pedersen, P.B. & Jandt, F.E. (1996). Culturally contextual models for creative conflict management. In F.E. Jandt & P.B. Pedersen (eds.), *Constructive Conflict Management* (pp. 3–28). London: Sage.

Perlmutter, H.V. & Heenan, D.A. (1986). Cooperate to Compete Globally. *Harvard Business Review* 64(2), 136–152.

Pološki Vokić, N. & Sonton, S. (2010). The relationship between individual characteristics and conflict handling styles – The case of Croatia. *Problems and Perspective in Management* 8(3), 56–67.

Pondy, L.R. (1967). Organizational conflict: Concepts and models. *Administrative Science Quarterly* 12(2), 296–320.

Pruitt, D.G. (1981). *Negotiation Behavior.* New York: Academic Press.

Ropeti, M. (2016). A pacific perspective on restorative justice: The power of saying 'sorry'. In A. Hayden, L. Gelsthorpe, V. Kingi & A. Morris (eds.), *A Restorative Approach to Family Violence: Changing Tack* (pp. 131–142). Oxon: Routledge.

Rousseau, D.M. (1989). Psychological and implied contracts in organizations. *Employee Responsibilities and Rights Journal* 2(2), 121–139.

Salancik, G.R. & Pfefer, J. (1978). Social information processing approach to job attitudes and task design. *Administrative Science Quarterly* 23(2), 224–253.

Sitkin, S.B. & Roth, N.L. (1993). Explaining the Limited Effectiveness of Legalistic Remedies for Trust/Distrust. *Organization Science* 4(3), 367–392.

Smith, W.P. (1985). Effectiveness of a biased mediator. *Negotiation Journal* 1(4), 363–372.

Stewart, F.H. (1990). Schuld and Haftung in Bedouin law. In T. Mayer-Maly, D. Nörr, W. Waldstein, A. Laufs, W.Ogris, M.Heckel, P.Mikat & K.W. Nörr (eds.), *Zeitschrift der Savigny-Stiftung für Rechtsgeschichte, Hundertsiebenter Band* (pp. 393–407). Vienna: Hermann Böhlhaus.

Tang, J. & Ward, A. (2003). *The Changing Face of Chinese Management.* London: Routledge.

Tinsley, C.H. (1998). Model for conflict resolution in Japanese, German, and American cultures. *Journal of Applied Psychology* 83(2), 316–323.

Todor, W.D. & Owen, C.L. (1991). Deriving benefits from conflict resolution: A macrojustice assessment. *Employee Responsibilities and Rights Journal* 4(1), 37–49.

Ury, W.L., Brett, J.M. & Goldberg, S.B. (1988). Getting Disputes Resolved: Designing Systems to Cut the *Costs of Conflict.* San Francisco, CA: Jossey-Bass.

Uzzi, B. (1997). Social structure and competition in interfirm networks: The paradox of embeddedness. *Administrative Science Quarterly* 42(1), 35–67.

Waikawa Marae (2005). *The Treaty of Waitangi: 1800–2005.* Wellington: Massey University.

Walker, A., Bridges, E. & Chan, B. (1996). Wisdom gained, wisdom given: Instituting PBL in a Chinese culture. *Journal of Educational Administration* 34(5), 12–31.

Wall, J.A., Sohn, D.W., Cleeton, N. & Jin, D.J. (1995). Community and family mediation in the People's Republic of China. *International Journal of Conflict Management* 6(1), 30–47.

Wang, C.L., Lin, X.H., Chan, A.K.K. & Shi, Y.Z. (2005). Conflict handling styles in international joint ventures: A cross-cultural and cross-national comparison. *Management International Review* 45(1), 3–21.

Wang, M. (2010). Are alternative dispute resolution methods superior to litigation in resolving disputes in international commerce? *Arbitration International* 16(2), 189–211.

Wehi, P.M., Whaanga, H. & Roa, T. (2009). Missing in translation: Māori language and oral tradition in scientific analyses of traditional ecological knowledge. *Journal of the Royal Society of New Zealand* 39(4), 201–204.

Wehr, P. & Lederach, J.P. (1991). Mediating conflict in Central America. *Journal of Peace Research* 28(1), 85–98.

Weir, D. & Hutchings, K. (2005). Cultural embeddedness and contextual constraints: Knowledge sharing in Chinese and Arab cultures. *Knowledge and Process Management* 12(2), 89–98.

Wheeler, L.A., Updegraff, K.A. & Thayer, S.M. (2010). Conflict resolution in Mexican-origin couples: Culture, gender, and marital quality. *Journal of Marriage and Family* 72(4), 991–1005.

Wikipedia. Treaty of Waitangi. (Available from: https://en.wikipedia.org/wiki/Treaty_of_Waitangi).

Witherspoon, G. (1975). *Navajo Kinship and Marriage*. Chicago, IL: University of Chicago Press.

Yazzie, R. (2004). Life comes from it: Navajo justice concepts. *New Mexico Law Review* 24(2), 175–190.

Yazzie, R. (2005). The Navajo response to crime. Paper presented at A National Symposium on Sentencing: The Judicial Response to Crime. San Diego, CA, The American Judicature Society. (Available from: https://jpo.wrlc.org/bitstream/handle/11204/1894/739.pdf?sequence=1).

Zhang, Y.B., Lin, M.C., Nonaka, A. & Beom, K. (2005). Harmony, hierarchy and conservatism: A cross-cultural comparison of Confucian values in China, Korea, Japan, and Taiwan. *Communication Research Reports* 22(2), 107–115.

Zhao, J. (2000). The Chinese approach to international business negotiation. *The Journal of Business Communication* 37(3), 209–237.

Zirin, J.D. (1997). Confucian Confusion. *Forbes*. (Available from: https://www.forbes.com/forbes/1997/0224/5904136a.html#445bbf9362dc).

Index

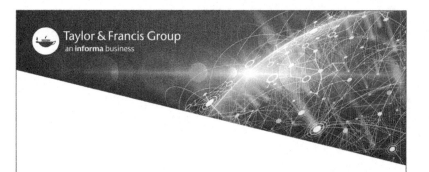

Made in the USA
Las Vegas, NV
18 February 2023

67746887R00103